THE

EPISTLE TO THE HEBREWS

AN EXPOSITION

BY

ADOLPH SAPHIR.

Author of "Christ and the Scriptures," "The Divine Unity of the Scriptures," etc., etc.

NEW AMERICAN EDITION.

VOL. I.

NEW YORK:
GOSPEL PUBLISHING HOUSE,
D. T. BASS, Manager,
24 & 26 WEST 22d STREET.

Printing Statement:

Due to the very old age and scarcity of this book, many of the pages may be hard to read due to the blurring of the original text, possible missing pages, missing text, dark backgrounds and other issues beyond our control.

Because this is such an important and rare work, we believe it is best to reproduce this book regardless of its original condition.

Thank you for your understanding.

CONTENTS.

VOL. I.

PAG

Introduction 1

CHAPTER I.

Comparison and Contrast between the Old and New Covenant; the Perfect and Ultimate Revelation in the Son 20

CHAPTER II.

The Glory of the Son of God 44

CHAPTER III.

Christ above the Angels 70

CHAPTER IV.

Christ above the Angels (continued) 94

CHAPTER V.

Jesus, the Son of Man, made lower than the Angels, for the Suffering of Death 118

CHAPTER VI.

Jesus, in All Things like unto His Brethren, through Sufferings and Death our High Priest 142

CHAPTER VII.

Christ the Lord, and Moses the Servant 167

CHAPTER VIII.

Unbelief in the Wilderness 188

CHAPTER IX.

Fear and Rest 209

CHAPTER X. PAGE.

The Word of God, Judging the Christian below; the great High Priest's Sympathy and Help above . . 232

CHAPTER XI.

Christ, as Son of Man, Called and Perfected to Be our High Priest 253

CHAPTER XII.

Growth in Grace and Knowledge 278

CHAPTER XIII.

The Danger of Apostasy; the Patience of Faith and the Anchor of Hope 308

CHAPTER XIV.

The Argument from Melchizedek; and the Inspiration of Scripture 338

CHAPTER XV.

Melchizedek a Type 363

CHAPTER XVI.

The Word of the Oath and the Son Perfected for Evermore 397

CHAPTER XVII.

Retrospect 416

INTRODUCTION

TO

AMERICAN EDITION.

To produce a satisfactory exposition of one of the most wonderful books of the New Testament, the Epistle to the Hebrews, is no small task. More than any other Epistle this Epistle goes to the Old Testament Scriptures, the Levitical institutions, historical events, and to the Psalms, and shows from all not only the fulfillment of types, sacrifices, prophecies, but proves throughout the completeness, perfection and glory of the New Covenant. It is the Epistle of Perfection, and the Perfection which it unfolds is Jesus Christ entered into the Holy of Holies, a Priest after the order of Melchizedek. Ephesians makes known to the heart the heavenly possessions which are ours in Christ Jesus, and Hebrews bids us to enter into the Holiest of all and worship there. The Epistle looks back to the blood which was shed, and shows all accomplished through it. However, it does not linger there, but its chief aim is the place in the Highest Heavens, where He lives—Jesus Christ the same yesterday, to-day and forever. Nor is this all. That Christ is coming again is a well known doctrine of the Word of God, and the Epistle to the Hebrews unfolds this precious Hope as many of the others do. The first and second chapters make it so clear that only one, who willfully turns away from the light does not see it. The first begotten is to be brought in again into the *habitable* earth (i : 6). The second chapter shows Him as Son of Man from the eighth Psalm, and that all things are yet to be put under His feet. Later in the Epistle we find the statement that He who was offered once, He who appears now in the presence of God for us, is to come the second time, without sin, to them that wait for Him. The exhortation in the tenth chapter (x : 22–25) has for its basis the approaching of the day, and the comfort for the tried and persecuted Hebrew Christians is in the same chapter: "For yet a little while and He that shall come will come and will not tarry."

The man who goes into this Epistle, this inexhaustible mine of God's revelation, to make known its unsearchable riches, must therefore be well furnished. He must have full grasp of the entire Old Testament Scriptures, especially the Levitical institutions. He must have heart knowledge of the Person and the Work of our Lord Jesus Christ, His work for us on the cross, His work for us in the Holy of Holies, and His future Glory. Without the knowledge of the latter the Melchizedek Priesthood of Christ (still future in its exercise), a Priest upon *His* throne, can hardly be understood.

Nor is this all. The Epistle was written primarily to Hebrew Christians, who were peculiarly situated, surrounded still by the shadows of a dispensation past and gone. It is almost impossible to understand certain parts of the Epistle, except the conditions and circumstances of these Hebrew Christians are understood and taken into consideration. It is here where many expositors have failed. This is especially the case with the vi. and x. chapters. Arminianism has built much of its unscriptural theory of "falling from Grace" upon the well known statements contained in these chapters. Many others are kept from a real enjoyment of the assurance of salvation by a misapplication of the exhortations contained in these two chapters. A correct understanding of the primary meaning makes these passages clear.

And now the man, who under God was fitted to unfold this Epistle and write a solid scriptural and spiritual exposition of it, we do not hesitate to say is Adolph Saphir.

Adolph Saphir, whose voice is no longer heard in the earth, was a Hebrew by birth. Brought up in an orthodox family, he had from childhood a good knowledge of the oracles of God committed to the Jews (Rom. iii: 3). When quite young he was saved by Grace and the dead letter became spirit and life in him. He soon developed through the Grace of God, into the man as he has often been described, "a man mighty in the Scriptures." His "Christ and the Scriptures" and "the Divine Unity of the Scriptures" are unanswerable arguments for the verbal inspiration of the Word of God. As a Hebrew Christian he had a grasp of Scripture, and of God's purposes such as few Gentile minds acquire. His exposition of Hebrews is a masterpiece in which all the wonderful knowledge of the Scriptures given to him by the Head in Glory is brought out. It is a joy to read this book. It has a freshness about it which refreshes. It is simple, clear, its language not only interesting, but eloquent.

The exposition was delivered in form of lectures in England during 1872 and 1873. Large crowds of all denominations, Episcopalians, Congregationalists, Methodists, Baptists, and others attended them, and wonderful blessing came through the lectures, which were shortly after issued in book form.

The English edition in one volume being exhausted it has been made possible to issue from the plates, imported into this country, a new edition in two volumes, and we shall not be at all surprised if the value and beauty of this exposition is once discovered, that other editions will become necessary. We bespeak a large sale for, and great blessing in the edification of the body of Christ through this work.

We like to call the attention of the reader to the introductory remarks. These ought to be carefully studied and read a number of times, for these remarks will greatly help in the understanding of the entire Epistle In these remarks he gives a short sketch of the Epistle and dwells especially on the Jewish Christians and their situation in

Jerusalem. We do not think another man has grasped so forcefully the circumstances in which these Hebrew Christians were when the Epistle was written by the Holy Spirit. He clearly shows them in their national relation, loving and hopeful, with an apostate Judaism fast ripening for its complete overthrow. They were still going to the ceremonial worship and upholding Levitical institutions. It was a transition period in which they lived. It was difficult to realize for them the new age of the church and all it meant. Thus we read in these introductory remarks: "Surrounded by temptations of a peculiarly sifting character, tested by persecution and reproach most fitted to shake their faith and loyalty to the Messiah, rejected by the nation, the apostle speaks to them, in language of intense and piercing earnestness, of the fearful danger of apostasy, and points out to them that it was a mark of the true Israel, and a necessary sign of the follower of Jesus, to be despised and persecuted—that the *proper position* of the God-chosen saint, of the believer, was *outside the camp, bearing reproach, enduring the cross, and despising the shame.*" We put the above words in italics because it seems to us they are heading up all the exhortations contained in the

Epistle. After all the doctrinal statements and proofs of the greater glory of the New Covenant and the passing of the old dispensation of shadow things, the Holy Spirit exhorts to go out of the camp, to have done with earthly tabernacles and earthly ceremonies. We call attention to this because of late both in Europe and America the teaching has been given, that a *believing* Hebrew should even now, not sever his connection with his nation and still continue with the law of Moses and practice certain ceremonies, as well as keep the seventh day. That such a position and teaching is altogether unscriptural and untenable needs hardly to be demonstrated here. The transition period is past long ago, the new age has come and is drawing to its close, but as long as it lasts and the church is being gathered out, it is no longer "to the Jew first," nor is there a distinction between Jew and Gentile in the body of Christ. The church complete and caught up to meet her Lord in the air, there will be once more a Jewish-believing remnant in the earth, which remnant is not a part of the one body, and that remnant, like the Hebrews in the transition period before the destruction of Jerusalem, will cling to the national Hope and they will not be disappointed. The believing Jew in Christ has no national Hope. His Hope is the blessed Hope of a coming Christ for His own.

Adolph Saphir brings this out very strongly in his exposition. Nor does he confine himself to the Jewish phase, but he is very pronounced against *Judaistic* Christendom. One of the finest and strongest passages in this exposition is the following: "Before the coming of Jesus the shadows symbolized truth to believing worshippers. After the coming of Jesus it must fade and vanish before the substance. If this is true of the Levitical priesthood, which was of *divine* appointment, how much more fearful is the assumption of any priestly title, position and function during the new dispensation. All Christians are priests. To imitate a revival of that which God Himself has set aside by a fulfillment, perfect and glorious, is audacious, and full of peril to the souls of men. It is not even the shadow of a substance, but the *unauthorized shadow of a departed shade.*"

There are a few interpretations, touching, however, none of the essential doctrines of the Bible, from which some of our readers may differ; to enter into some of these in a short preface would hardly be advisable. We fully believe, and know others share this belief with us, that Saphir on Hebrews is the best work on this Epistle in print.

Again and again in reading through the book the thought came to us how it is possible for other Hebrews to read such a sublime exposition of their Scriptures by one of their own and to remain indifferent. We hope and pray that through this new edition not only the body of Christ may be edified, but that some Hebrews may find Him of whom Moses and the Prophets speak.

May the blessing of our Lord rest upon it all.

A. C. Gaebelein.

80 Second Street, New York,
June, 1902.

The Epistle to the Hebrews.

INTRODUCTORY REMARKS.

COMMENCING in the style of a doctrinal treatise, but constantly interrupted by fervent and affectionate admonitions, warnings, and encouragements, this grand and massive book concludes in the epistolary form, and in the last chapter the inspired author thus characterizes his work: "I beseech you, brethren, suffer the word of exhortation; for I have written a letter unto you in few words."

We are attracted and riveted by the majestic and sabbatic style of this epistle. Nowhere in the New Testament writings do we meet language of such euphony and rhythm. A peculiar solemnity and anticipation of eternity breathe in these pages. The glow and flow of language, the stateliness and fulness of diction, are but an external manifestation of the marvellous depth and glory of spiritual truth, into which the apostolic author is eager to lead his brethren. The epistle reminds us in this respect of the latter portion of the prophet Isaiah,* in which, out of the abundance of an enraptured heart, flows such a mighty and beautiful stream of consoling revelations. In both Scriptures we behold the glory which dwelleth in Immanuel's land; we breathe the Sabbatic air of Messiah's perfect peace. Both possess the same massiveness; both describe things which are real and substantial, the beauty and strength of which is eternal; in both is the same intensity of love, and the same comprehensiveness of vision.

The central idea of the epistle is the glory of the New Covenant, contrasted with and excelling the glory of the old dispensation; and while this idea is developed in a systematic manner, yet the aim of the writer throughout is eminently and directly practical. Everywhere his object is exhortation. He never loses sight of the dangers and wants of his brethren. The application to conscience and life is never forgotten. It is rather a sermon than an exposition. Thus he himself describes the aim of his letter, and thus the Apostle Peter, writing to the same Hebrew Christians, refers to our book when he says, "And account that the longsuffering of our Lord is salvation; even as our beloved brother Paul also according to the wisdom given unto him hath written unto you."†

* Isaiah xl.-lxvi. Remark of Delitzsch. † 2 Peter iii. 15.

In all his argument, in every doctrine, in every illustration, the central aim of the epistle is kept prominent—the exhortation to *steadfastness.* Surrounded by temptations of a peculiarly sifting character, tested by persecution and reproach most fitted to shake their faith and their loyalty to the Messiah, rejected by the nation, the apostle speaks to them, in language of intense and piercing earnestness, of the fearful danger of apostacy, and points out to them that it was a mark of the true Israel, and a necessary sign of the follower of Jesus, to be despised and persecuted,—that the proper position of the God-chosen saint, of the believer, was outside the camp, bearing reproach, enduring the cross, and despising the shame. Representing to them the awful danger of drawing back, and the glory and blessedness of the cross, he entreats them, by the whole spirit of their history, and all the mercies of Jehovah, which in Jesus find their perfect manifestation and eternal fulfilment, to hold fast the beginning of their confidence unto the end, and to continue steadfast in the faith, and wait for the joy set before them.

It is worthy of notice and thought, that when the Hebrews were in such a dangerous condition of mind, when the apostle was afraid of their yielding to the strong temptations and persecutions of the temple, so that he felt it necessary to remind them that if after being enlightened they fell away, it was impossible for them to be renewed, that the method, which he adopts in his epistle, is to enter into the depth of Christian truth, to unfold before them all the glory of the eternal High Priest and the heavenly sanctuary, to leave behind the elementary doctrine, and to launch forth into the deep ocean of New Testament mysteries.* Thus it appeared to apostolic wisdom, that lukewarm, languid, and tempted Christians are to be roused, strengthened, and revived. The milk of simple gospel truth was not sufficient. It was necessary to declare unto them the whole counsel of God. As in the epistle which the exalted Saviour sends unto the church of Laodicea, there is the most glorious description of the person of Jesus, and of His overflowing and tender love, as in all His seven epistles† the self-revelation of Jesus is the basis and source of exhortation, thus in every age of the Church the renewal of strength, the rekindling of love, the deliverance from languor and inertness, bordering on death and destruction, can only proceed from a fuller and deeper knowledge of

* The apostle leads us also into the depths of Christ's humiliation. Nowhere in Scripture is the humanity of Christ so fully revealed ; nowhere are we so fully taught the sufferings through which the Son was made perfect, and the experiences of His earthly life, on which His sympathy with us is based.

† Rev. ii. and iii.

the Lord and His truth, from a renewed beholding of His countenance and of His glory. When the love of the majority shall wax cold, when iniquity shall abound, and the last struggle prepare, then let the church go on unto perfection, and behold with open face the glory of Christ; and, gazing on His brightness, she will be strong and courageous, and remain steadfast unto the end.

The circumstances in which the Hebrew believers were, at the time when this epistle was written to them, claim our attentive consideration. Perhaps Scripture is sometimes obscure to us, because we neglect the ordinary rules which are observed in the reading of uninspired books. We forget the human and historical element. We do not read consecutively and with the expectation, as well as the aim, to understand the scope and import of a whole book. And eager to arrive immediately at what we consider a practical application to our own circumstances, we do not sufficiently consider the primary meaning and bearing of the inspired Word.

The condition of the Hebrew Christians in the period of apostolic history, of which we now speak, is peculiarly difficult for Gentile believers in the present day to realise. As it was difficult for the believing Jews to realise during the transition period the new approaching age of the Church, of a body in which Jew and Gentile are united, which while different from and a contrast to the Theocracy (and yet filled with the same Spirit and glorifying the same Messiah), was to manifest its life and power apart from the law of Moses and the Jewish economy, so it is difficult for us now to think of the apostles Peter and John, and of thousands of Jews, observing the law of Moses, worshipping in the temple, and in every respect identifying themselves with the nation and her hope.

Jesus had, through suffering and death, entered into glory. Rejected by His people, He was exalted according to the promise to the right hand of God. He sent His apostles to Israel. They preached the death, resurrection, and exaltation of Jesus, and His second coming to judgment, and to establish His kingdom. They declared the gospel unto the nation, exhorting and beseeching them to turn to Jesus, who was sent first to them to bless them, by turning every one from their iniquities. Between the cross and the glory, when the Messiah would fulfil the promises unto the fathers, the apostles stood and testified to Israel. Their aim, their hearts' desire, their constant appeal, was Israel's national repentance and faith in Jesus. Thus was it becoming, and in accordance with the whole dealings of God. Thus the Saviour Himself came to the lost sheep of the house of Israel, as the minister of the circumcision. Thus in the marvellous love of God another opportunity was given to Jerusalem, even after her rejection of the divine Lord. And only when the Jews rejected the counsel of God, the apostles turned unto the Gentiles. Nor was it without difficulty that they entered into the full understanding of the divine counsel, according to which for a season Israel as a nation is left to itself, and the church, in which there is neither Jew nor Greek, receives the testimony and the blessing of God.*

While the apostles were thus as Jews preaching Jesus to the nation, many believed in the crucified Messiah. We read that when the apostle Paul and his companions came to Jerusalem, James, who was a pillar of the church, and all the elders received them, and said unto him, "Thou seest, brother, how many thousands (μυριαδες, ten thousands) of Jews there are which believe; and they are all zealous of the law: and they are informed of thee, that thou teachest all the Jews which are among the Gentiles to forsake Moses." It is evident that those believing Jews observed the statutes and ordinances of the law with great zeal and earnestness. They went daily into the temple; they appeared to the ordinary Jews as most diligent and scrupulous in their obedience to the p ecepts of Moses. And this observance of

* Acts iii. 26; xxvii. 25, &c.; Rom. xv. 8; Eph. iii.

the law did not conflict with their exclusive and explicit trust in Jesus as their Saviour. David and all the godly Israelites were saved by faith, and knew the grace of God, and righteousness without works, though it was God's will that unto them the law should be the rule and form of life.*

Nor must we be astonished, that even to these believing Jews it was difficult to receive such glimpses into the then future church dispensation as were given by the proto-martyr Stephen in his teaching about the temple, and the approaching crisis in Jewish history. After the death of Stephen, and the bitter persecution which then broke forth against the believing Jews, a lull seems to have succeeded. James, the brother of our Lord, according to tradition, revered by all the Jews as a just and devout man, Peter and John were pillars of the church at Jerusalem. Rejoicing in the work among the Gentiles, and acknowledging their freedom from the law of Moses, the apostles of the circumcision saw no reason and no right to alter the customs and observances of the Jewish believers. And the apostle Paul followed their suggestions, and showed to the Jews, both believers and unbelievers, his reverence for the law. That same apostle who, when the liberty of the Gentile Christians was concerned, and the truth of the

* Acts xxi. 20 ; Acts ii. 46 ; Rom. iv 6

gospel doctrine was endangered, withstood the apostle Peter, observes the law when he is among Jews; for herein he does not lose his liberty, but uses it. He became a Jew unto the Jews, as under the law, to them that were under the law; at all times and everywhere living in the love and liberty of the Son of God.*

Then arose another persecution of the believers, especially directed against the apostle Paul. Festus died about the year 63, and under the high priest Ananias, who favoured the Sadducees, the Christian Hebrews were persecuted as transgressors of the law. Some of them were stoned to death; and though this extreme punishment could not be frequently inflicted by the Sanhedrim, they were able to subject their brethren to sufferings and reproaches which were felt most keenly. It was a small thing that they confiscated their goods; but they banished them from the holy places. Hitherto they had enjoyed the privileges of devout Israelites; they could take part in the beautiful and God-appointed services of the sanctuary; but now they were treated as unclean and apostates. Unless they gave up faith in Jesus, and forsook the assembling of themselves together, they were not allowed to enter the temple; they were banished from the altar, the sacrifice, the high priest, the house of Jehovah.

* Acts xv.; Gal. ii. 14; 1 Cor. ix. 20–22.

We can scarcely realize the piercing sword which thus wounded their inmost heart. That by clinging to the Messiah they were to be severed from Messiah's people was indeed a great and perplexing trial; that for the hope of Israel's glory they were banished from the place which God had chosen, and where the divine Presence was revealed, and the symbols and ordinances of His grace had been the joy and strength of their fathers; that they were to be no longer children of the covenant and of the house, but worse than Gentiles, excluded from the outer court, cut off from the commonwealth of Israel,—this was indeed a sore and mysterious trial. Cleaving to the promises made unto their fathers, cherishing the hope in constant prayer that their nation would yet accept the Messiah, it was the severest test to which their faith could be put, when their loyalty to Jesus involved separation from all the sacred rights and privileges of Jerusalem.

The apostolic writer of the epistle enters fully and lovingly into their difficulties, and comforts them in his exhortation (παρακλησις) by showing them the unspeakably greater glory of the new covenant, in which they now stood by faith in the Saviour. Hence the subjects spoken of here are the priesthood, the sacrifice, the altar, the holy of holies. It is not, as in the epistles to the Galatians and Colossians, a question about circumcision, about things which are not lawful to eat, about ordinances—"Touch not, taste not, handle not." The Sanhedrim did not, and could not, interfere with their domestic and private religious life: it is the question of their Jewish citizenship—of their connection with the temple and its services—of their relation to the beloved city, and the chosen nation.

In order to establish and comfort them in this temptation, the apostle unfolds the glory of the new covenant; reminding them both of the unity and connection, and the contrast which subsists between the two dispensations.

He tells them that they are the true Israel, listening to the same God who spake of old by the prophets to the fathers, who had sent the perfect and ultimate revelation of Himself in His Son, who is Lord above all. Children of the law, which was given by the administration of angels, they were now reconciled and ruled over by the royal High Priest, whom the Father hath exalted above all principalities and powers. The disciples of Moses, who was faithful as a servant in all God's house, they were now partakers of Him who is the Lord and Master of the house, the Son, who abideth for ever. Brought into the promised land by Joshua, they had now, through faith, entered into rest, of which their history was but the shadow and imperfect type. And while the priesthood of Aaron was precious, as a picture and pattern of atonement and sympathy, Jesus was the true High Priest, who offered a perfcet sacrifice, whose intercession is all-prevailing, whose compassionate love is boundless, and whose power and glory are the substantial and infinite fulfilment of the prophecy of Melchisedec The tabernacle, with its symbols and services, was indeed glorious; but how much more glorious is the heavenly sanctuary, into which Christ has entered! and how much greater is the perfection, nearness, and liberty of worship, which He gives unto all His believers!

"We have," the apostle says so frequently, because the Hebrews imagined that they had *lost* treasures and blessings. Though deprived of the temple, with its priesthood, and altar, and sacrifice, the apostle reminds them, "We have" the real and substantial temple, the great High Priest, the true altar, the one sacrifice, and with it all offerings, the true access into the very presence of the Most High.

And having thus reminded them that the glory which pertaineth unto Israel (Rom. ix. 4) was truly and fully theirs, he exhorts them to steadfastness, and encourages them by their whole past history, throughout which for thousands of years the one golden thread of faith and the scarlet thread of reproach and suffering marked the presence of Jehovah. Nay, from the beginning of the world the true people of God were despised and persecuted. Righteous Abel believed the sacrifice, and became a sacrifice. Enoch testified to an ungodly generation. Noah was the only one who saved himself and his household. Abraham and all the patriarchs were strangers and pilgrims; they had to leave their home and kindred; they had to sacrifice what was dearest; Moses had to suffer the reproach of Christ; all your ancestors and prophets lived and suffered in faith, waiting for the city which hath foundations, whose builder and maker is God. And He who is the crown of Israel, as well as Israel's Lord, Jesus, the root and offspring of David, in whom all Israel's history culminates, the glory of the temple, the Lord of the Sabbath, the messenger of the covenant; Jesus the Lord Himself was rejected by His people, and as a malefactor, as one unworthy to live in the beloved city, He was cast outside the camp, and there He was crucified and nailed to the accursed tree. If you are the true children of Abraham, if you are the true disciples of Jesus, do not wonder that your place is also outside the camp; that you also are called to endure the cross and to despise the shame. Yet yours is even now the substance, and yours will be hereafter the joy.

Hence in this epistle the peculiarly large and

full meaning of the word *faith.* Throughout Scripture faith means more than trust in Jesus for personal safety. This is the central point, but we must take care that we understand it in a true and deep manner. Faith, as the apostle explains in the epistle to the Corinthians, is looking at the things which are not seen and temporal; it is preferring spiritual and eternal realities to the things of time, sense, and sin; it is leaning on God and realizing His word; it is the substance of things hoped for, the evidence of things not seen.

Thus every doctrine and illustration of this epistle goes straight to the heart and conscience, appeals to life, addresses itself to faith. It is one continued and sustained fervent and intense appeal to cleave to Jesus, the High Priest; to the substantial, true, and real worship; a most urgent and loving exhortation to be steadfast, patient, hopeful, in the presence of God, in the love and sympathy of the Lord Jesus, in the fellowship of the great cloud of witnesses.

Whoever is the author of this epistle, its value and authority remain the same. "We may compare it to a painting of perfect beauty, which had been regarded as a work of Raphael. If it should be proved that it was not painted by Raphael, we have thereby not lost a classical piece of art, but gained another master of first rank."* But let us see

* Thiersch.

how far the supposition of the Pauline authorship meets the circumstances.

The apostle Paul, according to his own testimony, which is abundantly borne out by his life and sufferings, cherished an affection for his brethren which finds its equal only in the devotion of Moses, and was surpassed only by the Lord, from whom all love descends into human hearts. Though he rejoiced in the calling and faith of the Gentiles, his heart was continually with Israel. It was no doubt a trial to him that Christian Hebrews regarded him with something like suspicion. Much as he desired to confirm and comfort them, he could not write to them as an apostle. We see how very modestly he justifies his writing an epistle to the Romans; in the same tone the author of the epistle to the Hebrews writes, "I beseech you, brethren, suffer the word of exhortation." Hence it appears natural that the apostle Paul should sink his individuality and apostleship as much as possible, and in harmony with the key-note struck in the first verse, "God spake," be to the Hebrews as the voice of one speaking truth and comfort to them in their hour of need and trial. In the concluding chapter it is difficult not to recognize the apostle Paul. A few expressions (as Heb. ii. 3)* seem such, as could

* According to a statement of Clement, Pantaenus, head of the Alexandrian school, held the apostle Paul to be the author, and

not have come from his pen,* and it is not unnatural to suppose that some Tertius was entrusted with more than the mere mechanical writing, with the formal and verbal arrangement of the argument.

But when we think of the depth and breadth of the epistle, when we remember the wisdom given to the apostle Paul, when we bear in mind that on this special point, the relation between the old and the new covenant, none was so fitted and

explained this difficulty by saying that he who was the apostle of the Gentiles could not speak of himself as apostle of the Hebrews, as the Lord Himself was the apostle of God to Israel.

* The question of the authorship of our epistle is difficult and complicated. The opinion that the apostle Paul is the author, though not the writer and composer, seems on the whole the most probable. The testimony of the ancient Eastern Churches is important. It is true that style and diction differ from that of the Pauline epistles, excelling it in purity, regularity, and smoothness. But this and other difficulties would be sufficiently accounted for by the supposition, already referred to, that the epistle was Pauline in thought, design, and argument, but not Pauline in its actual form. With regard to doctrine, the parallels with (other) Pauline epistles are striking and numerous, although the epistle contains several peculiarities of doctrinal statement. In no other portion of Scripture (not merely Pauline) is Christ represented as High Priest (the isolated passages, Psalm cx. and Zech. iii., excepted). The emphasis with which the humanity and the sympathy of our blessed Lord are mentioned requires also notice, as well as the peculiar importance attached to the ascension of Christ and the heavenly sanctuary. But the epistle itself accounts for these peculiarities, which are moreover in full harmony with the teaching of the apostle Paul.

The hypothesis, first started by Luther, that Apollos wrote the epistle, is ingenious, and meets to a large extent the difficulties real or supposed. But there is no historical foundation for it gifted to teach the church as he,* we find it difficult to waver in our decision, especially as so many collateral proofs seem to point to the same result. We have referred already to the testimony of the apostle Peter. We notice also the concluding benediction-mark of all Pauline epistles. Neither the Epistles of Peter, or John, or Jude, or James, conclude with words like these: Grace

Resemblances between our epistle in thought and expression and the writings of Luke have been pointed out.

The first impression of the simple reader, that he is listening to the words of him whom we so naturally call the apostle, is likely correct, though the question of the actual writer may remain unsolved. The following incidental remarks of Mallet are forcible: "Where do we find beside the apostle a theologian who could have written this epistle? Who beside him would have ventured to write it with such decided apostolic authority? And who had greater reason to write anonymously to Israel than the apostle who loved his people so fervently, and who was so hated by them that they refused to listen to his voice and to read his writings?" Although the authorship of Isaiah xl.–lxvi. is much more clearly and fully established, we may say both of that prophetic section and the epistle to the Hebrews, how could the authors of such writings, transcendently beautiful and glorious even among Biblical books, remain anonymous?

* "Comparing the manner of argument," says Lightfoot, "with the Talmuds Zohar, and Rabboth, and such like, you might easily tell with whom he is dealing, though the epistle was not inscribed to the Hebrews; the very style of it may argue the scholar of Gamaliel." And we may add the matter of it marks one "who had profited in the Jews' religion more than many;" and in my mind this sufficiently accounts for the writer's name being suppressed, not because the apostle of the Gentiles desired to address the Jews anonymously, but because he wished to sink his apostolic authority, and to argue with the Jews upon their acknowledged principles."—GEORGE VISCOUNT MANDEVILLE, *Horae Hebraicae. pp.* 5 *and* 6.

be with you all. (2 Thess. iii. 17.) The tradition of the Church in the East, where the Epistle was first received, is unanimous in asserting the authorship of the apostle Paul. And thus we believe, that according to the word of the Lord Jesus, when He appeared unto this chosen vessel, the apostle Paul, after testifying to the Gentiles and to kings, last of all in this epistle unfolds to the children of Israel the glory of the Messiah and His kingdom. However this may be, the epistle is in full and striking harmony with all Pauline teaching; it is in full harmony with all other portions of the Scripture; for it is not the word of man, but written by inspiration of God.

It is an epistle which enters deeply into the truth as it is in Jesus. It offers strong meat to them that are of full age; it goes on unto perfection. Let us approach this portion of the divine word with reverence, and with a deep sense of our dependence on the teaching and influence of the Holy Ghost. Our very weakness, and the peculiar trial of the present time, render this epistle more suitable to our need, and encourage us to hope that it will prove a word of exhortation to our hearts, establishing them in faith and love. Above all, let us bear in mind that, as the true difficulty throughout Scripture is our unwillingness to deny ourselves and to take up our cross, so this epistle, throughout, bears the inscription, "Outside the Camp." Every step of true progress is a step "outside the camp" with Jesus, who was crucified outside the gate. If we know the cross of Jesus, not merely as a doctrine, but a power of life, we possess the golden key which opens the treasuries of revelation.*

Jesus, the Son of God, exalted above all, infinitely high above us, and unspeakably near us in the power and sympathy of His High-priestly intercession, is set before us in this solemn and heart-stirring epistle. To look constantly and steadfastly unto Him, and with Him to be separated from the world, waiting for the glory of His second coming;—behold, here is wisdom and the patience of the saints.

* "The veil which is spread over the Scriptures for the Jews is also there for false Christians, and for all who do not hate themselves. But only let a man be sincerely disposed to hate himself, and how eager will he be to understand them, and to obtain the knowledge of Jesus Christ."—PASCAL'S *Pensées.*

THE

EPISTLE TO THE HEBREWS.

CHAPTER I.

COMPARISON AND CONTRAST BETWEEN THE OLD AND NEW COVENANT; THE PERFECT AND ULTIMATE REVELATION IN THE SON.

HEBREWS i. 1–4.

THE first four verses contain, as it were, an epitome of the whole epistle, and therefore it will be necessary for us to dwell more minutely on their weighty sentences. We consider the first and part of the second verse:

"God, who at sundry times and in divers manners spake in time past unto the fathers by the prophets, hath in these last days spoken unto us by the Son."*

* Literally God, who in many portions and in many ways spake in ancient times unto the fathers (or for the fathers) in the prophets. In many portions refers more to the matter, in many ways to the methods, of revelation. The Greek word λαλήσας denotes a confiding expression of inward thought, sentiment, and will.

The expression, *in* the prophets, reminds us of the condescension

The great object of the epistle is to describe the contrast between the old and the new covenant. But this contrast is based upon their unity. It is impossible for us rightly to understand the contrast unless we know first the resemblance. The new covenant is contrasted with the old covenant, not in the way in which the light of the knowledge of God is contrasted with the darkness and ignorance of heathenism, for the old covenant also is of God, and is therefore possessed of divine glory. Beautiful is the night in which the moon and the stars of prophecy and types are shining; but when the sun rises, then we forget the hours of watchful expectancy, and in the calm and joyous light of day there is revealed to us the reality and substance of the eternal and heavenly sanctuary. Great is the glory of the old covenant; yet greater is the glory of the new dispensation, when in the fulness of time God sent forth His own Son and gave unto us the substance of those things of which in the old times He had shown types and prophecy. When the apostle says it is God, the same God "who spake at sundry times and in divers manners unto the fathers by the prophets, who hath in the last days spoken unto us by His

of God, who clothed His thoughts in the garment of the prophet's individuality, and adapted His word to the peculiar character of the time and messenger. Hence in the prophetic books the words of the Lord and of the prophet frequently succeed one another and alternate.

Son," he confirms and seals the doctrine which was held by the Hebrews, that unto them had been committed the oracles of God; and that in the writings of Moses and the prophets they possessed the Scripture, which could not be broken, in which God had disclosed unto them His will—the counsels and purposes of His grace. "Unto them," as the apostle declares to us in the epistle to the Romans, "were committed the oracles" (or the outspeakings) "of God." And, as Jesus Christ Himself continually testifies, Moses and the prophets spake of Him. The Scriptures were that complete and infallible record of the revelation of God, from which all our knowledge of the grace and will of the Most High is derived.

This solemn acknowledgment of the fundamental importance and divine authority of the Scripture is from the very outset to gain the confidence and to establish the hearts of the Hebrew brethren. It is to give them the assured and trustful feeling of home. Thus the gospel narrative commences with a summary of Old Testament history, from Abraham to David and the Babylonian captivity, and to Jesus, the Immanuel predicted by Isaiah. Christ, or Messiah, is the comprehensive word, of which Moses and the prophets are the preparatory and expository heralds. The Saviour identifies Himself constantly with the Jewish Scripture—with the God of Abraham, Isaac, and Jacob. He, of whom the Jews confessed that He was their covenant God, was according to the declaration of the Lord His Father. And as the apostle of the Gentiles testifies to all churches, and most emphatically to the Church which was in the metropolis of the world, Rome, that unto Israel was entrusted the word of God, that Israel is the root, that the Jewish prophets and apostles are the foundation, so was it necessary and natural to remind the Hebrews that the God who spoke to their fathers was now speaking to them, that they heard the same voice, and were blessed by the same love.

"God hath spoken unto the fathers;" and by that expression "unto the fathers" the apostle reminds us that without a church, without a union of believers, without a manifestation of God in grace, historically, among a people whom He had set apart for His service, there would have been no Scripture; and that there was a congregation of the Most High from the very beginning of the world. "Unto the fathers" whom He had chosen that they might have fellowship with Him, that they might worship Him and rejoice in His name, God spake in old times, even as in the last times unto the Church—unto those who are called both from among Jews and Gentiles—He has made fully known His purpose in Christ Jesus.

This, then, is the great resemblance. The same

God in the old covenant and in the new covenant. He spake unto His church or unto His people. The Father is the author of revelation in both. The Messiah is the substance and centre of the revelation in both. The glory of God's name in a people brought nigh unto Him, to love and to worship Him, is the end of the revelation in both. The two are one. Martin Luther has quaintly compared it to the two men who brought the branch with the cluster of grapes from the promised land. They were both bearing the same fragrant fruit; but one of them saw it not, yet he knew what he was carrying. The other saw both the fruit and the man who was helping him. Thus is it, that the prophets who came before Jesus testified of Him, although they did not yet behold Him; and we who live in the fulness of times see both the Christ of whom they testified, and themselves who were sent by God to witness of Him.

But let us consider the marvellous unity of the two covenants.

"God hath spoken." This is the first point. Oh, how little do we think of the grandeur and majesty and all-importance of this simple declaration, "God hath spoken." A living God and a loving God must needs speak.* The god of the philosophers is a silent God, for he hath neither

* Compare my remarks on the necessity of Revelation in *Christ Crucified.*—Lecture v.

life nor affection; but our God, who created the heavens and the earth, who is and who loves, must speak. Even in the creation, which is an act of the condescension of God, He utters His thoughts; and when He created man as the consummation of the world, it was for this purpose, that man should hear Him and love Him, and should rejoice in His light and in His life. When sin enters into the world silence ensues. Man dreads God, and the melody of praise and prayer ceases; but the need of a revelation remains continually the same. God has created man, that out of the fulness that is in God, man may have living water wherewithal to satisfy his thirst. When man forsakes the fountain of living water he cannot get rid of the thirst, and he cannot divest himself of the nature with which God has endowed him; so that there is still within man the same absolute and utter necessity for a revelation of God from on high. He sees God's works in nature; he sees God's dealings in history; and when he examines his own mind, heart, and conscience, he reads there, although the letters seem almost obliterated, the record of the holiness and of the all-sufficiency of the only true and living God. Yet it is impossible for him to find in nature, history, or within himself that authoritative, living, and clear revelation and unfolding of the mind of God in which alone light and life can be brought to him. "Eye hath not seen, nor ear heard, neither have entered the heart of man" the things, which alone can satisfy the immortal spirit, whom God has created for the very purpose, that he should hear and with gladness obey the voice of God. Therefore it is necessary that God should speak.

And God does speak. It is a very simple declaration of Scripture that God has *spoken*, a grand truth expressed in simplest words, in order that we all may understand it. Often we read the words and do not realise what marvel of condescending love they reveal, what great and central mystery they unfold. "And God said to Abraham, to Moses, to the people of Israel." "The word of the Lord came unto the prophet." "Thus saith the Lord." Take a little child that has begun to think and to will, and even the thoughts and volitions of that little child remain an impenetrable mystery to you—an unknown land—unless that child chooses to express his thoughts and to utter his desires. And if this is true of a child, how much more is it true of Him who is unsearchable, the ever blessed and eternal God? Who knoweth the things that are in man except the spirit that is in man? And who knoweth the thoughts of God except the Spirit that is in God? For God's thoughts are not as our thoughts. As the heavens are higher than the earth, so much are God's thoughts higher than our thoughts. Who, then, can find out the Almighty by his own cogitations? or who can search the counsel of the Most High by the penetrating glance of his own intellect? Unless God speaks we do not know the thoughts of God.

But notice, secondly, man having by his own sin fallen away from God, and silence reigning now, it is only the infinite compassion and love of God that induces him to speak. If there was no redemption, there would be no revelation. If there was no blood of the Lamb, there would not be a single syllable uttered unto man by the Most High. It is because God is the God of edemption, that He is the God of revelation. It is because in Jesus Christ there is an atonement that God began to say to Adam in love, "Where art thou?" The love of the Father, and the blood of Jesus Christ, and the inspiration of the Holy Ghost; behold, these are the three necessary foundations upon which the Scripture rests. God, the Triune Covenant God, hath spoken.

And that God hath spoken is a very awful thing, full of power and life. We have got accustomed to it, to believe that we have the thoughts of God embodied in His word, and that He who is almighty and ever blessed in Himself, and against whom we have sinned, hath in His infinite love uttered unto us the thoughts of His compassion and of His mercy; but God Himself is astonished at it, and commendeth His love, and saith, "Hear, O heavens, and give ear, O earth: for the Lord hath spoken." And saith again, "For as the rain cometh down, and the snow from heaven, and returneth not thither, but watereth the earth, and maketh it bring forth and bud, that it may give seed to the sower, and bread to the eater: so shall my word be that goeth forth out of my mouth: it shall not return unto me void, but it shall accomplish that which I please, and it shall prosper in the thing whereto I sent it." And again, that He has magnified His word above all His name. And again, that He will come as a Redeemer unto His people, and that He will manifest Himself unto them by speaking. "I who speak am He.' "Therefore my people shall know my name; therefore they shall know in that day that I am He that doth speak." (Isa. lii. 6; comp. John viii. 25.) And throughout all the Scripture this wonderful indication is given unto us, that there is one who is the Word of God, and yet a person equal with Himself, the bearer of all His thoughts and purposes, His beloved, His only begotten Son. God hath spoken: in old times unto the fathers by the prophets; fully and perfectly unto us by His Son. In both dispensations the same God, on account of the same sacrifice, impelled by the same love and for the same sublime and gracious purpose.

Both Old and New Testaments are of God; the New Testament, as the Church-father Augustine said, is *en*folded in the Old, and the Old Testament is unfolded in the New.* Nor can we, who live in the times of fulfilment, dispense with the record of the preceding dispensation.† As an old author writes: "As the brilliancy of the sun appears far greater when contrasted with the darkness of the shade, so this epistle compares the light of the gospel with the shadows and types of the Old Testament, and by this means displays the glory of the gospel in full relief; for as shadows are images of bodies, so the ancient shadows are images of Jesus Christ, of His power and of His graces, and assist us to recognise more and more the substance and the truth; but from hence we derive also this additional advantage, that although the shadows of other bodies serve only to obscure them, the shadows of the Old Testament are so many reflectors, contributing light to the gospel."

* In Vetere Testamento Novum latet, in Novo Vetus patet. "What is the law, but the gospel foreshadowed? What the gospel, but the law fulfilled?"—HOOKER.

† This thought is more fully stated in my book, *Christ and the Scriptures;* and in chap. v. of my Lectures on *The Apostolic Commission.*

Is not this epistle another illustration of the truth, that they only who accept with reverence and faith the Old Testament under-

But now let us consider the contrast. Jesus Christ was not born till four thousand years after the creation of the world. He came in the fulness of time. Why were so many ages allowed to elapse before the Word was made flesh? Herein also is revealed the condescension of God. When it is said that "in the fulness of time God sent forth His Son, born of a woman," you must remember that this "born of a woman" refers also to the four thousand years, in which His goings forth were from of old to the whole history of the woman—of the daughter of Zion—of the Jewish nation. During all these years He who in the fulness of time came, and was born of the Virgin Mary, was going forth out of the human race—out of the chosen family—out of Israel, the covenant people of God, making Himself a little sanctuary unto us, as it were, condescending to our limited capacity, teaching us line upon line and precept upon precept, developing truth as the history of the nation developed. "At sundry times and in divers manners" did God speak unto the fathers by the prophets.

stand fully the peculiar glory of the New Covenant? Compare 2 Cor. iii. The neglect of the ancient Scriptures necessarily leads to a dim apprehension of the fulness, liberty, and joy of the gospel. While, therefore, the intention of many is to exalt the New Testament, they must necessarily fail unless they adopt the method of our Lord and of His apostles, which is to teach according to the Scriptures.

He chose prophets to be His messengers. The meaning of a prophet is one who is directly commissioned by God; one who, whatever his tribe, position, and dignity may be, is chosen by God according to His good pleasure, and is gifted with the Holy Ghost, and is entrusted with the message of God to utter it to the people. These three things constitute a prophet: direct commission from God Himself, gift of the Holy Ghost, and being entrusted with the very thoughts and words of the Most High. It is not merely *by* the prophets, that God spake. They were chosen not merely as the channels of separate and isolated revelation. God spake *in* them. They were the personal bearers of the message, the representatives and exponents of divine truth. Their words and typical actions were inspired, and in them the word of the Lord came unto Israel. When God in His infinite condescension sent prophets unto His people from the very beginning of the world (for by "prophets" we must understand all the messengers that God sent),* this was a great, good, and perfect gift in itself; and not only for one age, but for all generations, for the instruction and guidance of the whole Church.

* "God hath spoken by the mouth of all His holy prophets since the world began." (Acts iii. 21.) "Yea, and all the prophets from Samuel and those that follow after." (*v.* 24.) "And Enoch also, the seventh from Adam, prophesied." (Jude 14.)

Yet let us consider what were the imperfections of these messengers.

The first imperfection was this—that they were numerous; they were many. One succeeded another. They lived in different periods. Another imperfection was, that it was "in divers manners," in dreams, in similitudes, in visions, in symbols. Each prophet had his peculiar gift and character. Their stature and capacity varied. They were men of different temperament and tone of mind. The manner in which the revelation of God was given to them varied; even in the case of the same prophet the One Spirit appeared in various manifestations. Highest stands Moses, who therefore predicts, as in type so by direct announcement, the "prophet like unto me," to whom God spake not in vision, or in a dream, or in dark speeches. (Deut. xviii.; Num. xii.) Another imperfection was that they were sinful men. When Isaiah beheld the glory of God, he said, "Woe is me! for I am undone: I am a man of unclean lips." When Daniel, the "man greatly beloved," enjoyed communion with God, he felt and confessed that he had sinned, and transgressed, and done wickedly. All of them, from the greatest downwards, were men full of infirmities and sins. Another imperfection was that they did not possess the Spirit constantly. Of a sudden, after a long pause, the Spirit of God came upon them. God spake unto them, and gave unto them His message. But it was not like a continuous river. The word came to them from time to time; they did not *possess* the word. Another imperfection was this, that of that message that was entrusted to them they did not understand the heights and the depths. They themselves had to search diligently, and to enquire what the Spirit that was in them did signify of the sufferings and glory that should come. Another imperfection was, that, as they did not understand adequately that portion of the message that was given unto them, they could still less comprehend and contain the whole message. They saw only one aspect of it, only one portion of it in connection with the peculiar history and the peculiar trials of the people at the period to which they were sent. Another imperfection was, that they all testified, like John the Baptist, "I am not the light. I am only sent to witness of the light." They were only finger-posts directing the pilgrim, as he was in pursuit of the heavenly city, to go on further, until he would come to the pearly gates of the new Jerusalem.

We notice the imperfect and fragmentary character of the old dispensation, when we consider not merely the words, but the types, which are living prophecies. There was not a single one which could stand by itself, it had always to be supplemented. Abel shows to us that the righteous shepherd was to suffer and die; Enoch that the man of God would be lifted up into the heavens; Noah that there will be a Righteous One who will save not merely himself, but others, out of the destruction and judgment which sin draws down from a holy God. If we want to have an idea of the salvation of God we must combine the three—Abel, Enoch, and Noah—in one person; the Righteous Man, who suffers, saves, and enters into glory. Moses is a type of a mediator, prophet, priest, and king; but to obtain a view of the true Redeemer you must combine him with Joshua, for only Joshua leads the people into the promised land. Melchizedek is a priest and king, but we must combine him with Aaron in order to have an idea of atonement and of intercession, as well as of blessing and rule. David is a shepherd meek and lowly, a man who does not lift up himself above his brethren, and rules in love and in justice; but we must combine him with Solomon to get the idea of the kingship, both in its gentleness, sympathy, and suffering, and in its glory and extensiveness. Wherever we go we find it is in fragments. There is an altar; there is a sacrifice. There is a fourfold sacrifice, a sin-offering, a burnt-offering, a peace-offering, a meat-offering. There is a high priest; there is a tabernacle; there is a holy of holies; there is a candlestick; there is a shewbread; there is a veil. Everything a fragment; everything in itself showing unto us some aspect of truth, some portion of the treasure, without which we would be poor; but we must combine them all to see the full and blessed truth.

The old dispensation was imperfect. This is evident from the very fact that the message was sent in sundry fragmentary portions and in many different ways. It appears also from the nature of the chosen men, in whom the Lord spake. They were not merely finite and limited in their capacities, but sinful and fallen; and they witnessed of the perfect, ultimate, and all-comprehensive revelation of the light of Jehovah in the latter days. Great was the glory of the old covenant; for it was *God* who spoke. It was the Lord God of the covenant, of redeeming and sanctifying love, who for the sake of Christ and in Christ spoke unto His chosen people, and in the marvellous wisdom of His educating fatherly guidance taught them by a variety of types and of gradually unfolding prophecies.

But now the time of fragmentary, imperfect, and temporary revelation is past. God speaks to us now in another and more glorious manner.

Look now at the contrast. The whole contrast is in one word—in our language in one syllable—"by the *Son*." The prophets were many: the Son is one. The prophets were servants: the

Son is the Lord. The prophets were temporary: the Son abideth for ever. The prophets were imperfect: the Son is perfect, even as the Father is perfect. The prophets were guilty: the Son is not merely pure, but able to purify those that are full of sin and pollution. The prophets point to the future: the Son points to Himself, and says, "Here am *I*." God has spoken to us "by His Son."* He is the only Prophet. God asks, "Who is like unto me?" To whom then will ye liken me, or shall I be equal? "Who hath directed the Spirit of the Lord, or being His counsellor hath taught Him?" "With whom took He counsel, and who instructed Him, and taught Him in the path of judgment, and taught Him knowledge, and showed to Him the way of understanding?" God asks proud man, "Where wast thou when I laid the foundations of the earth?" Who is there that knows God, or is equal unto Him? None but the Son. He was with Him before the foundations of the world were laid. The eternal, uncreated Word was with God before the morning stars sang together and the angels shouted for joy. He is the true and faithful witness; for He speaks of that which He hath seen, and testifies of that which He

* Or more correctly in One who is Son. Notice here also the *in*. For the whole message of God is only *in* Christ; and Him we only seek to know (Phil. iii. 10), and know only ἐκ μέρους in part. (1 Cor. xiii.)

knows. "No man knoweth the Father but the Son. No man hath seen the Father. The only begotten of the Father He hath declared Him." He is the true and faithful witness, whose testimony is co-extensive, if I may so say, with the counsel and the things of God: the Prophet whose mind is adequate to understand the mind of the Father. He is not merely the true and faithful witness because He is from everlasting, He is also *the beloved of* God. Notice this in the word "Son." "The only begotten," says John, "who was in the bosom of the Father," who is His treasure and delight, the infinite object of His love, in whom from all eternity was His rejoicing, who shares with Him all His counsels. This beloved one of God—oh, surely He is the true messenger who will reveal all the secrets of the Father's heart, and who will tell unto us all the fulness of His counsel, and all the purposes of His grace! God hath spoken to us by His Son.

Now contrast Him with the prophets. Were the prophets sinful? Behold our blessed Jesus, born of the Virgin Mary, conceived by the Holy Ghost, true man, yet growing up from His infancy in the love and fear and knowledge of God, without spot and blemish, not merely sinless but gifted with every perfection, showing forth true humanity according to the mind of God. Were the other prophets dependent upon momentary visits of the

Holy Ghost? Look at Jesus. You never read in the gospels that the Spirit came upon Jesus, or that the word of God came unto Him. The Spirit was always in Him; for He had the gift of the Spirit without measure. The word of God was alw ys in Him, abiding, living. Oh, how beautiful is that expression of the apostle Peter, "Lord, to whom shall we go? Thou hast the words of eternal life." Not, "Thou utterest the words of eternal life;" but, "Thou *hast* them: they are thy property, thy possession. Thou art Lord of the words, master of the words, fountain of the words." Notice again, the prophets say, "Thus saith the Lord." Jesus says, "Verily, verily, I say unto you;" and yet He spake nothing except what He heard the Father say; for He is the Son of the Father. The Son, and therefore equal; the Son, and therefore subordinate; yet whether the Father speaks or Jesus speaks, it is one voice, one love.

And not merely does He say, "Verily, verily, I say unto you;" but He Himself is His message. Not like the prophets does He testify of one that was to come after Him;* but He says of Himself,

* Jesus does indeed speak of the Comforter, the Holy Ghost. But what is the mission of the Comforter? Is it not to glorify Christ? to bring to the remembrance of the disciples all that the Saviour had taught? to take of the things of Christ and of the Father, and to show them unto us? The Holy Ghost is not a substitute for Jesus, but by Him the real presence and indwelling of the Father and the Son are vouchsafed. Jesus is the Son, manifesting foth His glory. (John ii.)

"I am the bread of life. I am the resurrection and the life. I am the way, the truth, and the life. I give unto every one that cometh unto me rest and the water of life." And thus, dear friends, we ascend to the marvellous truth, that Jesus, the Son of God, not merely declares unto us the message of the Father, but He Himself is the message of the Father. All that God has to say unto us is *Jesus.* All the thoughts and gifts and promises and counsels of God are embodied in Jesus. He is the Light, the Peace, the Life, the Way, and the End. And this leads us still higher. How is it that the message and the gift are one? Because Jesus is the Word of God. "In the beginning was the Word, and the Word was with God, and the Word was God." How mysterious and intimate is the union, how deep and essential the relation between the Son of God and the revelations of God in Him and in the Scripture! Christ, the Son, is the real, substantial, eternal Word, by whom the worlds were made, by whom all things are upheld, by whom God speaks unto us, and reveals His saving love. Christ is the Word of the written Word,* the substance and spirit, the centre and life of Scripture; and as the Word He quickens and blesses

* "The Scriptures and the Lord
Bear one most holy name:
The written and the incarnate Word
In all things are the same.'

us with eternal blessings. How comprehensive and simple is the declaration, "God speaks in His Son."

Let me remind you how in the Son all the message of God is contained. I appeal to your remembrance of the teaching of Scripture. You who know the Scripture, and you especially who have come through the law unto the gospel, will understand me when I say that if the sinner knew nothing else but this, "God has sent a messenger, and this messenger is His own Son," he might discover in this the whole gospel, good news, glad tidings; *for*, in order to send unto us condemnation, in order to give unto us the knowledge of our sin and of our desert, in order to send unto us the message of impending judgment, His own Son is not needed. Any angel would suffice for this work; any servant could proclaim this message. Moses is able to utter it; even our own conscience is sufficient messenger. When God sends His own Son into the world, when God makes the stupendous sacrifice of allowing His only begotten to take upon Him our flesh and blood, there can be only one meaning in it—SALVATION.* It can only have one purpose—our

* It need scarcely be added that the teaching and the life of the Lord Jesus, and even His death on the cross, proclaim the law of God, and reveal to us our guilt and lost condition; and that in one aspect, the Father sent Jesus to Israel as a preacher of repentance, "peradventure they will reverence my Son." But the primary, as

redemption. It can only have one motive—the overwhelming love of God. In the fulness of time God sent His own Son—to teach, to preach, to announce judgment? Oh, no, a thousand times no. God sent His Son to redeem us. Behold, I declare unto you tidings of great joy. Unto you is born this day a Saviour. Eternal life is in Christ Jesus the Son before the world began. These two ideas are always connected in the teaching of the apostle Paul—*the law* and time—that which passes away and man, *the gospel* and eternity, and the Son of God and the everlasting counsel. So Paul says "in promise of eternal life which God gave unto us before the foundation of the world," because it is not human, but divine; not temporary, but eternal; not connected with man and his works and efforts, but entirely and exclusively connected with the mission of the Son of God. God has spoken to us by His Son, and therefore we know that He has spoken *peace* to us.*

But notice, secondly, as the Sonship is the beginning of the gospel, so it is also the end and

well as the ultimate object of His mission, was to seek and to save that which is lost, to preach the glad tidings of salvation.

* To preach Jesus is to preach peace, joy, life. The evangelist, that is, the bearer of the glad tidings, "opens his mouth, and beginning at (whatever) Scripture, preaches *Jesus*." (Acts viii. 35.) "The word which God sent unto the children of Israel, *preaching peace by Jesus Christ* (He is Lord of all)." (Acts x. 36.)

purpose of God's message. God, speaking to us by His Son, shows unto us that we also are to become the sons of God. He that receiveth a prophet in a prophet's name shall receive a prophet's reward; he that receiveth Him in a righteous man's name, a righteous man's reward; but he that receiveth the Son of God as the Son of God shall become a son of God. Jesus will give him power to become a son of God, born of the Spirit unto eternal glory. "Whosoever shall confess that Jesus is the Son of God, God dwelleth in him, and he in God." Such is the marvellous declaration of the apostle John. "Thou art the Christ, the Son of the living God," was the confession of Simon Bar-jona. Jesus replies, "Flesh and blood have not revealed this unto thee, but my Father which is in heaven." So great a thing is it for a poor sinner to know that the only begotten of the Father was made flesh and dwelt among us, and died for our salvation, that whenever any one among the Jews or the idolaters said, "I believe that Jesus is the Son of God," the apostles said: "Come, let us baptize him. What need we more? He has discovered the secret. The secret has been revealed to his soul. God has come to him: God dwelleth in him, and he in God. Let us baptize him." This is the rock upon which the Church is built—"Thou art the Christ, the Son of the living God." God has spoken to us by the

Son, and in knowing the Son we receive sonship, the adoption. And this is the peculiar glory of the new covenant, this the distinguishing feature of the Pentecostal Church. In the Incarnate Son the Father has brought many sons unto glory. The only begotten of the Father has, after His death on the cross, become the firstborn among many brethren. The Holy Ghost, coming through the glorified humanity of Jesus, unites us to Him, who is the beloved Son, and in whom the eternal and infinite love of the Father rests upon all His believing people. In the Son we know and have the Father; in the Son we also are the children of God.

Lastly, brethren, remember this is the ultimate revelation. There can be nothing higher; there can be nothing further. In "these last days" He hath spoken unto us. "Little children, it is the last time." The Saviour testifies in the book of Revelation: "These things must shortly come to pass." Surely, I come quickly. We are hastening unto the coming of Christ. Oh that we may know Him who is coming,—as the Son of God! If Christ is our life, then, when the Son of God shall appear, we also who are the sons of God—now in weakness, suffering, temptation—shall be made manifest with Him in glory. Amen.

CHAPTER II.

THE GLORY OF THE SON OF GOD.

HEB. i. 1–4.

WE have considered the contrast between the Old and New Dispensation, which is brought before us in the words of the first and second verses, God speaking in time past unto the fathers by the prophets, and God speaking in these last days* unto us by His Son. When

* The contrast between the time before the first advent and the last days will be again referred to in connection with ii. 5. The expression, "last days," occurs Gen. xlix. i.; Jer. xxiii. 20; Ezek. xxxviii. 16; Hosea iii. 5; Micah iv. 1; Isaiah ii. 2; Daniel ii. 18. According to the Jewish canon of interpretation, the last days denote the days of the Messiah. Now, according to the perspective of Old Testament prophecy, whenever some obstacle which stood in the way of the fulfilment of the Messianic promise was removed, the immediate advent of the time of blessedness was expected, and then a new revelation was given which disclosed some further delay, and enlarged the vista of God's expectant people. Thus 2 Sam. vii. points to a son of David; Daniel ix. to seventy sevens after the return from exile. But since the day of Pentecost the apostles

the apostle arrives at that word, "by His Son," he has reached the central and culminating point of all the revelations of God. The Son of God has come. In this all things are summed up. For what other purpose could the Son of God come but for salvation? Judgment, the preaching of the law, mere teaching, are works indeed high and important, but which may be executed by any creature chosen and sent by God. The message of law needs only human and angelic mediators. But when the Son of God Himself comes, surely it must be for the purpose of a new creation; it must be for the purpose of the manifestation of infinite love and boundless compassion, bringing deliverance and life. Again, if the gift is salvation, who else can bring it but the

knew with a perfectly assured clearness that the days of Messiah had commenced, as the exposition of Joel's prophecy by the apostle Peter distinctly declares. (Acts ii. 17.)

In "these last times" the beginning, or the first advent, and the consummation, or the second coming of the Lord, are viewed sometimes as coincident, or at least as lying very close together, and this in harmony with Old Testament representation; for instance, Isaiah lxi., the acceptable year of the Lord and the day of vengeance of our God. And at other times the two advents are viewed as separated by the period of the Church, and the second coming of Christ is viewed as the transition between our days and the "world to come." Thus in one sense we live in the day of fulfilment ("the darkness is past, the true light *now* shineth"); in another sense, in the days of expectation and waiting, the Son of God Himself on His Father's throne expecting and looking forward. While we are thus contrasted with the fathers of old we are also like them (and like God's ancient people at present), looking forward to the *Hope of Israel.* (Acts xxvi. 6.)

Son of God? Prophets have announced the will of God. Moses has declared unto us His holy commandments. By the law cometh the knowledge of sin and condemnation. By the prophets is kindled the hope of redemption. But no man, no angel, no creature, can restore us. If we know the depths of the fall, we know also the grandeur of the remedy that is needed. As soon as we hear the Son of God is come, we may expect salvation; as soon as it is announced to us that salvation is to appear, we may expect none but the Most High can bring it; for Jehovah is Redeemer; He only is our salvation. Not like a gift from heaven, as sunshine, and rain, and bread; not as a servant, or angel, or messenger, does Jesus come to this earth, but the Son of the Father, equal with Him in glory and majesty; the Lord from heaven, unto whom all things belong, who abideth in the house for evermore. Thus was it that the apostle Paul, from the very commencement of his Christian life, from the very moment of his conversion, saw these two ideas combined. He is Lord from heaven above all; He is Jesus, who died for the sinner, and identifies Himself with the church. And therefore, throughout all his epistles, as throughout the whole experience of the children of God, these two wonderful facts are seen together. How can we sufficiently adore Him who is the Son of God! How can we sufficiently love Him who shed His precious blood to deliver us!

The moment he says "the Son," the apostle has reached a mountain-height from which a vast and most extensive view opens before his eye. We are accustomed, in the epistles of the apostle Paul, to have him take us, with the mighty wings of faith and love, unto high, lofty peaks, and show unto us the wonderful land of Immanuel, boundless and infinite, as well as full of beauty and sweetness, and perpetual harvest.

Thus is it in the epistle to the Ephesians, where he begins by ascribing praise to God the Father, who hath "blessed us with all spiritual blessings in heavenly places in Christ Jesus." Having gained this wonderful position, "with Christ Jesus in the heavenly places," he shows unto us the eternity before the foundation of the world, when God chose us in Him; and he points out to us the ages that are to come, when God shall be glorified in Christ Jesus, and in the church whom He has given unto His Son, when we who first trusted in Christ shall be to the praise of the glory of His grace. Thus is it in the epistle to the Colossians (chap. i. 14–29). The moment he speaks of the redemption which we have through faith in the blood of Jesus, He opens unto us the glory of the Lord Jesus who died for us, and leads us back to the very beginning of things, when all things were made in Him, and to the end of things, when all things shall be summed up in Him. God's eternity has become our home. All things are ours, because in Jesus we behold the Son of God.

But accustom yourselves always, when you hear of Jesus, to think of Him as divine and human —two natures in one person. When you hear of the Son of God, think of that glorious and loving One who was born of the Virgin Mary; who lived for thirty-three years upon earth in poverty and lowliness; who died upon the accursed tree; who rose with the self-same body out of the grave, and appeared unto His disciples, and spoke unto them, and ate with them broiled fish and of an honeycomb; who ascended in His body into heaven, and who shall so come again—the man Christ Jesus, the Son of God—to reign upon the throne of His father David, and to show forth the majesty and the love of God throughout all His creation.

It is of the incarnate Son of God that the apostle speaks; and showing unto us His glory, he leads us, in the first place, to the *end* of all history, He is appointed the heir of all things; (2) to the *beginning* of all history, in Him God made the ages; (3) *before* all history, He is the brightness of His glory, and the express image of His being; (4) *throughout* all history, He upholdeth all things by the word of His power.

(1) The end of all history. The Father has appointed the Lord Jesus Christ, His Son, the heir of all things. Him, the Son of Abraham and the Son of David, the theocratic Son, the Messiah; not in His abstract Deity, but as the Son who became man; as the Word made flesh; as the Lord God, visiting and redeeming His people; as the Son who became the servant to fulfil all Jehovah's good pleasure. Thus He promised unto Abraham that his seed should be the heir. Thus He promised unto the Son of David, who is also David's Lord, and the only-begotten of the Father. "Ask of me, and I will give thee the heathen for thine inheritance, and the uttermost ends of the earth for thy possession." He ratified it through all the prophets; and finally the angel who appeared unto the Virgin Mary declares unto her that the holy child shall be called the Son of the Most High, and the Lord God shall give unto Him the throne of His father David, and He shall reign over the house of Judah for ever; and of His kingdom there shall be no end. The Father hath appointed Him, in the everlasting covenant, according to the good pleasure of His will, in the infinite love and delight which He had to Him who is His equal, to be "heir of all things." What great expressions these are in Scripture! What wonderful conceptions, far transcending anything that men ever could have imagined!

The Old Testament speaks of heaven and earth, summing up all things by these two words. The New Testament speaks of the creation of God—all things which He by the word of His power and in His wisdom hath called forth; or it speaks of the ages—ages upon ages, worlds upon worlds, in which the manifold fulness of the divine thoughts come gradually into existence. All things He hath given unto Jesus to inherit;* as the Messiah, the theocratic Son, according to the promise to the fathers, and this only on the basis of His eternal and essential sonship. Because He is the Son of God, therefore is He the Messiah. "The Father loveth the Son, and hath given all things into His hands." According to His deity there is no necessity for any gift, reward, or transfer. According to His deity incarnate, the Messiah, in the everlasting covenant, is appointed Heir, and all things are given into His hand.

What are these "all things"? It is clear that there is nothing excepted that is not given unto

* Compare Rom. iv. 13; viii. 17; Gal. iii. 29; Zech. iii. 7. The Lord has not yet entered fully into the actual possession of the inheritance which, according to the Father's eternal counsel, and as a reward of His obedience unto the death of the cross (Phil. ii.), is appointed unto Him. Notice how the promise is given unto Him, as our Saviour and Head. We are joint-heirs with Him. He and His people will be *glorified together*, according to the blessed mystery that we were crucified together with Christ. What glory! and yet a glory which always reminds us of our sin and unworthiness, and of the grace and love of the Lamb that was slain.

Him. So said the risen Saviour,—"All power is given unto me in heaven and on earth." In His intercessory prayer before His sufferings He had said, "Thou hast given Him power over all flesh." This is the first thing. The whole human race is given unto Him. Since He took upon Him our flesh and blood, God has given unto Him the whole human race—power over all flesh. And out of this whole human race, which belongs unto Him by eternal right, and by the right of His incarnation, by the right of His perfect and holy humanity, by the right of His unspeakable love, and of His death,—out of this whole world of humanity God has chosen in Him a people, that the Son should give eternal life to "as many as thou hast given Him." "Thine they were, and thou gavest them me." All these are His in a special sense. That innumerable multitude which no man can number from among all nations, peoples, and kindreds, and tongues—the chosen family in whom God has manifested His love, who have been renewed by the Holy Ghost, who have been washed in the blood of Jesus, who have been trained, educated, sanctified—all the lively stones, who by the Spirit have been built on the only foundation, who have been chiselled, beautified, perfected by the all-loving Divine Spirit, through experiences and sufferings most precious, appointed by perfect wisdom and grace, who have become the members of His wonderful mystical body, they all are His. He not merely rules over them; He lives, He moves in them. He thinks, and they think; He feels, and they feel. His will is the power which energizes in them. As a man who is in perfect health and strength has control over all the members of his body, so the whole church is the body of the Lord Jesus Christ, each member in his separate sphere, each according to his peculiar preparation and gift of nature and grace, each shadowing forth some feature of Christ's beauty, and echoing some syllable of the Divine Word—all perfect, all beautiful—organized into one harmonious, living, and glorious whole—"the fulness of Him that filleth all in all." They belong unto Jesus. God has given us unto Him as His inheritance.

And this church Jesus Christ has obtained as the first and central part of His inheritance. As the material sun is placed in the firmament to be a source of light and heat and joy unto the rest of the creation of God, so God appoints the church to be the first-fruits of His creatures—the body of Christ, wherewith He influences and blesses, whereby He guides and controls all things. Even over angels they shall rule: even unto powers and principalities more ancient and majestic than our race He shows forth by them the good pleasure of His will and the fulness of

His counsel and love. And the material creation which God hath made in Jesus Christ He hath also given unto His Son, that Jesus, through the glorified church, and by the angels in heavenly places, as well as through Israel and the nations dwelling on earth, should be glorified in the whole realm, which is His portion and His inheritance. How rich is our adorable Jesus! The blessed Lord, when He was upon the cross, had nothing. He had not where to lay His head; even His very garments were taken from Him. He was buried in a grave which belonged not to Him or to His family. On earth He was poor to the very last; none so absolutely poor as He. He rose again, and then declared that all power is *given* unto Him by the Father in heaven and in earth. He has appointed Him the "heir of all things." As man, He is to inherit all things; as Jesus, God and man in one person. All angels, all human beings upon the earth, all powers in the universe, when asked, "Who is Lord of all?" will answer, "Jesus, the Son of Mary." Our poor earth, Bethlehem-Ephratah, little amidst the thousands of this world, has been chosen that out of us should come He who is the heir of all things.

"All things." Nothing shall be lost. You remember that apparently startling word in the parable of the talents, "Take from him that hath the one talent, and give it unto him that hath the ten talents." What is the meaning of it? Whatever has been dispensed in the kingdom of grace—whatever seed has gone forth from the divine sower—whatever thought, whatever beauty, whatever element that is valuable, and good, and true—can never be lost. The unfaithfulness of man will never lose it to Jesus and to His beloved church. It must remain in the family; it must be secure and permanent. The one talent that the unfaithful steward did not use is not to be wasted and to be lost unto the commonwealth; but it is to enrich the chosen people; for all things are given unto Jesus. He has appointed Him heir of all things.

And lest any one should mistake or misinterpret the truth of God, as if any passage in Scripture encouraged the hope that all beings should be finally brought unto happiness and into the love of God, let us remember that the "all things" includes also that dark and fearful region of which we know so little (enough only to be filled with terror and dismay)—that awful region where the light and the love of God can never penetrate, where there is uttermost darkness. Even under the earth, in hell, in the abyss, Jesus has power. (Phil. ii.) He has power over death, and shall ultimately destroy it. He has power over Satan, and shall ultimately bruise him under our feet, banish him and imprison him where he can no more send forth the influences of sin and of injury. And all everywhere—friends and foes, saved and lost—shall acknowledge that Jesus is Lord; for He who has power in heaven and on earth has also the keys of Hades and of death. He is "appointed heir of all things."

All things are His. And this is so natural; because, in the second place, God has made "all ages," or "all worlds,"* by Him. It is natural that He who is the Alpha should also be the Omega. Scripture teaches us creation as the work of the triune God. God is triune, and therefore in everything that God does we behold the Father, the Son, and the Holy Ghost. You read, in the first article of the creed, of "God, the Creator of heaven and earth;" in the second, of Jesus as the Redeemer; in the third, of the Holy Ghost. But as in Jesus, the Redeemer, we must behold the Father, even as we receive through Him the Holy Ghost; as when we speak of the Holy Ghost we must behold the Father and the Son, of whom the Spirit testifies, and by whom

* "By *αἰῶνες* ages is meant the same as by the 'all things.' Scripture has various modes of expressing the idea of the universe. In the Old Testament there is no comprehensive word; there the two great divisions are mentioned heaven and earth. In the New Testament we have the terms—*creation* (κτίσις, Mark x. 6; xiii. 19; 2 Peter iii. 4; Rev. iii. 14), the world being viewed as created by God; all things (1 Cor. viii. 6; xv. 27) as the totality of all finite being, *ages*, or (αἰῶνες) as that which exists and moves in time. The most common expression is kosmos, but without reference to the classical idea of an artistic work."—KAHNIS' *Dogmatik*, i. 247.

He is sent; so when we think of the Creator, we must not think merely of the Father, but we must think of the Word by whom and the Spirit through whom all things were made. "The Word was with God," equal with God, and in love and continual intercourse and communion with the Father. And this Word was the beginning of the creation of God (Rev. iii.; Col. i.), Himself eternal and uncreated; that is to say, in the Son of God all the creation was planned and summed up from all eternity. In Him was life; in Him was light; and God in Him beheld all things that were to come into existence. He is bef re all things (not merely as before and above time, but) as the idea and cause of all things. He is that eternal wisdom of which we read in the book of Proverbs, which was with God before the foundations of the world were laid. God has made all things by Christ according to Christ, and for Christ. What more natural, then, that He by whom and in whom all things were made should be also the inheritor of all things?

(3) But the apostle goes still further. Before all history He is "the brightness of the Father's glory, and the express image of His being." Wherever He looks He sees Christ, the light. Without Christ, there is darkness. Think of the end of history, and you are lost in amazement; think of the beginning of the world, and you are

lost in ignorance; think of before the beginning, and you are altogether lost in an element transcendent and incomprehensible, because it is not for our finite minds to contemplate such wondrous heights until the heavenly, divine light of revelation comes to our aid. And who is the light? Christ is the light. The eternal, infinite God reveals *Himself* in Christ. The Son is the light, which maketh manifest; *God* is manifest in Him. Christ is "the brightness of His glory, and the express image of His being." By the glory of God, His own inapproachable, infinite light is understood.* We must not imagine that Jesus Christ is the light illumining something which is not light; for God is light. The Father is light, yet not to us without the mediation of the light, which is Christ. Without Christ *He* is darkness by excess of brightness. It is because that Sun is so exceeding glorious, so exceeding bright,

* **ἀπαύγασμα**, occurs only in this passage. (Compare 2 Cor. iv. 6; Col. i. 15.) In Christ we behold Him, whom none can see. But Christ is not merely a reflection of the Father, but is Himself light. God covers Himself with light, as with a garment; but the apostle speaks here of the essential glory of God, which appears to us in the person of His Son. The two aspects of truth, that the Son is equal with the Father, and that the Son is begotten of the Father, are expressed in the old creed "Light of light." The Father hath life in Himself, and hath given unto the Son to have life in Himself. (John v.) "Who is so void of understanding as to doubt concerning the eternal being of the Son? for where has one seen light without effulgence?" (ATHANASIUS) "The Sun is never seen without effulgence, nor the Father without the Son." (THEOPHYLACT.)

so exceedingly unbearable in its majesty, that it shines forth in another sun—and yet not another, but one with Him—which God, in His wonderful wisdom and power, hath given unto all worlds; that in this sun they may behold the brightness, the effulgence, the outflow of His glory. The glory of the God of Israel appeared between the cherubim; the tabernacle itself was called the glory; and when the tabernacle was removed, God's people exclaimed, "Ichabod"—the glory has departed. These were symbols. but when Jesus was born of the Virgin Mary, we beheld the glory of the only-begotten—the glory of God in the face of His Son Jesus Christ.*

And this brightness of the glory is the express, substantial, true, living image of His being; so that he that seeth the Son seeth the Father. In Jesus we behold infinite power, wisdom, goodness, holiness, compassion, truth. All things that are

* Compare Ezek. i. 26 and 28, x. 4, xliii. 2: Exod. xxiv. 16; where glory of the Lord appears evidently to be a person. Thus the Messianic promise is often expressed, as in Isaiah xl. 5: "The glory of Jehovah shall be revealed." In Exod. xxiv. 16, after stating that the glory of Jehovah abode upon mount Sinai. the verse continues, "And *He* called unto Moses." Notice also (Exodus xxxiii. 19) the request of Moses, "Show me thy glory," is answered "I will make *all my goodness* pass before thee. This harmonises beautifully with the Scripture teaching, that in the Son, the Saviour, glory is beheld, as the full manifestation of *grace;* as, for instance, "The Word was made flesh and *tabernacled* among us, and we beheld His glory, the glory of the only begotten of the Father, full of grace and truth."

in the Father are in the Son. The divine substance is revealed to us in the Son, who is the image of the invisible God. It is as the Son that the eternal life, which was with the Father, was manifested unto us. He who declares unto us God, whom none hath seen, the Word, is God (John i.), He is truth, substance ; and the beloved disciple testifies of Him : He is the true God and eternal life.

And as the Lord Jesus is the heir, the end and consummation of all things and the beginning of all things, and the eternal Word before all things, the apostle Paul tells us (4) that throughout the course of history, in providence, he beareth all things with the word of his power.* If it was not for Jesus and for the atonement, if it was not for the Lamb foreordained from the foundation of the world, the history of this world would never have been continued after the fall of man. The reason why God in patience and long-suffering continues the ages, delays judgment, and sends forth the gracious and life-sustaining influences of His Spirit to arrest the process of decay and disintegration ushered in by sin, is that Jesus the Lord is the restorer ; and it is the good pleasure of the Father's will to reconcile in Him all things to Himself, having made peace through the blood of His Cross. But not merely are all

* "The Son of God is a person ; for He has the word." (BENGEL.)

things upheld for the sake of Christ, but also through and in Him. He by whom all things were made is the life of all things. "My Father worketh hitherto, and I also work." He is the inherent energy, truth and beauty of all things. He is as it were the spirit, the symmetry, the logic and substance of all that exists. By Him princes rule and senators decree justice. In Him every truth is rooted. By Him everything that is firm stands. By Him all things are continued; for He is the Word of God—the expression of the eternal thoughts and truths of the Most High.

Although the history of Israel is in many respects unique, yet it is also to be viewed as a specimen of the history of all mankind. If we had an inspired record of the history of nations, we should see that in all history Christ is the centre and the moving as well as the upholding power. Moses saw from the beginning that the heathen would not possess this light of knowledge, and would ascribe to themselves what is manifestly only the work of Jehovah. (Deut. xxxii. 27–38.) Thus it happened literally in the case of Ashur, which ought to have recognised the hand of Jehovah in their victory over the surrounding nations and their gods, as well as over Israel and Juda, but who ascribed glory to themselves, and boasted in their praise. (Isaiah x. 8–15.) The examples of Nebuchadnezzar, Darius, and Cyrus show how the heathen might have traced the guidance of Jehovah in their own history."* It is easy for us to see how the great victories of the Greeks, by which they conquered the Eastern Power, before which the whole world trembled, how the establishment of the Roman Empire, and the unity and communication thereby established among many nations—how all the great movements of the past were subservient to the spread of Christ's gospel and the gathering of His church. All nations must be evangelised (Matt. xxiv. 14); and hence doors, which for centuries seemed hopelessly closed, are opened through events which apparently are quite secular in origin and spirit, but which are only instruments in the hands of Him who openeth, and no man shutteth. †

It is the Lord Jesus who is moving all things, carrying on by His wisdom and power the development and progress of all things, restraining and overruling, guiding and blessing, that the purpose of God may be accomplished, and that ultimately the kingdom may come.

Christ is Lord of all The whole universe centres in Him. A star appears at the time of the Messiah's advent. The sun loses his splendour

* BAUMGARTEN, *Apostelgeschichte*, i. 350.

† Think, for instance, of the way in which China, only a few years ago, was opened to the Christian missionaries.

when Jesus Christ dies upon the cross. There shall be again wonders and signs in the heavens when the Son of man shall come in power. In the material world we know that there have been many and great cycles of development. And both science and revelation teach us to look forward to a new earth. It is the Lord Jesus who shall make all things new. And all developments are borne up and moved by the word of His power. Oh, I know that the general conception which the world has of Jesus is that He is Lord of a spiritual realm, of thought and sentiment, bishop and head of ministers and pastors for edifying souls! But the world does not know that He is moving all things by the word of His power; that all politics, all statesmanship, all history, all physics, all art, all science, everything that is—all that has substance, truth, beauty, all things apart from that cancer of sin which has attached itself to it, consist by Jesus the Son of God.

Now, when the apostle has given us this idea of the wonderful glory of the Lord Jesus, the Son whom God has appointed Heir of all things, by whom He has made the worlds, who is "the brightness of His glory, and the express image of His being," who "upholdeth" and moveth "all things by the word of His power," He continues by stating something still more marvellous. Why has this wonderful and glorious being, in whom all things are summed up, and who is before all things the Father's delight and the Father's glory; why has this infinite light, this infinite power, this infinite majesty, come down to our poor earth? For what purpose? To shine? To show forth the splendour of His majesty? To teach heavenly wisdom? To rule by His just and holy might? No! He came *to purge our sins.* What height of glory! what depth of abasement! Infinite is His majesty, and infinite is His self-humiliation, and the depth of His love. What a glorious Lord! And what an awful sacrifice of unspeakable love, to purge our sins by Himself!

Sin has brought Him down from heaven. Our defilement has drawn Him from the height of His glory. Oh, what an expression, what a climax! "Who being the brightness of His glory, and the express image of His being, and upholding all things by the word of His power, when He had by Himself *purged our sins.*"

Sin may be viewed as a transgression of God's good, just, and holy law, deserving punishment. and bringing down the curse of God. Sin may be viewed as a disease unto death which requires healing. Sin is also defilement, and this view seems both the deepest and the most painful. Her perhaps we see most clearly and feel most painfully the difficulty, the utter impossibility, as far as man or angel is concerned, of being delivered from sin, and brought nigh unto the source of life, love, and blessedness.

Sin is a great and heavy burden. It is a departure from the Father's house into a far country. It is ingratitude and rebelliousness, yea, even hatred of God. Power can lift and remove a burden. Compassion can seek the wayward and lost sheep, and follow it across hill, and moor, and wilderness until it finds it. Grace can stoop to declare unto an enemy the message of peace and good will. But sin is *defilement.* It is that which is loathsome to God, which fills His inmost being with repulsion. Think of our sins as defilement. Think of their number, of their heinousness! Who will remove this fearful and utte ly loathsome iniquity which separates us hopelessly and infinitely from God in His holy and righteous love? Who will touch the leprosy? Who can take it out of the way, and cleanse the sinners, so that they appear pure and spotless in God's sight? The Son of God came to make the purification of our sins; and this, oh marvel of marvels! by Himself. Not like the high priest in Israel, offering something as a sacrifice; not with the blood, the life of another, but by Himself. He came into contact with this sin. He was the only one who could properly understand the true nature, depth, and guilt of sin. God of God, Son of the Father, He perfectly sympathized with the Father in His loathing and abhorrence of sin; but having befriended us, and having become one with us, He could not bear the thought of our being lost. So this loathsomeness of our iniquity, as loathsome to Jesus as to the Father, He takes upon Himself, as Joshua the high priest is seen by the prophet Zechariah. Jesus, perfect in His love to the holy and righteous Father, perfect in His love to the sinful and guilty people whom He came to save, with infinite hatred of sin and with infinite love of the sinner, enters, alone and unassisted, into that awful wilderness where, as our substitute and sin-bearer, He feels the Father's face turned away from Him. As the expression of His agony, in which faith and love endured all things and triumphed, He utters the cry, "My God, my God, why hast thou forsaken me?" Then Jesus the Son of God purged by Himself our sins.

The manner and power of this purification form the subject of this whole epistle. But in this short expression, "By Himself He purged our sins," all is summed up. By Himself: the Son of God, the eternal Word in humanity. Himself: the priest, who is sacrifice, yea, altar, and everything that is needed for full and real expiation and reconciliation. Here is fulfilled what was prefigured on the day of atonement, when an atonement was made for Israel, to cleanse them from all sin, that they may be clean from all their sins before the Lord. (Lev. xvi. 30.) Thus our great High Priest saith unto us, Ye are clean this day before God from all your sins. He is the fulfilment and reality, because He is the Son of God. "The blood of Jesus Christ His Son cleanseth us from all sin." (1 John i. 7.) The church is purchased by the blood of Him who is God. (Acts xx. 28, with His own blood.) Behold the perfection of the sacrifice in the infinite dignity of the incarnate Son!*

Sin is taken away. Oh, what a wonderful thing is this! When once you see that Jesus the Son of God died upon the cross, and purged your sins, and that because of His obedience unto death God hath exalted Him at His right hand, that, having effected by Himself this purification, He entered into heavenly glory, you have no more conscience of sin. You do not require day by day, as it were, to receive the forgiveness of your sins. You have been washed, you have been made clean, you have received full absolution and remission. Nay, more. In the heavenly sanctuary where Jesus is, sin no more can rise; and as you were crucified and buried with Him, so you are raised with Him, and seated together

* Although the addition *by Himself* might at first sight seem superfluous, the thought being already indicated by the medial form ποιησάμενος, yet this full and emphatic declaration is most frequent in the apostolic writing, and both befitting the importance of the subject as well as confirmatory to our faith. (Com. 1 Peter ii. 24.)

with Him in heavenly places. You need only to confess day by day, and with great humility, and contrition and sorrow, your continual transgressions and trespasses, that your feet may be washed. " He that is washed needeth not save to wash his feet, but is clean every whit: and ye are clean." But conscience of sin you have no longer. And although, as Christ becomes clearer and dearer, we see and feel more our sinfulness and unworthiness, although with increasing sorrow and mourning we confess our unbelief and ingratitude, we have no longer conscience of sin, the conscience is free from the burden, and purified from the defilement of sin. As forgiven and accepted, as pure and spotless, as worshippers within the holiest of all, we appear before God: in the light of His love we behold, and acknowledge our sin.

Christ, the Son of God, the Lamb that was slain, is our High Priest, our Righteousness.

What other—man-invented and appointed—priest will intrude here? What other sacrifice can be mentioned? What works, offerings, or tears of our own can be thought of? Jesus, the Son of God, the Son of man, *by Himself* hath cleansed us from our sins.

The apostle has thus spoken of the greatness of Christ. Why does Jesus reveal His majesty and His glory? Not that we should tremble, and not merely that we should reverence and adore, but that our hearts should be drawn out to Him in love. The wo ds of Jesus Himself in Matthew xi. are quite a parallel to our passage. Jesus first shows that no man knoweth the Father but the Son, and no man knoweth the Son but the Father, and that all things are given into His hands. Why does He say this? Why does He, as it were, exalt Himself, and reveal His dignity, and His divine authority over all creation? It is only that He may embrace us in His arms; it is only that He may add immediately, "Come unto me, all ye that are weary and heavy laden, and I will give you rest." Oh, the more majestic and glorious Jesus appears to us, the sweeter will be our peace, and the more childlike our confidence! This great, this infinite, this glorious Jesus was attracted by your very sin, and by your very guilt, and by your very helplessness. It was to purge our iniquities that He came down from heaven. Let us know, that we have obtained mercy, and that we have received the forgiveness of our sins, even through the redemption by the blood of Christ. Let us know it, that henceforth we may no longer be the servants of sin, that henceforth we may no longer walk in darkness; but, being delivered from all fear, and brought nigh unto God in Jesus, we may walk in love even as the Saviour God has loved us, and that we who have obtained mercy may show in our daily walk that we are merciful, forgiving one another, and forbearing one another, and introducing into every branch of our life and every sphere of our activity the new principle of love, even the holy, forgiving, and renewing love of God. Amen.

CHAPTER III.

CHRIST ABOVE THE ANGELS.

HEB. i. 3-6.

"WHEN He had by Himself purged our sins, He sat down on the right hand of the Majesty on high; being made so much better than the angels, as He hath by inheritance obtained a more excellent name than they. For unto which of the angels said He at any time, Thou art my Son, this day have I begotten Thee? And again, I will be to Him a Father, and He shall be to me a Son? And again, when He bringeth in the first-begotten into the world, He saith,* And let all the angels of God worship Him."

* Literally, when He shall have brought in again the first-begotten into the habitable earth. The time is future; and the place, not the world in general, but this earth of ours, which is the chosen sphere, where Christ is to be manifested and to reign.

The opening verses of this epistle contain, as it were, a summary of doctrine.* They set forth the glory of the Son of God. We behold Him as the Christ, the true *Prophet*, in whom is the perfect and ultimate revelation of God; the true *Priest*, not merely fulfilling all that was prefigured by Aaron (who purged by Himself our sins), but also fulfilling that which was prefigured by Melchizedec, *king* of righteousness, at Salem, seated in heavenly glory, and crowned with majesty at the right hand of the Power on high, exalted above all angels and principalities. We behold in these verses the nature of Christ. He is the Son, the brightness of the Father's glory, and the express image of the Father's being. We behold the work of the Son: by Him all worlds were created; by Him all things are upheld; by Him the atonement was made; and as He is appointed the heir of all things, history shall find its consummation in His manifestation and kingdom. And here

* They contain a summary of the first chapter and the germ of all truths expounded in this epistle. The following analysis of Bengel is useful. "His Majesty is set forth (1) *Absolutely* by the very name 'Son,' and by three glorious predicates, 'Whom He hath appointed,' 'By whom He made the worlds,' 'Who sat down on the right hand of the Majesty on high;' thus His course is described from the beginning of all things till He reached the goal (*vv.* 2, 3). (2) *Relatively*, in comparison with the angels (*v.* 4): the *confirmation* of this follows, and the very name 'Son' is proved at verse 5; the 'heirship,' verses 6–9; the 'making the worlds,' verses 10–12; the 'sitting at the right hand' of God, verses 13, 14."

we behold also the exaltation and the future glory of the incarnate Son, given unto Him as the fruit of His obedience. He is seated at the right hand of the Father, and all things are put in subjection under Him.

Is it more wonderful to see the Son of God in Bethlehem as a little babe, or to see the Son of Man at the right hand of the Father? Is it more marvellous to see the Counsellor, the Wonderful, The mighty God, The Prince of Peace, the everlasting Father, a child born unto us, and a Son given unto us—or to see the Son of Man, and in Him the dust of earth, seated at the right hand of God? The High Priest entered once a year into the holy of holies; but who would have ventured to abide there, or to take up his position next to the Cherubim, where the glory of the Most High was revealed? But Jesus, the Son of Man, ascended, and by His own power, and in His own right, as well as by the appointment of the Father, He is enthroned, crowned with glory and majesty. On the wings of omnipotent love He came down from heaven; but to return to heaven, omnipotence and love were not sufficient. It was comparatively easy (if I may use this expression of the most stupendous miracle) for the Son of God to humble Himself, and to come down to this earth; but to return to heaven, it was necessary for Him to be baptized with the baptism of suffering, and to die the death upon the accursed tree. Not as He came down did He ascend again; for it was necessary that He who in infinite grace had taken our position should bear and remove our burden and overcome our enemies. Therefore was His soul straitened to be baptized with His baptism; and therefore, from the first moment that He appeared in Jerusalem, He knew that the temple of His sacred body was to be broken, and He looked forward to the decease which He should accomplish on that mount. Not as He came did He ascend again; for He came as the Son of God; but He returned not merely as the Son of God, but as the Son of God *incarnate*, the Son of David, our brother and our Lord. Not as He came did He ascend again; for He came alone, the Good Shepherd, moved with boundless compassion when He thought of the lost and perishing sheep in the wilderness; but He returned with the saved sheep upon His shoulder, rejoicing and bringing it to a heavenly and eternal home. He went back again, not merely triumphing, but He who had gone forth weeping, bearing precious seed, who Himself had been sown, by His sacrifice unto death, returned, bringing His sheaves with Him. There had been given unto Him in His resurrection the Bride, the Church; she was raised with Him to be seated with Himself in heavenly places. It was when He had by Himself purged our sins that He sat down at the right hand of God; by the power of His blood He entered into the holy of holies; as the Lamb slain God exalted Him, and gave Him a name which is above every name.

"The Father said unto Him, Sit thou at my right hand." But it is equally true that the Lord Jesus Himself ascended, entered into the most holy sanctuary, and took His place at the right hand of God. He *sat down:* this expression shows that it was not merely the exaltation by the Father, but His own act and right; for Scripture is careful to teach us not only the subordination of the Son, but also His equality with the Father. Thus are we taught that the Father raised up Jesus, and also that Jesus had power to lay down His life, and He had power to take it again: "The Good Shepherd giveth His life for the sheep." "No man taketh it from me, but I lay it down of myself. I have power to lay it down, and I have power to take it again."

For this purpose the Son of God came down to earth, that through suffering, and after having purged our sins, He might return to glory, that in His transfigured humanity He should have the glory, which as the Son He had with the Father before the foundation of the world. The cross was the only way to the throne. The session at the right hand of God is spoken of in Scripture *exclusively* as of the Messiah, the Son of David, the Lord, who is God and man. And now, the God-Man, the Son of God incarnate, Jesus who is the Christ, being exalted to the right hand of the Father, the apostle teaches us that God has given to Him a more excellent name than the angels, and that He has obtained this name by inheritance. He does not speak here merely of the Son of God in His deity; for if He spoke of Him as the Son of God merely, would it not only be superfluous, but would it not be also blasphemous and irreverent, to speak of Him who is Lord over all as greater than the angels? But when he speaks of Jesus the Son of God and the Son of Man, then is it necessary, salutary, and comforting for us to know that this Jesus, who was born of the Virgin Mary, formed in fashion as a man, in all things tempted like as we are, yet without sin, that Jesus in His humanity is now exalted, and that a name is given to Him above all angels. We who live in the West think a name of slight importance; but God always taught His people to attach great importance to names. The first petition in the Lord's Prayer is, "Hallowed be Thy name;" and all the blessings and privileges which God bestowed upon Israel are summed up in this, that God revealed unto them His name. The name is the outward expression and the pledge and seal of all that a person really and substantially is; and when it says that the Son of God has received a higher name than the angels, it means that, not only in degree, but in kind, He *is* high above them. He has obtained it by inheritance; that is to say, God decreed from all eternity to give that name unto Him, as the Son and Mediator.

In the book of Revelation we are told that the Son has a name which no man knoweth. There is an infinite, incomprehensible depth and mystery in the Son as there is in the Father; and as no man knoweth the Father save the Son, so no man knoweth the Son but the Father. But an excellent name, a name which is above every name, has been revealed unto us; and such is the loving-kindness of God, that Christ's highest name and His sweetest name are identical; even *Jesus*, "who saves His people from their sins."

Now, in order to prove this truth, the apostle reminds the Hebrews of a number of passages in which the Messiah is spoken of. And here let us briefly consider the method according to which the quotations are given. We must notice that the author of the Epistle to the Hebrews always quotes the Scriptures *as the Word of God.* He does not say, 'as David says,' or 'as Isaiah says,' or 'as Moses says,' but whenever he quotes from Moses and the prophets he always quotes their words as the words of God, or "as the Holy Ghost saith," or "as One saith;" because among the Hebrews it was well known and firmly believed that "all Scripture was given by inspiration of God," and that every word of God is pure. Our Saviour, when He quotes the Scriptures, sometimes says "the Scripture," sometimes "the prophets," sometimes "David," sometimes "Isaiah." And so also the apostles do not always introduce quotations from Scripture in the same manner. The human and the divine character of the word must both be acknowledged and remembered. According to the spiritual condition of the persons addressed, and according to the purpose of the speaker, is the manner in which the words are introduced as God's or the words of Moses, &c. Sometimes the words, which are manifestly the utterance of Jehovah, are quoted: Well doth Isaiah say, and Isaiah is very bold, and this both by the Lord Jesus and the apostles. So fully and freely is the human channel in all its individuality and spontaneity acknowledged, though the divine authority and the inspiration of the Holy Ghost are always maintained and presupposed. Our Lord appeals even to the books of Moses as "your law;" when Israel does not recognise the Word incarnate, He refers them to the document which they held as their own, and in which they trusted, not knowing its power and spirit. To him who has not the word abiding in him, the books of Isaiah, Matthew, Paul, are simply the writings of these men. To us they are the word of God. In this epistle all quotations are traced direct to the Lord Himself, thus corresponding with, and carrying out, the key-note struck in the first verse of this epistle: "God, who at sundry times and in divers manners spake in time past unto the fathers by the prophets, hath in these last days spoken unto us by His Son."

Jesus, after His resurrection, opened unto His disciples the Scriptures. He spoke of Moses and of the prophets, and specially mentioned the Psalms; and we read, "Then opened He their understandings that they might understand the Scriptures;" and after the day of Pentecost the Holy Ghost brought all things to their remembrance, all the words and instructions He had given to them; and we see from the Acts of the Apostles that they saw, as it were, the whole edifice of Scripture in the grandeur and symmetry of its structure. Now they were full of light. These very men who before were not able to understand what they saw with their own eyes, still less to comprehend His words, remembered and understood now that all these things happened that the Scripture might be fulfilled. (John ii. 22; xx. 9.) The infallible instructions of the Son of

Man were brought back to their remembrance by the Great Teacher's aid. And shall we not therefore attach the greatest value and the greatest importance, as well as the most implicit and docile faith, to the explanations given in the Acts of the Apostles, in the Epistles, and in the Revelation, of quotations from the Scriptures? We are bound by a blessed tie to their interpretations.*

David is called a "patriarch" on account of the position which he held in the history of Israel; a "prophet" because, as he tells us, "The Spirit of the Lord spake by me, and His word was in my tongue." (2 Sam. xxiii. 2.) But he was also a type in his own character and history of that One who was to come. Many people read the Scriptures without considering the perspective of Scripture. It appears to them as a picture, so to speak, upon a flat surface, in which there is no perspective; they do not see the gradual unfolding and development; they do not perceive the historical basis upon which prophecies rest, and the varying shades and tints which their peculiar position and distance in reference to the

* Notwithstanding many plausible objections to and limitations of this assertion, I cannot think and say otherwise. I believe also in the inexhaustible, many-sided, and eternal meaning of Scripture above the capacity and measure of the prophet, or of any individual or any period of the church. This has been expressed by Stier as the "Vollsinn," and by another in the quaint and somewhat paradoxical sentence—Whatever Scripture *can* mean, it *does* mean.

fulfilment gives them. They do not remember that the Lord Jesus Christ had His goings forth from of old, from everlasting; that His condescension goes back far into the ages, and that the whole Jewish nation was, as it were, the mother out of which the Messiah proceeded. Thus their history not only *contained* prophecy, but their history *is* prophecy. The evangelist Matthew gives us the key to the whole Jewish history in the first chapter, when he tells us that the infant Jesus was taken by Joseph and His mother Mary into Egypt, "that it might be fulfilled which was spoken of the Lord by the prophet, saying, Out of Egypt have I called my Son." Israel and Israel's history are typical; they are instalments as well as shadows of the great history.

It is very wonderful how, in God's ways, fixed necessity and liberty go hand in hand. In a way which we cannot understand, but which we can admire and adore, God's counsel must stand fast; while His people act and move in perfect liberty, and His enemies are left to freedom and dealt with in patience and justice. From all eternity Jesus is appointed the Son of David; but the development of history goes through liberty, the exercises of faith, of hope, of patience, of love, of joy, of suffering. Everything that is human is in sweetest harmony with that unfailing and unchangeable purpose of God's love which must surely come to pass, even as in the greatest sin—the crucifixion of our Lord—the determinate counsel of God was fulfilled; and yet it was "with wicked hands," and of their own free choice, that the Jews crucified the divine and loving Saviour. This same blending of liberty and necessity is seen in the history of the patriarch. By a free choice of faith Abram, who was chosen to be the father of Israel, and of all who are blessed in the Messiah, left his father's house, and followed God. By faith he received the promise of Isaac, and, as a reward of his implicit confidence in the truth of God and in his death-conquering power, the eternal promise was renewed and sealed to him. And the inward clinging of the soul to the word of the Redeemer God, which amidst many struggles and failings characterized Jacob, who is Israel, breaks forth, interrupting the inspired (objective) predictions, when on his death-bed he exclaims, I have waited for thy salvation. Quietly and gently God fulfilled His counsel, hidden as yet to David, when the son of Jesse was taken from the sheep-folds. He did not know the wonderful significance of that morning when Samuel came to his father's house, and all his brothers passed before him, and David, in the simplicity and unconsciousness of his youth, was chosen and anointed to be king over Israel.

It took some time—it took many years of bitter sorrow, of painful conflicts—before the meaning of that act was explained to David himself. And at last, when through all the varied and profound discipline which he underwent, and by the inward teaching and the heart-renewing work of the Holy Ghost, God brought out in David, according to his limited and human measure, what in perfection is only in the Son and Lord of David, he went forth a true king of Israel—a man after the heart of God, strong in faith and love to the Most High, gentle and meek toward men, anointed by the Spirit, upheld by loyal and free Israelites, who loved him intensely and were willing to die for him, and yet not lifting up his heart above his brothers, but desiring to rule with the righteousness of meekness, and to show forth judgment and truth; to found his kingdom upon the word of God, upon knowledge and light, justice and love, concord and brotherly affection; building his dominion more upon the hundred golden pillars (as we might call them) of the Psalms, founding his throne on the firm foundation of his union with all the godly in the land, of their harmony in the praise and joy of Jehovah. Think of him thus as a parable, as it were. Think of this shepherd king, by the grace of God and the loving and free choice of God-fearing men—a king whose power rests upon invisible pillars, not upon outward authority, and pomp, and splendour. He gathered round about him not that which was high and lofty and lifted up; he looked not, like Saul, to that which seemed strong and mighty, but to the meek of the earth, the excellent, who put their trust in Jehovah, those who knew how to praise and to serve the God of their fathers. Thus was David a true king after the heart and mind of God; and when he thought of building a house of God, then God sent unto him the prophet Nathan, and confirmed to him the promise, that as he was king over Israel, so his seed was to rule after him; that the throne of David was to be an everlasting throne. Of that seed of David it was also said that God would be a Father unto him,* and he should be God's son. David is quite overcome with the condescension

* 2 Samuel vii. A very important chapter; commencement of a new phase of Israel's history; one of those turning-points with which commences a new period. The promise refers primarily to Solomon, who built the temple, who reigned in peace, and who extended the kingdom in manifested and acknowledged glory. The typical character of Solomon is set forth clearly in Psalm lxxii., where the Messiah, the Prince of Peace, the Divine King and Lord is described, and his reign of truth and prosperity. In 1 Chron. xvii. 17 also it is evident that David knew the fulfilment was in the distant future: "Thou hast also spoken of thy servant's house for a great while to come, and hast regarded me according to the estate of a man of high degree, O Lord God." Luther translates, "Thou hast regarded me in der Gestalt eines Menschen, der in der Höhe Gott der Herr ist," in the appearance of a man, who in the height is God the Lord. Stier renders, "And this is the manner of a man, who is God the Lord."

and love of God, and, being filled with the Spirit, he saw that Solomon was not the completion of this prediction, and that he to whom God had thus promised to be a Father was to be One infinitely greater and higher than himself or his own children; that God spake of that One for whom all the fathers looked, and waited as the revelation and full realization of God's salvation. I may say of David as it was said of John the Baptist—"He was not that Light, but was sent to bear witness of that Light"—He was not that King, but was sent to witness and to prefigure that King—the Son of the Most High. And thus, in all the sufferings and exaltations of David, in all the events and experiences of his life, he felt and saw that the lowest and deepest foundation of his own life was the Messiah, Christ Himself; that his own sufferings were ultimately to be fulfilled in the Son, who was above all. And therefore it is that in the Psalms of David we find David; his very heart and soul, the man himself; but we find also Christ. David and Christ are completely identified. David, according to his limited measure, is an instalment of Christ. He is a type of Christ; and therefore that psalm which was an expression of David's experience, in which he cried, "My God, my God, why hast thou forsaken me?" is also the expression of the experience which no finite mind can fathom; the Lord Jesus on the cross utters these very words! What marvellous poetry is here, not in words merely, but in life and history! What wonderful condescension! He who is Jehovah, David's Lord, is mirrored forth by the son of Jesse. David's Son is none other than the Son of God, and He shall rule over Israel for ever. "I will give you the sure mercies of David." There is no other man in Scripture thus identified with Jesus Christ;* and therefore He is emphatically called "the Son of David." It is in this light that we must read the expressions quoted here by the apostle from the second psalm.

Most majestic is the book of Psalms. Very significant and striking is the commencement of this book, so grand and sweet, so precious to all the children of God, even as it was peculiarly near and dear to the Lord Jesus during His life on earth. The book of Psalms commences with two psalms, which have no superscription. The first chapters in the books of Scripture are often, as it were, the expressive announcement of the subsequent chapters; the countenance of the whole; the short, compressed key-note is struck; out of the abundance of the heart the inspired author seems to utter immediately the sum and substance of his commission.

In the first two psalms we have a summary of

* David therefore often stands for Messiah. Hosea iii. 5; Ezekiel xxxiv. 23, &c.

the whole book. The first word is 'Blessed,' and the conclusion of the second psalm is, "Blessed are all they that trust in Him."* For God's thoughts are always thoughts of love. And though by reason of our disobedience, and the corruption of our heart, we cannot obtain the blessing which the law promises to all who keep it (Psalm i.), the promise of David's son was given in order to bring unto us new and greater blessing through the marvels of redemption. (Psalm ii.) As the apostle Peter said, "Unto you first, God, having raised up His Son Jesus, sent Him *to bless you.*" All the thoughts and purposes of God toward His people are blessings.†

The psalmist represents in the second psalm all the world united against God; He describes their determined, inward, and zealous opposition to Him. He describes God in His holy calmness, in His quiet majesty. He has laid the foundation, He has ordered the method, rule, and

* Psalm i. was viewed as a prologue of the whole collection. Comp. Acts xiii. 33, where the words, "Thou art my Son," are quoted as the first psalm. The ancient Jewish view is expressed in the beautiful saying—The first psalm begins and ends with blessing. That is because the first and second psalms are one. The first psalm is didactic, a response, as it were, to the law of Moses (David's Bible); the second prophetic, Messiah's kingdom.

† Luther on Psalm ii. 7: "Here the whole law is abrogated, and the office of Christ most clearly and distinctly described. He teaches not what *we* are; for this the law doeth; but He teaches who *He* is, the Son of God, that we may receive Him, and use His gifts with rejoicing and delight."

triumph of His house from all eternity. He can afford to give centuries and thousands of years to His enemies to mature all their plans, to utter all their thoughts, to bring forth all their objections, and to try all their experiments. He is patient also, and long-suffering; not willing that any should perish, but that sinners should turn unto Him and live. But He has anointed His holy King. He has appointed One—that wonderful person, Who is His representative and the sceptre of His might—God and man, through Whom the power and the pleasure of the Lord are to be established on the earth. And this Son is now declaring to us the decree, the counsel according to the good pleasure of His will, the purpose which cannot be changed, the promise which standeth firm from eternity to eternity: "Thou art my Son; this day have I begotten Thee."

Now what this passage means is evident from the exposition given to us by the apostles. It refers to the resurrection of Jesus. He was the Son of God before the incarnation. We must ever hold fast the fundamental truth of the eternal, essential sonship of our Lord. It was the Son who was sent into the world, and given unto us by the Father. Thus Scripture teaches; and not that He who was sent and was born of the Virgin Mary thus and then became the Son. At the incarnation the Son of God became man. (Gal.

iv 4.) But the truth specially taught here is, that the Son of David, the Theocratic King, the Messiah, who is to subdue all ungodliness on the earth, and to exalt all who trust in Him, is "declared to be the Son of God with power."

Let us consider the apostolic interpretations of this psalm. In the book of Acts (xiii. 32) the apostle Paul, speaking of the resurrection, said: "And we declare unto you glad tidings, how that the promise which was made unto the fathers, God hath fulfilled the same unto us their children, in that He hath raised up Jesus again; as it is also written in the second psalm, Thou art my Son, this day have I begotten thee. And as concerning that He raised Him up from the dead, now no more to return to corruption, He said on this wise, I will give you the sure mercies of David." Here the general and comprehensive view is taken of Jesus as the Messiah and fulfiller of all God's promises; and the "to-day" of the second psalm is referred to the resurrection. In like manner the apostle writes to the Romans, with evident reference to our psalm: "His Son Jesus Christ our Lord, which was made of the seed of David according to the flesh; and declared to be the Son of God with power, according to the Spirit of Holiness, by the resurrection from the dead." Analysing now the comprehensive term Messiah into its constituent parts—Prophet, Priest, and

King—we notice, besides the above reference to His kingship, that Peter in his address to the Jews quotes the prophecy of Moses—"A Prophet shall the Lord your God *raise up* unto you of your brethren" (Acts iii. 22); even, as he says, that "God, *having raised up His Son Jesus*, sent Him to bless you." (*v.* 26.) And as to the priestly office, Paul declares that Christ glorified not Himself to be made a High Priest, but He that said unto Him, "Thou art my Son; this day have I begotten thee." *

Thus in the resurrection of the Lord Jesus, when as Messiah He was fully brought into His prophetic, priestly, and regal dignity, was fulfilled the word—"Thou art my Son." Unto which of the angels said God this at any time? What angel has a name like this name? What angel can be compared with our Lord, the Man Christ Jesus, who was crucified and liveth for evermore?

The apostle passes on to another passage, which has no reference to the first coming, but to Christ's

* In Rev. ii. 27 we see that the second psalm, though applying directly to the resurrection, extends to the time of the second advent, when Messiah shall declare the decree to the Gentiles. "Now" (Psalm ii. 10) the time of grace, "then" (*v.* 5) the day of judgment. Although the words are thus connected with the resurrection of Christ, we must still view them as referring also (implicitly and fundamentally) to the eternal, essential sonship. Both aspects, the eternal and historical, are found in the prophetic writings: Prov. viii. contains the germ of the doctrine of the eternal generation of the Son. "To-day" is thus viewed by the church fathers to refer to the timeless and eternal generation.

second advent, when God shall bring in again into the inhabited earth the First Begotten. The 97th Psalm speaks of the (return or) coming of Jehovah to the earth to subdue His enemies, and to be the rejoicing of His people.

The psalm commences with a call to the inhabitants of the land, and to all the earth, with the multitude of isles, to rejoice at the coming of the Lord Jehovah, who shall reign and deliver the godly, and manifest His glory. It is the advent in which, as Zechariah almost in the same words predicts, Jehovah shall be King over all the earth. (Zech. xiv.) The period between the first and second advent is not beheld by the prophetic psalmist. The world during this interval seeth Jesus no more. He is hid. The heavens contain Him, and only His people see Him by faith, and know His presence by the indwelling Spirit. He is ruling the world; but He is not known, not recognized. But God shall bring Him in again, He shall bring Him into sight and manifestation. Not as the only-begotten, mark; for as the only-begotten He came in His incarnation (John i.), but as the first-begotten; that is, as the risen Lord, the second Adam, the first-begotten of the dead, the first-born among many brethren. Thus the prophet is supplemented by the apostle. Jehovah, of whom the psalmist speaks, is identified by the apostle with the risen

Jesus, the Son of God. Now at His coming (the second, as we Christians know, not coincident with the first, as according to the prophetic perspective ancient Israel believed) the world is divided into the righteous, the upright in heart, who worship and love God; and idolaters, that serve graven images, and boast themselves of idols Just as in the Apocalypse we read the world is divided into the saints of God, and those who worship the beast and his image, and receive his mark upon their foreheads and in their hands.

The advent of Jehovah brings judgment and confusion to the idolaters, and a *harvest* of light and joy to the godly. (*v.* 11.)

Now, bringing in the glorified Son, God the Father, who alone has the right to command creatures to perform acts of worship and adoration, saith unto the angels, "Worship Him."*

Thus is humanity in the person of Messiah exalted far above any creature. Thus the consummation of all history, and the perfect manifestation of God's glory to the rejoicing adoration of angels and men, will be in the Lord Jesus, who is not ashamed to call us brethren, who is one with us by a link which can never be severed.

Who then is like unto Jesus? Who like Him

* The angels are mentioned frequently in connection with the second advent. (Matt. xvi. 27; xxv. 31; 1 Thess. iv. 16; 2 Thess. i. 17.)

is adorable? Holiness and goodness are worthy of adoration only in their *essence and source.* He, whom holy angels are called by God to worship, must be essential holiness, goodness, love—must be none other but the infinite and eternal, the ever blessed and coequal Son of the Most High.*

How near is Jesus unto us, although He is so high above us! This is the very reason why God has exalted Him. This is the reason why He is so high above everything, above all powers and dominions; that He who has all power and love may be visible and accessible; that every one may see Him, and draw near to Him; that out of the lowest depths we may behold Him; and that from the utmost corner of the land we may cry unto Him, and be saved. Jesus is exalted for the very purpose of being a Prince and a Saviour, to give repentance and remission of sins. If Jesus was not so high, would He be so nigh? He who is omniscient, omnipotent, all-wise, all-loving, whose sympathy is full of human tenderness, is in the holy of holies for the very purpose that He may succour, comfort, and uphold us during the days of our trial and sorrow, that He may be a present help in time of trouble. Jesus is exalted above all, that He may fill us with His

* We shall consider in our next lecture the reason why the apostle Paul institutes this comparison between the incarnate Son of God and the angelic creation.

power and love. He is high above us, that, looking unto Him, the author and finisher of faith, unto Him who through the cross entered into glory, seeing Him constantly above us, the Lamb in the midst of the throne, we may run with patience the race set before us. With all the holy angels and all the saints of God we look unto Him, we worship and rejoice as an old father of the German Church says—"Jesus is in heaven; therefore it is easy for a poor sinner to have his heart in heaven. Let Jesus dwell in the heart, and then heaven will be in the heart." Amen.

CHAPTER IV.

CHRIST ABOVE THE ANGELS.

HEB. i. 5–ii. 4.

I CONTINUE the argument of the apostle to prove that Jesus is exalted above the angels. He began with the second psalm, in which, based upon the promise which God gave unto David, and which is recorded in the second book of Samuel, the glory of the Messiah, as the omnipotent King of all nations, appointed and upheld by the Father, is described, founded as it is upon the eternal and essential Sonship which was manifested in His resurrection from the dead. Well known was this psalm among the Jews, and well understood was it that it spoke of the divine dignity of the Messiah; for it was in the light of this psalm that Nathanael, as soon as Jesus manifested Himself unto Him as the searcher of hearts, exclaimed, "Rabbi, thou art the Son of God;

thou art the King of Israel." It was on the basis of this psalm that the high priest adjured Jesus to tell him whether He was the Christ, the Son of the living God.* Nathanael and all Israelities knew that the Messiah, who was to be King, was to be in the dignity and glory of the Son of God. As in the second Psalm the Son of David is addressed in a way in which God never spoke to any of the angels, so in the 97th Psalm, which describes the coming, or in New Testament light the return, of Messiah to earth, He is said to be Lord and King, and all angels are commanded to worship Him. The 97th Psalm speaks of the advent of the Messiah, which is yet in the future, to which both the believing synagogue and the Church of the Lord Jesus Christ are looking, when He is to be manifested in great power, and to be acknowledged as King

* Hales says the sole application of this illustrious prophecy to the Messiah was the unquestionable doctrine of the primitive Jewish Church. He adds a few quotations: "Our masters deliver, that the blessed God said unto Messiah, Son of David (who is shortly to be revealed in our days), 'Ask of me somewhat, and I will give it thee,' as it is said in Psalm ii. 7, 8." The Midrash Tillim understands the Gentiles of Gog and Magog, and states that Messiah is styled "my Son," and not "a Son to me;" that is, absolutely and not relatively, as in Nathan's prophecy.

Jarchi affirms, that whatever is sung in this psalm our masters interpreted of Messiah the King; but "according to the sound of the words, and for the confusion of the heretics (*i.e.* Christians), it is convenient that we expound it of David."—From Visc. MANDEVILLE'S *Horæ Hebraicæ.*

of the whole earth. Fire and darkness go before Him, and He shall execute judgment upon the nations, and divide the idolaters from the faithful, and the wicked from the godly. For in this psalm the world is described as in the same condition as that referred to in the book of the Revelation. When Jehovah comes, the man who is to be the Lord and King of the whole earth (as is said also in Zechariah and all the prophets), then shall all idolaters be confounded, and they that are upright in heart shall enter into the harvest of light. And so in the book of Revelation, His own people are they who have not worshipped the beast and yielded to idolatry; whereas all the rest of the world shall have fallen away both from the Son and from the Father. In our own day, religious questions begin to concentre on this point—Is God the Creator? or is there no God? Men who deny that Jesus is the Son, begin to deny the Father also.

The apostle reminds us, that while Jesus is thus spoken of, as the Son, the angels are only the swift and penetrating messengers in obedience to the power and will of God. He proceeds to another psalm, the 45th, and he asks the question: "To which of the angels said He at any time, Thy throne, O God, is for ever and ever: a sceptre of righteousness is the sceptre of thy kingdom?" That 45th Psalm is unique among all the Psalms of David. It is the germ of the Song of Solomon. If there is a doubt whether the Song of Solomon refers to Jehovah in His covenant relation to His people, then it must likewise be doubtful whether this 45th Psalm refers to the Bridegroom, who is to be the divine Man, the Lord of Israel; and if not, it is impossible to explain how this psalm finds its way into a collection of hymns, whose great and constant theme is God as King and Lord of Israel and the nations. But we see from the opening verses that it is a mysterious psalm, and that here, as in all the Scriptures, we have to search and dig below the surface, that we may discover the hidden treasure of pure gold which rewards those who pray to behold the wonders of God's teaching.

The author of the psalm is himself astonished at the wonderful, beautiful, and multitudinous thoughts which rose within his heart, and looks upon them as given to him by a higher power, he feels that he is carried away by a mighty afflatus, by a powerful tide, that he is only the pen of a ready writer; and he begins to consider the thoughts which are *in* him, but not *of* him. His heart is overflowing with the abundance of the revelation which the Lord God is giving unto him. Then he beholds in the Spirit one who is beautiful and fair, a true and real man, yet free from all imperfection and all defilement; in whom there is that true beauty of holiness and uprightness which manifests itself in words of truth and grace, poured into His lips. And this holy and lovely One, although He belongs to the human race, is yet not of them, but stands quite by Himself, and towers high above them, even as heaven is above earth. He is One with us, yet above all the children of Adam. He is also the mighty One, El Gibbor, the mighty God, who (compare Isa. ix. 6) subdues all enemies by that meekness and righteousness which He introduces into the world. And because He loved righteousness and hated iniquity, therefore God anointed Him with the oil of gladness above His fellows; or, in New Testament language, "because He was obedient unto death, even the death of the cross, therefore God highly exalted Him." The Son of man is the Christ; He is anointed with the Holy Ghost, the oil of gladness, above all His equals. As He speaks also in the prophet Isaiah, "The Spirit of the Lord God is upon me, because He hath anointed me to preach the gospel to the poor; He hath sent me to heal the brokenhearted, to proclaim liberty to the captives; to give to them that mourn beauty for ashes, the oil of joy for mourning, the garment of praise for the spirit of heaviness." The psalm thus reveals unto us the mystery of the Trinity—the Son, God and man in one person, "fairer than any of the children of men," obedient unto death, exalted by the Father, and anointed by the Holy Ghost. God the Father thus addresses the Son of man—"Thy throne, O God, is for ever and ever; a sceptre of righteousness is the sceptre of thy kingdom." *

To which of the angels was ever language addressed as unto this One, who indeed is born of a woman, the Son of man, a descendant of David, who lived upon earth the servant of God, honouring the law of Moses, and obedient to all the commandments of God? But to Him the Father has given a throne and a sceptre for ever, and speaks to Him as His equal from all eternity unto all ages.

But the apostle continues by quoting another psalm. Christ is in all the psalms; they speak of Him. The divinity and humanity of the Lord are set forth in all the Scriptures. It is the delight of the Father, in all the Word, to honour the Son, even as it is the delight of the Son continually to

* There is abundant evidence to prove that the Jews applied this psalm to Messiah. Stier says: "We cannot enter into controversy with those who see in this psalm only a marriage song or hymn to an earthly king, without first discussing the general principles of Scripture faith. . . ." This psalm is not isolated in the Bible. (Comp. Isa. liv. 5; lxii. 5; Jer. iii. 1; Ezek. xvi. 8; Hosea and Canticles *passim;* John iii. 29; Matt. ix. 25; Matt. xxii. xxv.; Eph. v. 32; 2 Cor. xi. 2; Rev. xix. 21.)

Gibbor is a title of Messiah. He is mighty to save.

Compare also with verse 6 the Jewish tradition: "We have heard that Christ abideth for ever." (John xii. 34.)

point to the Father that we may see His glory. The apostle refers to the 102nd Psalm—a psalm which, without apostolic teaching, I doubt if any of us would have had the boldness so to apply; for in many respects it is the most remarkable of all the psalms—the psalm of the afflicted One while His soul is overwhelmed within Him in great affliction, and sorrow, and anxious fear. He has been righteous, He has been holy; but men persecute Him. He is forsaken, His tears are His meat day and night, and yet God had exalted Him. God had shown unto Him that He was His chosen One; God had prospered Him up to a certain point; He upheld Him, carried Him through, sustained and honoured Him, caused His work to prosper and His word to bring forth fruit. But then, instead of entering into glory, He felt that His path was shut up, that all His people forsook Him and rejected Him; that instead of light there was darkness; that instead of a throne there was the cross before Him. God had lifted Him up, given Him power, given Him the hearts of His people. God had for thirty-three years continually said unto Him, "Thou art my Son. Thou art my servant, whom I uphold; mine elect, in whom my soul is well pleased;" and at last, in the middle of His days, before His work was completed, He was to be cut off. Persecution and dismay, and the unbelief of the people, m.t Him; and His soul was "exceeding sorrowful, even unto death." The shadow of the cross fell into His heart, and His soul was straitened within Him.

Thus, in the 12th chapter of the gospel of John, we read that His soul was sorrowful in the anticipation of that hour, for the sake of which He had come into the world. Thus it was in the garden of Gethsemane, and yet He knew and believed that God would deliver Him. And when this afflicted One pours out His heart He says, "Thou wilt arise, and have mercy upon Zion. The time to favour her, the appointed time, will come." He rests with firm faith on the promises of God, in which light and glory are secured to Israel. God's counsel must stand, His counsel must be fulfilled. Then it is that God the Father replies to Him, "Thou, Lord, in the beginning hast laid the foundation of the earth; and the heavens are the works of thine hands."* Then it is that God the Father replies with this word of assurance to this afflicted, mourning, distressed One, reminding Him that although for a little season He has become a servant, and entered into darkness and sorrow, though He

* Stier: The Messiah receives here the mighty answer of God, 'It is impossible for Thee to succumb; for Thou art the Living One with me from all eternity.' Christ is here presented as Creator; He is Lord (Jehovah); the earth is His and the fulness thereof.

has humbled Himself, and feels like David, "I am a worm and not a man," yet is He none other but the Lord, the Word, the Creator of heaven and earth. He was in the beginning with the Father, when the word went forth from God to lay the foundations of the earth. By Him also the heavens were framed. He is the Eternal, the First and the Last, who shall remain the same for ever. Although the elements shall melt away, and the heavens and earth be moved; although the world in its present phase shall pass away and be put off like an old vesture, yet this suffering One is the Lord; He is the same, and His years fail not.*

How marvellous is this! how incomprehensible this union of divine and human, of eternity and time, sadness and omnipotence! Do not wonder that such language of anguish, faintness, and sorrow, of agonising faith, is attributed by the Holy Ghost to Jesus. Remember that the life of Jesus was a life of faith, a real, true, and earnest conflict;

* In *Horæ Hebraicæ*, already quoted, interesting extracts are given (pp. 100-102) to prove that the ancient Jews referred this psalm to Messiah and His days. On verse 27, "But thou art He," the Jews say that Ani and Attah and Hu, I and Thou and He, are names of God denoting three persons; and their anthem, publicly sung on the last day of their feast of tabernacles, is, "For thy sake, O our Creator Hosanna; for thy sake, O our Redeemer Hosanna; for thy sake, O our Seeker Hosanna!" as if, says Bishop Patrick, they beseeched the blessed Trinity to save them and send them help.

that "He is the author and finisher of faith;" and that, although He continually took firm hold of the promises of God, yet His feeling of sorrow, His sense of His utter dependence on God, His anxious looking forward to His last sufferings, all this was a reality. He gained the victory by faith; He knew that He was through suffering returning to the Father; He knew that as Son of man and Redeemer of His people He would be glorified with the glory which He had with the Father before the foundations of the world were laid. To which of the angels said God at any time, as He said to the meek and lowly Jesus, "Thou, Lord, in the beginning hast laid the foundations of the earth"?*

And lastly the apostle quotes the short but most comprehensive 110th Psalm. Of all the psalms it is most frequently quoted in the New Testament. Martin Luther says this is "Der Haupt Psalm"—the chief psalm, the head psalm, the psalm which was the greatest strength and consolation to him, as it ought to be to all God's people. "The Lord said unto my Lord, Sit thou at my right hand, until I make thine enemies thy footstool."

* Kurtz sums up the contrast between the angels and the Lord Jesus: (1) The angels are servants in the kingdom; the Son has a throne, and is therefore Ruler. (2) They work in the shape or power of the lower elements (wind and fire); He by the moral power of righteousness. (3) Their work is changing and transitory; Christ's rule immutable and eternal.

The Jews in the time of Jesus all knew that this psalm referred to the Messiah. There was not the slightest doubt about this. Hence our blessed Saviour asks them this question—How is it that David, speaking of the Messiah, in the Spirit, by the Holy Ghost, calls Him Lord, if He is his Son? Here was a dilemma. The 110th Psalm refers to the Messiah; how then does David call Him Lord? In three of the gospels is this passage quoted; and the question of our Saviour is so important and so much a leading central one that all the (synoptic) evangelists reported it. Christ always referred the Scripture unto the Holy Ghost, and in this passage He does so explicitly—"David in the Spirit;" that is to say, when by the Holy Ghost there were revealed to him eternal truths. It was impossible for man's mind, unassisted, to know what is declared in this psalm, to rise to this height, and to have the comprehensive view opened to us here. Peter, in his sermon on the day of Pentecost (and it is to be noticed that that great model and typical sermon was nothing else but unfolding of Scripture), says to the Jews, "David did not ascend into the heavens." The Jews regarded David with the most profound veneration. They felt that Messiah was, in a peculiar sense, connected with their great king. The apostle is almost afraid to refer to David's death and burial. And therefore he says, "Let me freely speak unto you of our father David; that he is dead and buried, and his sepulchre is with us unto this day." But as a prophet, and knowing the promise of the Son of David—the Messiah—he said, "The Lord said unto my Lord, Sit thou at my right hand." This is the passage* that the apostle Paul afterwards expounds so fully in our epistle, showing from it the peculiar glory of the priesthood of Jesus as the true Melchizedec. On this psalm are based the expressions of the epistles on the ascension of Christ.† What does it mean? That the Son of man, the Son of David, was to be exalted by God high above all things, and that He was to be placed upon the throne as His equal, endowed with all might and all dominion. And thus it is that our blessed Saviour says, "All power is given unto me in heaven and in earth;" and thus is it that

* "A Moonshee in India noticed that David, though himself a prophet and king, spoke here of another as his Lord. He was anxious to know who was meant. He afterwards read in Isaiah of One who suffered on account of our sins. He was anxious to know who was meant by this description. When some time after he read the creed of the Christian Church—'Crucified, dead, and buried; the third day He rose from the dead, ascended into heaven, sitteth at the right hand of God,' it flashed across his mind that Jesus is He of whom David speaks in the 110th Psalm."—Quoted in RICHTER'S *Hausbibel*. (Ps. cx.)

† Eph. i. 20: "When He raised Him from the dead, and set Him at His own right hand in the heavenly places." And again, 1 Cor. xv. 27—"For He hath put all things under His feet."

He ascended high above all heavens, in order that in His humanity as well as in His divinity He might govern and fill all things. "Unto which of the angels said He at any time, as unto Jesus, Sit thou on my right hand?"

But now you may ask, Why does the apostle speak about the angels? He has shown from the 2nd Psalm, from the 97th Psalm, from 2 Samuel vii., from Chronicles, from the 110th Psalm, most clearly that this man Jesus is none else but God, Lord, of infinite and eternal Majesty; and that, therefore, in His humanity also He is highly exalted above all angels. But what is the point of this comparison? what is its importance and the inference to be drawn from it? The argument is simply this: the old dispensation, the law, was given by the mediation and administration of angels. I Jesus was above angels, then His dispensation, the new covenant, His priesthood, are high above that of the law.

The Jews thought much about the angels. As Stephen said, and the apostle teaches in the epistle to the Galatians, the angels were connected with the giving of the law: "The chariots of God are twenty thousand, even thousands of angels. The Lord is among them, as in the holy place of Sinai." The chariots of God do not consist of anything that is material and inanimate. Intelligent living worshippers, loving and obedient spirits, are the chariots upon which God moves. Thus, in the ancient prayer of the synagogue, the angels are called the *Ophanim*, or the *wheels*. Stephen says, "You have received the law by the disposition of angels." In the epistle to the Galatians, Paul reminds them that "the law was given through the administration of angels."

Scripture speaks often of the angels. Let me remind you of some of the doctrines which the Bible contains concerning them.

In the first place, human beings know nothing about angels, except what God pleases to tell them. Hence all that human poets have imagined about them is of no importance or value, unless it agrees with the record of the divine Scripture.

With regard to the angels, I may notice three tendencies to error. The first tendency to error we see in the epistle to the Colossians, and we may call it "the Gnostic error," when men, following their own speculative reason, endeavour to penetrate mysteries which are not revealed to us, and form erroneous views of the angels as to their nature, and their relation to God and to Christ.

Secondly, the Romish error, according to which the angels are placed in a false mediatory position, and are invoked, when men rely upon their intercession, or call upon their aid. The only case recorded in Scripture of the angels being invoked in any way is when David calls upon them to bless the Lord, and with His other creatures to exalt Him, their God and our God. And the third tendency is what I may call the Protestant one—to think too rarely and in too isolated a manner about them; not to consider sufficiently what is said about them in Scripture, and not to feel and remember vividly that they are constantly with us, that we and they are members of one great Family, and that the angelic worship and the worship of the church are harmonious.

Now Scripture tells us of the angels only, as it were, incidentally. It is as if some one who dwells in a great and vast realm, but who does not think it wise, necessary, or salutary to give us full and systematic knowledge of it, occasionally, as we require it, lifts the curtain, and gives us a glimpse of the perfect and harmonious whole of that world in which He is enthroned.

Notice the *multitude* of angels: "We have come to an innumerable company of angels." In the book of Revelation it speaks of "myriads, tens of thousands, and thousands of thousands," millions of angels. In the gospel of Luke "the multitude of the heavenly host" praise God, and announce in songs of gladness the Saviour's birth to the shepherds. An immense, countless multitude of angels! Let our minds expand to the idea. Let the innumerable company of angelic beings who have loved and served God for thousands of years show us how grand is that world in which we live, and in which this poor earth, on account of the blood of Jesus—the Son of God—which redeemed it, is the dearest spot. This innumerable multitude is a polity, a state. There are gradations in it, groups, orders, legions of angels. "Jacob called the name of the place Mahanaim." There are the cherubim and the seraphim; thrones and dominions. There is Michael the defender, the champion of God's people, especially called forth in the latter days. We read of the archangel, whose voice shall be heard when the Lord Himself shall descend from heaven. There is a kingdom with gradations, with order. This kingdom is intimately connected with the kingdom of grace. Jesus tells us every day to think of this connection and harmony. He teaches us to pray, "Thy kingdom come. Thy will be done in earth, *as it is in heaven.*" When a sinner is converted, the angels rejoice; and when Jesus comes again, the angels will come with Him. There is only one kingdom of angels and men; and all that God has created form one wonderful united whole. We cannot see the angels; not because they are invisible; for we could see them at this moment if God saw fit to open our eyes. The things which are true, substantial, lasting, and real, are things as yet invisible, and apprehended only by faith. They will last for ever, though they are not yet seen by us; and when all that is unreal and shadowy shall disappear, then they shall be made visible at the appearing of our great God and Saviour. Whenever there is a crisis in the history of God's kingdom the angels appear, as at the giving of the law, and at the incarnation of the Son of God. Thus we read of angelic manifestations before and after the birth of Jesus. The Son of man often speaks of and always beholds the angels. In the garden of Gethsemane an angel appears to strengthen Him, and angels appear to the disciples at the resurrection and at the ascension of the Saviour. When He comes again multitudes of angels shall come with Him and separate the evil from the good; before the angels Jesus shall confess His people.

Angels are connected not merely with salvation and with the spiritual kingdom of God, but with *all* the kingdom of God; with all physical phenomena. There was an earthquake at His resurrection. Why? Because angels had been and rolled away the stone. The Pool of Siloam had miraculous powers; "for an angel came down at certain seasons and troubled the water," and endowed it with healing power. The angels carry on every development in nature. God does not move and rule the world merely by laws and principles, by unconscious and inanimate powers, but by living beings full of light and love. His angels are like flames of fire; they have charge over the winds, and the earth, and the trees, and the sea. Through the angels He carries on the government of the world. And these angels, whom God has made so glorious, who excel in strength, hearken to the voice of His commandment and obey Him, while they in worship continually behold the countenance of the Father. They are always ascribing glory and praise, and constantly adoring with joy and wonder the glory of God as it is revealed in the Lamb that was slain, and made manifest in the Church of Christ. For as Christ is the centre, so the church is exalted in Him, that in the church the manifold wisdom of God may be made known to principalities and powers.

Now, glorious as the angels are, they are in subjection to Jesus as *man;* for in His human nature God has enthroned Him above all things. Their relation to Jesus fixes also their relation to us. In a great house there may be many servants who are honoured, trusted, and beloved; but the position of the little child who is the heir is different, though as yet he is inferior in knowledge, strength, and attainments. "Are they not all ministering spirits, sent forth to minister for those who shall be heirs of salvation?" You who are the children of God, begotten by the Holy Ghost, you are the brethren of Jesus; for "He took not hold of angels, but in His great love He took hold of the seed of Abraham." You are the future kings and rulers, and unto man in Christ all things are put in subjection, as it is said in the 8th Psalm: "Are they not all ministering spirits?" They love us. We know it, because they showed a most unselfish and tender interest in our salvation. When Jesus descended from heaven, and visited our earth, so far from being filled with envy, they rejoiced, and with great alacrity came down and brought the glad tidings to the shepherds. With joy they also announced that Jesus is risen, that He is exalted, that Son of man whom—O mystery of mysteries!—they had seen agonizing in the garden, who was then strengthened by an angel; whom they had beheld on the cross. How glad were they to roll away the stone; how rejoiced when they saw Him exalted above the heavens; how tenderly they expressed their sympathy with the sorrowing women; "for I know that ye seek Jesus which was crucified. He is not here: for He is risen, as He said." We know they love us; for they rejoice when a poor, fallen, degraded sinner turns from ungodliness and takes hold of salvation as it is in Jesus. They watch us in our dangers, in our difficulties. "God has given His angels charge over us, to keep us in all our ways, lest we dash our foot against a stone." They are astonished, and marvel when they see Lazarus in his poverty, in pain, in distress, despised and forgotten by man. Day by day they watch his patience, his faith, his trustful cleaving unto God, and eagerly they learn from him more and more of the mystery of suffering, and of man's fellowship with Jesus; and lovingly they wait for the appointed hour, when, delivered from the body of pain and death, they carry him safely, and gently, and swiftly into Abraham's bosom. And after having ministered unto God's people to the end of this age, they shall rejoice when they hear His voice saying unto the children, "Come, ye blessed of my Father, inherit the kingdom prepared for you from the foundation of the world."

For Jesus' sake, "are they not all ministering spirits?" Oh, how great is Jesus! How great is the covenant of grace! How great is the glory of the Son, and how wonderful is our position as children of the Father!

And now, brethren, the apostle is not able to continue his argument without first giving vent to his feeling of solemn anxiety about our salvation, and exhorting us earnestly and affectionately. We ought to give the more earnest heed to the things which we have heard. So great a salvation has been revealed to us; salvation which has its origin in eternal depths of love; salvation which is built upon the rock, even the sufferings and resurrection of Jesus the Son of God; salvation which is consummated in glory, greater and higher than that of the angels, by which the highest position is given to us among all creatures in the kingdom of God. If so great salvation is *neglected*—I do not say rejected or treated with contempt and unbelief; but if it is neglected; if we do not rise to the height of this argument; if the love of God does not melt our hearts; if we do not think salvation the one thing that is necessary, important, essential; if we do not devote to it our whole heart, our whole soul, all our energies; if we do not strive to grasp it with all our might, concentrating all our earnestness and strength, how shall we escape? Jesus has Himself declared and brought it; God the Father has ratified it and sealed it; the Holy Ghost has confirmed it with His gifts and wonders. It is the ultimate revelation of God; it is the unspeakable gift of His love, according to His eternal purpose.

Have we this first chapter? Is it ours? Do we possess it? Can we say, "I will go with this into eternity;" I believe it from my heart; it is a treasure to my own soul; I stand upon this rock; I hear His voice in *the Son*, and therefore I can go to Him with child-like confidence? Let me sum up, and apply the teaching of this chapter in four questions. Do we worship Jesus? In this chapter He is called by divine names, the *Son, Lord, God.* Divine works are assigned to Him; the creation of the world, the upholding of all things, the atonement upon the cross, and the government now from the right hand of the Majesty. Divine attributes are given to Him; He is omniscient, He is omnipotent, He is unchangeable, He is eternal. Divine worship is accorded to Him. God the Father Himself commands the angels to worship Him. Do you worship Jesus, Jesus the Son of David, who was crucified upon the cross? Have you learnt, like Thomas, to say unto Him, "My Lord and my God"?

The second question is this: Do you know *truth?* Do you belong unto the generality, the majority of this world, who think that one religion is as good and true as another, one religious opinion not more valuable or certain than another? Have you the *truth,* the *one* truth? Do we know that God, who has spoken in times past by the prophets, has now spoken unto us fully, clearly, and finally in His Son? Jesus saith: "I am the truth;" we have received the true, real, full, perfect, ultimate revelation of the mind of God in Jesus Christ His Son. Oh, what a blessed thing it is when, instead of being tossed to and fro by every wind of doctrine, and instead of depending upon the wisdom and ingenuity of human reason, we have this rock—God hath spoken; in Jesus hath God spoken!

The third question I ask—Are you free from all your sins? Are they all forgiven? Are you forgiven? Jesus has purged away our sins by one sacrifice upon the cross. "The blood of Jesus Christ, the Son of God, cleanseth from all sin." Of Him all the prophets witness, all the apostles witness, and the angels witness, and God the Father, God the Son, and the Holy Ghost witness, that "Whosoever believeth in Him has," that moment, "the perfect absolution, remission, and forgiveness of all sins," and is pure and spotless in the sight of God. Do you believe that Jesus who died on the cross is now at the right hand of God? Oh, then, understand also the full meaning of David's word—"*With God* is forgiveness of sins, that He may be feared!" As we were crucified together with Jesus, so, in consequence of our justification, Jesus was raised and we are accepted in the Beloved. We are now free from sin, and in the presence of God. In Christ we *have* redemption, the forgiveness of sins. He hath taken away all our transgressions.

Lastly, Do you know that Jesus, your Saviour, your Lord, your God, is at the right hand of God, and that you are the brethren of Jesus and the children of the Father, and the heirs of the kingdom? Do you live in the hope that you will behold Him, that you will see Jesus as He is, and that then you will be like Him? And having this hope in you, do you purify yourselves even as He is pure? Oh, live *in* the love of God! Live *on* the love of God! Live *from* the love of God! Start with the fulness of God's love in Jesus Christ! Never be tempted to go back again to the terrors or to the method of the law! Never be tempted to look again to anything else but the blood of Jesus, which taketh away all sin! And each time you go to the Lord's table and commemorate the dying love of Christ, say to yourself, "Now I am showing to all the world the death of the Lord; that He has finished the work, that salvation is perfect, that He has offered a complete, all-sufficient, and full atonement." Rejoice that Christ is here who was crucified, yea, rather, who is risen again, and that we who believe are the body of Christ, one with Him for evermore. Who is he that will condemn or that will separate us from the love of God, which is in Christ Jesus? He who died for us is none else than the Son of the Most High!

May the Lord grant unto us "that we may know Jesus, and the power of His resurrection, and the fellowship of His sufferings; that we may be made conformable unto His death;" and that we may attain unto the glory of the first resurrection when the heirs of salvation shall be made manifest with Jesus Himself. Amen.

CHAPTER V.

JESUS, THE SON OF MAN, MADE LOWER THAN THE ANGELS, FOR THE SUFFERING OF DEATH.

HEB. ii. 5-10.

THE apostle now enters into the holy of holies. He approaches the great subject of the epistle—Jesus Christ exalted through sufferings; by death, even by His own blood, entering as a great High Priest into the heavenly sanctuary. He has reminded us already that Jesus as the Son of God hath by inheritance obtained a more excellent name than the angels. He now wishes to show us what humiliation and sufferings He endured upon earth, and that these did not merely not interfere with His glory, but are the meritorious cause of his exaltation.

"Unto whom hath God put in subjection the world to come of which we speak?" The world to come was a topic of instruction and conversation among all God-fearing Jews; and when they came to believe in Jesus, their attention was still more directed to the fulfilment of prophecy, and their affections more deeply interested in that future of which all the prophets had testified. Jesus Himself had spoken of the regeneration of the world, when the twelve apostles should "sit upon twelve thrones, judging the twelve tribes of Israel." The world to come evidently does not mean heaven, because heaven is a present kingdom, in which the glory of God is manifested, and in which the worship of the angelic and the beatified hosts continually ascends to the throne of God. It is evident from Psalm viii., in which the world to come is described, that it has reference to earth and to the future dominion of Messiah, the Son of man. The world to come does not mean the gospel dispensation; for that began with the preaching of Jesus and the outpouring of the Holy Ghost on the day of Pentecost. But this world to come is something future, to which all the apostles were looking; for Peter testifies, "We look for new heavens and a new earth, wherein dwelleth righteousness;" and again, that the heavens must receive Jesus "until the times of the restitution of all things." The world to come, according to the opinion of the ancient synagogue, means the renovated earth under the reign of the Messiah; it means the time predicted in the prophets, when the kingdom shall be given to the Son of David, and Israel shall dwell in their own land in peace and righteousness, and all the heathen nations shall walk before Him and worship the God of Jacob; when abundance of food and raiment shall be for all the poor and needy; when oppression shall cease on the earth, and the voice of cruelty shall no longer be heard; when even the outward creation shall manifest the presence of the peace of God and of the blessing of the Most High; when from the river even unto the great sea the King shall reign; when war shall be learnt no more by the nations; when the will of God shall be done upon earth as it is done in heaven.

This world to come, which is so fully described in the prophets, must be under subjection, under the government, and under the rule of some one. It has not been put in subjection unto the angels; but, as the word of God teaches us continually, it has been put in subjection under the Messiah, the Son of David, the Son of God. He it is who is to be the beloved of God, to reign upon earth, fulfilling the whole counsel of God; in whom all the promises given unto the fathers were to be "yea and Amen."

Now the testimony of one concerning this reign

upon earth in the world to come is given in Psalm viii., and in speaking of it the apostle does not say "David said;" for, as we have already noticed, all his quotations in this epistle are given in this impersonal way, and reference is immediately made to the source of all Scripture, even the Lord God Himself. Although it is very instructive for us to know what David saw, and what Isaiah thought and felt, and in what peculiar circumstances they were placed historically when the predictions were given to them, yet it is important for us to see the higher truth, that these men were the medium and channel of a higher revelation which they themselves did not fully understand.

The apostle Paul reminds us that these things happened and were written for our instruction. The apostle Peter reminds us that the prophets enquired diligently into the things they were enabled to write, and that they described them not for themselves, but for us, to whom the gospel is now preached in clear fulness. Scripture is thus spirit-breathed and eternal; and it is for us to enter in faith and reverence, and meditate on the breadth, and length, and depth, and height of the counsel of God. How marvellous, when we remember that David and Isaiah did not understand fully what through their inspired lips was uttered! How wonderful when we think of it, that all the great periods of the church, from the first to the second coming of Jesus, were to a very large extent hidden from them, so that they saw the first coming in suffering and the second in glory, as if they were two continuous events, scarcely separated by any interval, and that they beheld at Messiah's coming, Israel on the restored earth in peace and blessedness. And the Gospels, and Acts of the Apostles, and the Revelation, fill up that great and wonderful interval, during which Christ gathers from Jews and Gentiles a body for Himself. And, notwithstanding this great distinction between the prophetic and apostolic writings, there is such a harmony of truth and of sentiment, such a oneness of spirit, such an interpenetration of the two portions of Scripture, that, wherever we go in this grand and spacious temple of God's word, we see the one central idea and the one pervading thought; we feel that the Builder is the Lord of ages, who was, and is, and is to come. What is it that we see? The glory of God Himself. In the morning of the world's history, in the early dawn, all was mysterious, dark, and dim. The truth was only given in a fragmentary manner, yet the manifestation of the glory was continually assuming more distinct features. Glimpses are given unto us of a wonderful human countenance, like the son of Abraham, Isaac, suffering in meekness; like Joseph, entering through humiliation unto glory; like David, ruling in lowliness, beloved, though persecuted. We behold a heavenly, divine One, appearing as the Messenger of the covenant; the Angel, in whom is the Name, the Rock that followed them in the wilderness; the Captain of the host of Israel; the Son of David; until in the gospel of Matthew we see the glory of God "in the face of Jesus Christ"—the same countenance and the same character; all these various luminous streaks breaking through the darkness; all these various and occasional approximative manifestations; all these beams of light, if I may so speak, condensing themselves at His appearing, and showing themselves at last in perfect distinctness and brightness; so that what many prophets and kings desired to see and to look into is, in God's great condescension, come unto us. We behold unveiled, what they beheld afar off.

If such is the unity of Scripture, it is a very important subject to dwell upon. We can easily understand the difficulties which outsiders find in perceiving how thoroughly convinced we are of the truth of Scripture; how no shadow ever crosses our minds about the divine authority of the word of God; how the objections and discrepancies which science and criticism bring forward, and the difficulties in the interpretation of the word of God do not affect our faith; how we have an inward perception and conviction of the inspiration by beholding the perfect unity of the Scriptures, from Genesis to Revelation. "One"—whether David, or Zechariah, or king Solomon—one in a certain place "testifies." He is a *witness* to what God has revealed.

Now, what is the testimony of Psalm viii.? Look at the psalm. What does it mean? David praises the goodness of God, and the condescension of God to man. The name of God is known all over the earth; the glory of God is high above the heavens. He who has made the heavens, and the moon, and the stars, condescends to frail and feeble man, and to the son of man. He is mindful of him, only placed a little below the angels, but crowned with glory and honour. He has given him power over all things in the world, over the beasts, and over the cattle, and over the fowls of the air. This psalm is evidently responsive to the original investiture of man with power when first created by God. God created him in His image, and appointed him to be the ruler upon earth. But does this explain the psalm? Let us look candidly, and say if this key is sufficient to open it. God's name is not now known over the whole earth; and this man, of whom the psalmist speaks as ruler, is it Adam? It cannot be Adam, because he does not speak of *man*, but the "son of man." He speaks evidently of the descendants of Adam. "Out of the mouth of babes and sucklings thou hast perfected praise." Is it fallen man? True, he is lower than the angels, inasmuch as he inhabits a mortal body, and is limited and finite in many ways. But where is his power over creation? As it says in the epistle to the Hebrews, "We do not see all things yet put under him." But the apostle gives to us the key, that the psalmist speaks of the world to come, and of Jesus the Son of man; and when we think that this psalm is written by the Holy Ghost, and when we take in connection all the passages referring to it in the word of God, we shall understand that this is one of the most comprehensive and far-reaching predictions that the word of God contains.*

God created man to be the ruler of the earth; he was to be the representative of God and king here below. All things were to be subject to

* Luther: "This psalm speaks entirely of the sufferings of Christ, and the glory which He obtained through suffering, as Heb. ii. 9 clearly testifies." It is quoted as referring to Christ: (1) Matt. xxi. 16; (2) 1 Cor. xv. 27; (3) Eph. i. 20-22; (4) Heb. ii. Luther has beautiful remarks on the spiritual teaching and consolation of this psalm. On verse 3 he adduces 1 Cor. ii. 1; i. 21-23; on verse 6 the glory and honour of Christ. (Isaiah liii., lxi.; Psalm xlv.)

The designation "son of man" is given, with the exception of Ezekiel, to none but Messiah. In Daniel vii. 13 the expression is Ben-Enosh, which brings before us more vividly that He who was crucified through *weakness* is now exalted and glorified. In this psalm Ben-Adam is more appropriate—"the Adam above," "the Adam on high, who has dominion over all things," an expression occurring in the Talmudic writings and the Zohar. Compare also Rom. v. and 1 Cor. xv.

him. This is the very idea of a king, as we find in the book of Daniel. "Thou, O king, art a king of kings: for the God of heaven hath given thee a kingdom, power, and strength, and glory. And wheresoever the children of men dwell, the beasts of the field and the fowls of the heaven hath he given into thine hand, and hath made thee ruler over them all. Thou art this head of gold." (ii. 37, 38.) The idea of kingship is that it is not an authority entrusted to man by man. It does not come from below. It is a power and sovereignty given by the supreme Lord of heaven and earth Himself. And the kingship of Nebuchadnezzar, as it comes from God direct, so it involves everything upon earth. Not merely are all peoples and nations and languages to render allegiance to him, but the beasts of the field and the fowls of the air, which move on and over his territory, are also subject to him. He is invested with power by God Himself, and over all things is his dominion. Now this kingship which Adam lost by his sin is to be given unto one who is called the "Son of man." Jesus our Lord evidently referred to this passage also, when He called Himself the Son of man. It is in this expression that the passages in Daniel are rooted. "From henceforth ye shall see the Son of man coming in the clouds of heaven." He is called the Son of man because He is the sum and substance of the human race, the representative and restorer of humanity—the man Christ Jesus. He is the second Adam; in Him there is a new commencement of humanity given unto us. He is the Son of man not merely in that He is a partaker of flesh and blood, and that, born of a woman and appearing in the likeness of sinful flesh, He has become one with our race; but because it is given to Him to be the head of the new humanity: He is to be Lord and Ruler, the King of the earth. This Son of man, made a little lower than the angels, is to be the King; and through Him the knowledge, love, and life of God shall be brought to the ends of the earth. All people that on earth do dwell, all people to the furthest islands of the sea, shall know and worship the God of Israel. God's name shall be excellent on the earth while He has exalted His glory above the heavens; that is, the whole earth shall see the manifestation of grace in the church which is to the praise and glory of His name; the manifestation of salvation-glory, which is above all angels and all things belonging to the first creation.

"Out of the mouth of babes and sucklings thou hast perfected praise." This was fulfilled at the time when the children sang "Hosanna" to the Lord; it is a symbol, and it is fulfilled now continually when out of the mouth of babes are declared the mysteries the Father reveals to them (Matt. xi.); and it shall be fulfilled when it shall be found that by the foolishness, and weakness, and nothingness of believers, God brings to nought the wisdom of the wise, and the power and glory of the world.

But this Son of man whom God chose for Himself was made a little lower than the angels that He might taste death; for through this death was He to enter into the glory and honour with which the Father decreed to crown Him for His obedience and humiliation.

Let us consider what it is that the Son of man, humbling Himself for us, has endured. There are two expressions used—to suffer death, and to taste death. Let us remember that between Jesus, as He was in Himself, and death there subsisted no connection. He was conceived by the Holy Ghost, and born of the Virgin Mary. He was without sin, without spot and blemish. He had never transgressed the law. In Him Satan could find nothing. Death had no personal or direct relation to Him. Do we look upon death as being the punishment of the transgression of the law? Christ fulfilled all righteousness. The Lord Jesus Christ, as far as His humanity was concerned, was free from the power of death. No power could kill the Lord Jesus Christ. "No man taketh my life from me; but I lay it down of myself." The Lord Jesus Christ, the Prince of Life, of His own power and will, laid down His life. The death of the Lord Jesus Christ in this respect is different from the death of any human being; it was the free, voluntary, spontaneous act and energy of His will. When the Lord Jesus Christ died He put forth a great energy. He *willed* to die. And so in one sense we may say that His death was a great manifestation of His power.

Let us consider that the Lord *tasted* death. A man may die in a moment, and then he does not taste death. John the Baptist was beheaded; it was in the twinkling of an eye that the severance took place between body and spirit. Men may die in a moment of excitement, and, as extremes meet, almost in unconsciousness, or with calmness and intrepidity, with lion-like courage, as many a warrior; but that is not *tasting* death. The death of our Lord Jesus Christ was a slow and painful death; He was "roasted with fire," as was prefigured by the Paschal Lamb. But it was not merely that it lasted a considerable time, that it was attended with agony of mind as well as pain of body; but that He came, as no other finite creature can come, into contact with death. He tasted death; all that was in death was concentrated in that cup which the Lord Jesus Christ emptied on the cross. During His lifetime He felt a burden, sorrow, grief; He saw the sins and sorrows of the people; He had compassion, and wept. In the garden of Gethsemane He realized what was the cup which He would have to drink upon Golgotha. He was in great agony, not instead of us, but because He shrank from that impending substitution on the accursed tree. There is no substitution and expiation in the garden—the *anticipation* of the substitution was the cause of His agony; but on the cross He paid the penalty for the sins of men in His own death. But what was it that He tasted in death? Death is the curse which sin brings, the penalty of the broken law, the manifestation of the power of the devil, the expression of the wrath of God; and in all these aspects the Lord Jesus Christ came into contact with death, and tasted it to the very last. He tasted it as the consequence of sin, though He knew no sin in Himself personally; but He, as the perfect, pure, and spotless Son of God, and Son of man, had an infinite appreciation of the evil of sin in its loathsomeness, in its cruelty, in its apostasy from God, in its contrariety to the will of the Holy One. He saw the true nature of sin Godwards and manwards; upwards to the throne of holiness, and downwards to the bottomless abyss; in its depths, and in its everlasting consequences, did He perceive it. We do not see the real consequences of sin, not knowing the exceeding sinfulness of sin. We find it difficult to realize that such awful infinite results should come from it; but He saw sin in all its mystery, in all its reality.

Death is the penalty of the transgression of God's law. He had magnified the law and fulfilled the law all the time that He was upon earth. In His heart the law was written as upon the tables in the ark of the covenant. He delighted in the will of God, not as something external to Him, but as something that lived within Him, the music and rhythm of His soul. He saw death as the result of the transgression of the law, and the curse and punishment of the law. He was made under the law, and now He was made a curse for us.

Satan has the power of death. Jesus says, "This is your hour, and the power of darkness;" and it was Satan, the prince and the power of darkness, whom Jesus vanquished upon the cross. He came into contact with the prince and the power of darkness, whose right it was to insist upon the hand-writing of ordinances, which is against the transgressors, and who can fix the sting of death by applying it with the strength of law. (1 Cor. xv. 56.)

And last of all, and most fearful of all, it was the expression of the wrath of God. The just displeasure and indignation of God against sin makes itself felt in death. Death is being forsaken of God; it is the expression of the withdrawal of God's favour and strength Death is to be left without God. The Lord Jesus Christ came into contact with death as the wrath of God. He tasted death with full and perfect consciousness. Therefore He said, at the end of the three mysterious hours during which the Sun lost his light,* "My God, my God, why hast thou forsaken me?" With fulness of faith He continued clinging to God; for in all this He acknowledged the truth, the righteousness, and the faithfulness of God, and called Him "my God." Thus did He taste death. Thus did He who was life itself come into contact with death; thus did He who was holiness itself come into contact with sin; and thus His love to God and to man was sublimated, as it were, to the highest perfection. Thus He satisfied the holiness, justice, truth, and faithfulness of God; and thus He took away the sting of death as the penalty of sin and the strength of Satan.

Christ was made a curse for us; He was forsaken of God, and left alone with the power of darkness. But though He emptied the cup of wrath, though all the billows and waves of death

* "These were three mysterious hours. The time of this desertion corresponds with the 4th verse of Psalm viii., in which the Sun is not mentioned (Matt. xxvii. 45)."—BENGEL, *Gnomon.*

went over Him, He continued to *live*, to trust, to love, to pray: He gained the victory in the lowest depth of His agony. His love was stronger than death, and in His death He brought life to all those whose sins He bore. He tasted death by the grace of God. It was the grace of God that gave Him up unto death. "It pleased the Lord to bruise Him." The ultimate reason of Christ's death is the love of God to Jesus and the children given to Him; its ultimate purpose, the manifestation of God to angels and to men. "That He, by the grace of God, should taste death for every one." Scripture throughout refers to the sacrifice of Jesus as the consequence of the love of God; and as the manifestation of divine love ' God was in Christ reconciling the world unto Himself." It is only the enemy, the unbeliever, who represents the Scripture doctrine to be that the anger and the wrath of God the Father had to be appeased by Jesus, in whom there is greater clemency and mercy than in the Father. This is a false witness. It is the love of God that Jesus revealed; nay, it is *God's* love that Jesus died for the guilty. Christ did not die in order that God might love the world; but it was because God loved the world that Jesus died. Through Christ crucified we behold God as Father.

But what love would it be if Christ's death

was only an example? What if there had been no *necessity* for that unspeakable gift—for that stupendous sacrifice? What if sin could be forgiven without the character of God being vindicated? without the manifestation of His justice, truth, and holiness? if the law could have been set aside, and its penalty and condemnation passed over? if the favour of God could rest immediately on the sinner who recognizes the love of God, and the real obstacles between God and the transgressor remain as they were, untouched, unremoved? And these objective obstacles are the hatred of God against sin, the wrath of God against evil—wrath as a necessary and essential manifestation of love, which is in perfect holiness and justice—the condemnation of God's law, which is holy, just, and good, the power of death, and Satan, the prince of darkness. The subjective obstacles (in man) are not less real—his hardness, hatred against God, and death in trespasses and sins. If Jesus died only as a martyr and example, or as manifesting the love of God, who was willing to receive repentant sinners, we cannot understand the reason of agony and sacrifice so awful and of miracle so transcendent as the incarnation. Nor would such a death bring us nigh unto God. There would still be the infinite distance between God and the conscience; and the mountains of our guilt, the condemnation and curse of the law, and the righteous displeasure of God, would still separate between Him and us. Christ would be no mediator; for He would, on this supposition, never have entered into our real position, difficulty, and death. The lost sheep would still be in the wilderness, and the Good Shepherd would have only shown His willingness to rescue it, His compassion, self-denial, love, but would not actually have *found* and *saved* it. Only when we believe the Scripture testimony, that He laid down His life for and instead of us—that He became sin and a curse in our stead—that His blood was shed as a ransom for the remission of our sins—only then do we see that in Jesus we have the love, favour, and blessing of God, that in Him we have redemption, and are brought nigh to the Father.

And notice, He tasted death by the grace of God *for every one.* We speak about the pardon of sins. *We* are pardoned; but all our sins have been punished. God forgives *us*, but *our sins* He never forgives, never pardons, in the sense of remitting their punishment. All our sins were laid upon Jesus, every one was punished. "God condemned sin in the flesh." He executed judgment upon all our sins, for every one of us, for all the children of God. For each of them Jesus tasted death. Here there is not merely the forgiveness of sin, but there is the actual putting away of all our sins; and the apostle explains to us that this great and marvellous mystery of the death of Jesus as our Substitute, bearing our sins, bearing our curse, enduring the penalty of our sins, and overcoming all our enemies (that is the law, and Satan, and death), that this is in order to manifest unto us the fulness of the perfection of God.

"For *it became Him,* of whom are all things, and by whom are all things, to make the Captain of our salvation perfect through sufferings." What a marvellous declaration! "It became Him." It is in accordance with the divine perfections. All divine attributes are harmonised here—His wisdom and His mercy, His justice and His holiness, His power and His truth. "It became Him because of His love, it became His justice, it became His wisdom that thus it should be. There was in it no triumph of one attribute over another, no prodigality which infinite wisdom could reprove, no facility which infinite holiness could challenge; there was a common rejoicing of all God's attributes in their common and harmonious exercise." God's attributes (we speak humanly and with great imperfection) are all *simultaneous.* They all move together, because they are all-perfect and all-glorious. In His mercy He must be righteous, in His justice merciful; in His wisdom there is strength, in His power patience.

Everything that is in God is beautiful and perfect. "Of Him, and through Him, and to Him, are all things;" and that in which He has concentrated the revelation of Himself must *become Him*. The more we look upon Jesus as our Redeemer, and contemplate the atonement upon the cross, the more do our thoughts expand, and the more do we see the image and glory of the Most High; the more do we dread sin, the more do we enter into the knowledge of God and into fellowship with Him. Who brings out the perfection of God but the Lamb slain? Well then may it be said, "It became Him to make the Captain of our salvation perfect through sufferings."

If I may so say, God is never so Godlike as when He reveals Himself in Jesus crucified for sins. Oh, how did the Jews shrink from the mystery of the Crucified One! How did every thought in them rebel against the idea of their King being hanged upon the tree! How hard is it for them to believe that the Messiah was the Crucified One! They turn away from the cross of Jesus, and rest, in what they believe a spiritual faith, in the one incomprehensible, invisible, glorious God. They forget that throughout the Old Testament times God *revealed* His glory, and that the promise is the appearing of the glory, the manifestation of Jehovah. They do not understand the mystery—God revealed and glorified in the death of His Son. It became Him, in bringing many sons to glory, to make the Captain of their salvation perfect through sufferings. He brings many children to glory. We use the word glory often in a superficial and thoughtless way. What is glory? What glory do we possess? Are our bodies glorious? Soon they will be in the grave, the food of worms. Are our minds glorious? We may, in a moment, lose the light of reason, and forget all the information we have acquired, and be unable to think connectedly. Are our hearts glorious? They are polluted with sin. Are our souls glorious? We have no strength or life in ourselves. Then what is the glory? What glory is ours? What do you expect when you are laid in the grave? You remember that Jesus said to Martha at the grave of Lazarus, when the signs of corruption were so evident and repulsive, "Only believe, and thou shalt see *the glory of God.*" Ah! *God's glory.* Not the glory of Lazarus. Not *our* glory, but *His own* glory. "We rejoice in hope of the glory of God." Now see how easy it is to believe that there is no other righteousness but God's righteousness. A mortal, sinful, and weak creature, I expect glory, though my body is laid in the grave, and mind and heart fail me. The glory I hope for is Christ's—to be glorified together with Him. It is divine glory. We rejoice in hope of the glory of God. What righteousness have I? I have no righteousness but Christ's righteousness. Just as God will give me His glory, so He hath given me His righteousness; not the righteousness which is by the works of the law, the fruit of my own endeavours, not partly mine, and partly the result of looking to the Lord Jesus Christ. The sinner is guilty, lost, and imperfect; but, clothed in the righteousness which is from above—God's righteousness—he is perfect, glorious, beautiful. Then I understand what the apostle Paul says—"Whom He justified, them He also glorified." If He has given me Jesus as my righteousness, then He has also given me Jesus as my glory. It is His purpose to bring many children unto glory, and it was necessary to make the Captain of their salvation perfect through sufferings. The apostle touches here only briefly on what forms one of the chief themes of the epistle to the Hebrews—the connection between Christ's sufferings and glory.

Without entering now on this truth, I conclude with this remark: Most of us last Lord's-day commemorated the dying love of Jesus. The Lord's Supper is the connecting link between the first and second coming of Christ. Looking back we see the finished work of Jesus, the sacrifice which He has made; by which one sacrifice, once for all, He hath perfected for ever them that are sanctified. By faith we are sanctified, separated unto God; our sins are forgiven, our righteousness is divine, we are complete in Christ. Looking forward, we expect the world to come; we show the death of the Lord till He come. That same Jesus whom now, in His personal absence, though we see Him not, we love and trust, in whom we rejoice, and who is specially with us while we commemorate His dying love, shall return to take the kingdom and the power. Now during the interval we live by and on what Jesus has done for us when He died upon the cross. We are *always* celebrating the Lord's Supper. And this is His wondrous love, that day by day He gives us His body to eat, which is meat indeed, and His blood, which is drink indeed. This is outwardly expressed at the Lord's table. The daily, hourly, secret but most real life of the Christian, which is nothing else but eating Christ and living by Him, even by Him who gave His body and shed His blood for us; this is manifested to ourselves, the Church, and the world, by the ordinance of the Lord's Supper, in which the union between Christ and the believer is renewed, confirmed, and sealed. The spiritual Lord's Supper is for every day and all the day; for this is our life, to feed on Jesus, who died for us. This is the glorious consequence of His death—"I am He that liveth, and was dead; and, behold, I am alive for evermore." And this is, if I may so speak, His blessed occupation now—to feed and strengthen the children until He shall come again in glory. He continually renews and imparts to us that love which died for us upon the cross.

Oh that we may know what it is to be justified and what it is to be glorified! that we may be clothed with God's righteousness now, and that we may be glorified together with Christ at His coming! Let us take the cup of salvation, behold Christ crucified, but now exalted, our righteousness and glory. Amen.

CHAPTER VI.

JESUS, IN ALL THINGS LIKE UNTO HIS BRETHREN, THROUGH SUFFERINGS AND DEATH OUR HIGH PRIEST.

HEB. ii. 11-18.

JESUS CHRIST as the Son of God, and according to that glory into which in His humanity He has entered through His sufferings and death, is high above the angels. It was necessary for Him to pass through sufferings and through death; it was in accordance with the divine plan, and in harmony with all the divine attributes and perfections. Through His sufferings and death He glorified the Father. He put away sin; He abolished death; He destroyed the power of the devil; and for Himself, and for all those who are His, He has obtained that high position in which, as the 8th Psalm testifies, all things are put under His feet; and not merely this, but He Himself has become a merciful and faithful High

Priest, able to succour us who are tempted, and to sympathise with us in all our sorrow and in all our trial.

Now, the first truth which is brought before us in the verses which we have read is, that Jesus, who is not ashamed to call Himself brother, and us His brethren, is one with us. We who are sanctified by Him, and He who sanctifies, are of one. Christ is He who sanctifies. The source and power of sanctification are in Jesus the Son of God, our Saviour. We who were to be brought into glory were far from God, in a state of condemnation and death. What can be more different than our natural condition and the glory of God which we are awaiting? Condemned on account of our transgression of the law, we lived in sin, alienated from God, and without His presence of light and love. We were dead; and by dead I do not mean that modern fancy which explains death to mean cessation of existence, but that continuous, active, self-developing state of misery and corruption into which the sinner has fallen by his disobedience. Dead in trespasses and sins, wherein we *walked;* dead while living in pleasing self. (Eph. ii. 1, 2; 1 Tim. v. 6.) What can be more opposed to glory than the state in which we are by nature? And if we are to be brought into glory, it is evident we must be brought into holiness; we must be delivered and separated from guilt, pollution, and death, and brought into the presence of God—in which is favour, light, and life—that His life may descend into our souls, and that we may become partakers of the divine nature.

Christ is our sanctification. "By one offering He hath perfected for ever them that are sanctified." By the offering up of His body as the sacrifice for sin He has sanctified all that put their trust in Him. To sanctify is to separate unto God; to separate for a holy use. We which were far off are brought nigh by the blood of Christ. And although our election is of God the Father (who is thus the author of our sanctification, Jude i.), and the cleansing and purification of the heart is generally attributed to the Holy Ghost (Titus iii. 4, 5); yet as it is in Christ that we were chosen, and from Christ that we receive the Spirit, and as it is by the constant application of Christ's work and the constant communication of His life that we live and grow, Christ is our sanctification.

We are sanctified through faith that is in Him. (Acts xxvi. 18.) By His offering of Himself He has brought us into the presence of God. By the Word, by God's truth, by the indwelling Spirit, He continually sanctifies His believers. He gave Himself for the Church, "that He might sanctify and cleanse it with the washing of water by the

Word." (Eph. v. 26.) "Sanctify them through thy truth." (John xvii. 17; xv. 3.) Through sanctification of the Spirit unto obedience and sprinkling of the blood of Jesus Christ. (1 Peter i. 2.)

Christ Himself is the foundation, source, method, and channel of our sanctification. We are exhorted to put off the old man and to put on the new man day by day, to mortify our members which are upon earth. But in what other way or method can we obey the apostolic exhortations, but by our continually beholding Christ's perfect sacrifice for sin as our sufficient atonement? In what other way are we sanctified day by day, but by taking hold of the salvation which is by Him, "the Lamb that was slain"? Jesus is He that sanctifieth. The Holy Ghost, the Comforter, is sent by Christ to glorify Him, and to reveal and appropriate to us His salvation. We are conformed to the image of Christ by the Spirit as coming from Christ in His glorified humanity.

"He that sanctifieth and they who are sanctified are all of one;" namely, of God the Father. And here we are reminded of the teaching of Scripture, that all things are of the Father, and to His glory. Christ is the vine, we are the branches; but the Father is the husbandman. Christ is the bridegroom, and we are the church, the bride; but it is the Father who is the King, which made a marriage for His Son. Christ is the head, we are the members; but as we are Christ's, so Christ is God's. "The head of Christ is God." (1 Cor. xi. 3.) "He that sanctifieth and they who are sanctified are all of one." Christ is of the Father; we are of the Father. As the Lord Jesus Christ Himself says, "Thine they were, and thou gavest them me;" and as in the epistles of John, we are taught that we are of God, and the seed of God abideth in us. What a wonderful brotherhood is this, rooted in the mysterious election of eternal love! Christ, the only begotten of the Father, and we who by nature are children of wrath and disobedience, are eternally and indissolubly united with Him. Therefore He is not ashamed to call us brethren. As it is said also in the 22nd Psalm, in which the sufferings of Jesus upon the cross and His exaltation are described: "I will declare thy name unto my brethren: in the midst of the church will I sing praise unto thee." Notice how literally that was fulfilled; for it was immediately after His resurrection, and in reference to this Psalm, that Jesus said, "Go to my brethren, and say unto them, I ascend unto my Father, and your Father; and to my God, and your God." The risen Saviour, as the first-born among many brethren, hastens to declare the name Father unto His disciples, and to assure them, that He who sanctifieth and they who are sanctified are both of one.

Christians, if Jesus is our brother; if Jesus and

we are both of one; if Jesus says, "I will sing thy praise in the midst of the congregation;" if He is the leader of our prayers and praises before the throne of God, then we may approach the Father without fear and without doubt! Christ's peace is our peace, and our worship is the worship of perfect acceptance, of perfect trust and love in union with the Head of the Church, Jesus crowned with glory after His sufferings. Thus do we praise and pray in the name of Christ; thus does Christ Himself praise and pray in the midst of the congregation. Where is doubt now? For is Jesus in doubt of His acceptance with the Father? Is not His atonement upon Golgotha most glorious in the sight of God? It is Jesus who is our representative and spokesman. As on that night on which He was betrayed He sang the hallelujah with His disciples, so now He presents to the Father our sacrifice of thanksgiving, our adoration, our petitions, and the Father hears the voice of Jesus in the voice of the church.

The apostle illustrates the relationship which subsists between the Lord Jesus and His people by another typical prediction. The prophet Isaiah is not merely an eminent evangelist of the Old Testament, but his position in the important crisis of Jewish history is typical. The judgment which was then threatening Israel, the judicial blindness and hardness of heart which fell upon the great majority of the nation, was a type of that culminating sin and obstinate rejection of Jehovah which is described in touching and solemn words in Matthew xiii. 13–15, John xii. 37–41, and Acts xxviii. 25–27. But Jehovah promises protection and grace to those who trust in Him. The prophet by faith has his refuge in God, and looks with confidence to the future. He and the children whom God has given unto him are types of the Redeemer and His people. The children of the prophet are signs and wonders. The application of this typical prediction by the apostle to Christ and His people is bold, but beautiful, and in harmony with the whole spirit and scope of the prophecy.

The Lord Jesus all the time He was on earth exercised faith in the living Father. Even His enemies bore witness at the crucifixion, "He trusted in God." All His lifetime He was one of those peculiar people who, instead of being guided by what is called "common sense," instead of being influenced by public opinion, prudence, and the power of the world, was always beholding Him who is invisible; was always walking with God, and doing His will. "I am not alone, because the Father is with me." He was continually leaning upon the Father. Thus we understand these two quotations: "I will trust in Him," and "Behold I and the children whom thou hast given me." Christ is represented as Brother and as the everlasting Father. The promise was given to the Messiah:—"He shall see His seed. Who shall declare His generation?" Christ who sanctifies and we who are sanctified are both of one—the Lord Jesus, who is not ashamed to call us brethren, who hastened to declare to us the Father's name after His resurrection, who during His lifetime exercised to the fullest extent faith in God, at the last shall acknowledge us as the children given to Him of the Father. Brotherhood is now the relationship subsisting between Him and us, a relationship which can never be altered. We may lose friendship; but brotherhood is fixed and unchangeable. Thus our Lord Jesus and we are rooted and united in God the Father.

Christ is the Elect of God, and we are chosen of the Father in Christ Jesus. In Him we are predestinated unto the adoption of children. Of God are we in Christ; and of God Christ is made unto us wisdom, and righteousness, and sanctification, and redemption. God the Father gave us to Jesus, even as the Father gave Jesus to us. And because Jesus and the Father are one, the union between the Lord Jesus, given unto us by the Father and the children, given unto Jesus by the Father, can never be broken.

The Son of God being appointed to be the Captain of our salvation, it was necessary that

He should become partaker of flesh and blood. "Inasmuch as the children are partakers of flesh and blood, He also Himself likewise took part of the same." What is the meaning of "flesh and blood"? The human race, in its creature dependence and weakness, is described in Scripture by "flesh." "O Thou that hearest prayer, unto Thee shall all flesh come." Christ said in His prayer, "As Thou hast given Him power over all flesh." "Flesh and blood" describe us in our present earthly condition. "Flesh and blood cannot inherit the kingdom of God." A change must take place to fit us for the heavenly region. The flesh and blood which the Lord Jesus Christ took shows that He became truly and really man. "The Word was made flesh, and dwelt among us." This seems a wonderful contrast. The Word, eternal, all-perfect, all-glorious, the Son of the Most High, who was with God from the beginning, and was God, He became flesh, He was born of the Virgin Mary. "The flesh" shows the weakness of which the Lord Jesus Christ became partaker. It is written that He was crucified through weakness; that He came in the likeness of sinful flesh. When people saw Him, they did not notice in His outward appearance anything superhuman, glorious, free from earthly weakness and dependence. He did not come in splendour and power. He did not come in the brightness and strength which Adam possessed before he fell. "In all things He became like unto us." In everything; in His body, for He was hungry and thirsty; overcome with fatigue, He slept. In His mind, for it developed. He had to be taught; He grew in wisdom concerning the things around Him; He increased, not merely in stature, but in mental and moral strength. In His affections, He loved. He loved the young man who came unto Him, and was not willing to give up his riches. He loved Lazarus, Mary, and Martha — the disciple who leaned on His bosom. He was astonished; He marvelled at men's unbelief, and said to the Syro-Phœnician woman, "O woman, great is thy faith." Sometimes He was glad, and "rejoiced in spirit;" sometimes angry and indignant, as when He saw the hypocrisy of the Jews, who accused Him of having broken the Sabbath. Zeal, like fire, burned within Him: "The zeal for the house of God consumed me;" and He showed a vehement fervour in protecting the sanctity of God's temple. He was grieved; He trembled with emotion; his soul was straitened in Him. Sometimes He was overcome by the waves of feelings when He beheld the future that was before Him. In all things He was made like unto us. Do not think of Him as merely *appearing* a man, or as being a man only in His body, but as man in body, soul, and spirit. He exercised faith; He read the

Scriptures for His own guidance and encouragement; He prayed the whole night, especially when He had some great and important work to do, as before setting apart the apostles. He sighed when he saw the man who was dumb; tears fell from His eyes when at the tomb of Lazarus He saw the power of death and of Satan. He wept over Jerusalem, as He foresaw the fearful results of their grievous sin. His supplications were with strong crying and tears; His soul was exceedingly sorrowful; He was sorely pressed, and He agonized in Gethsemane.

"He suffered being tempted." The temptation was a reality to Him. He felt most keenly and painfully the weight and the pressure of the test. His soul was full of love to Israel, and eager to gather children of Jerusalem. The broad road, easy and attractive to the flesh, would have led to immediate recognition and reception by Israel: the way of humility and obedience, of faith and suffering, was narrow to Jesus also. He *felt* hunger, reproach, hatred; Satan was permitted to test Christ's most sensitive heart, with the most penetrating and painful trial.

When His sweat was as it were great drops of blood falling down to the ground, His soul was shrinking from the awful cup of Golgotha; and to strengthen Him in this most real, and to us unfathomable, conflict, an angel from heaven appeared unto Him. The world also was a temptation to Him. The spirit of the world was enmity against Him, and came into collision with Him every moment. His own brothers said, "Why do you not go up to the feast and shew yourself?" His own disciples said, "Far be it from thee to suffer, Lord." But He saw Satan in all this; and said, "Get thee behind me, Satan." Not for a single moment did He yield—erect He stood. But, nevertheless, and by this very perfection of His victory, He felt every moment all the burden of the weight. If He had given in, that very moment the pressure would have been relieved. Because He remained without sin, He *suffered* being tempted. Jesus, as Messiah, felt the sorrow of love rejected, of instruction refused, by the people to whom He came in mercy infinite; He felt keenly the pain of being called a blasphemer in His own beloved city. As the prophet describes it, He mourned and wept before God, that He had spent His strength and labour in vain. He felt that Satan could give unto Him the allegiance of the nations, if He would only yield to him on one point. The narrowness of the path He chose was a reality to Him. "He *suffered* being tempted;" and His *suffering* was again a temptation to Him. "This," He said, "is your hour, and the power of darkness." In the garden of Gethsemane, and on the cross, He saw in His sufferings the power of Satan's temptation He felt the fearful strength of the adversary, endeavouring to make Him swerve from His loyalty to God. "He that sanctifieth, and they that are sanctified, are one." Mysterious brotherhood! "He became in all things like unto His brethren." "He suffered being tempted," and was tempted in all His sufferings.

Now we advance a step further. By death He took away the power of him who has the power of death, that is, Satan. We considered the expression, Christ *tasted* death,—that He did not merely die, as it were, in a moment of enthusiasm, as many a warrior has lost his life courageously. But, laying down His life, He came into contact with the whole sting of death; measured its length and breath and intensity, the power of Satan, the wrath of God, the condemnation of the law. How clear it is from this passage what Jesus Christ *suffered* in death!

But which death did He die? That death of which the devil has the power. Satan wielded that death. He it was who had a just claim against us that we should die. There is justice in the claim of Satan.* He stands upon the

* It is quite true that Satan is only a usurper; but in saving men God deals in perfect righteousness, justice, and truth. According to the Jewish tradition the fallen angels often accuse men, and complain before God that sinful men obtain mercy. Our redemption is in harmony with the principles of righteousness and

justice of God; upon the inflexibility of the law; upon the true nature of our sin. But when Christ died our very death, when He was made sin and a curse for us, then all the power of Satan was gone. It was of the grace of God that He tasted death for every one. This is often set before us in Scripture, lest we should imagine that the Lord Jesus loved us more than the Father loves us, or that the Father did not love Him with the most intense love at the very moment He hid His face from Him as our Substitute. In the expiatory death of Jesus all the attributes of God are in sweetest harmony; but grace shines brightest through all. "By the grace of God He tasted death."

And now what can Satan say? The justice, majesty, and perfection of the law are vindicated, more than if all the human race were lost for ever. In the sufferings of Christ there was not merely punishment endured, but there was faith and love; the highest and deepest obedience; the law was magnified. There was a burnt-offering in this sin-offering. The penalty due to the

equity, on which God has founded all things. The prince of the world is *judged;* he is conquered not merely by power, but by the power of justice and truth. That Messiah is to vanquish the angel of death was held by the Jews, according to Isaiah xv. 8: "When Satan saw Messiah he was afraid, and fell upon his face and said, He is the Messiah, who shall cast me and all nations into hell; as it is written, The Lord will swallow up death for ever."

broken law Jesus endured, and now, as the law is vindicated, sin put away, death swallowed up, Christ has destroyed the devil. In connection with this word, I must refer to the extraordinary delusion of supposing that "destroy" means to annihilate. Christ did not annihilate the devil; Satan still exists, and will exist for ever and ever. But the Lord has taken his power from him: He "bruised his head." Satan, we are taught here, has the power of death, even as Satan introduced sin into the world. While we are without Christ we are under the power of darkness (Col. i. 13); we walk according to the prince of the power of the air, the spirit that now worketh in the children of disobedience. (Eph. ii. 3.) But when we come to believe, by Jesus we are delivered from the power of Satan, and brought into the liberty of the children of God. (Acts xxvi. 18.) Only through the death of our Lord Jesus Christ upon the cross can men be delivered from Satan. As we are delivered from the dominion of Satan, who has the power of death, we are also delivered from the fear of death. And this is to some extent the special privilege of believers living in the new covenant. Now, being delivered out of the hand of our enemies, we may serve God without fear. The children of God in the old dispensation had faith in God and the Messiah. and lived in the hope of everlasting blessedness. They enjoyed the peace of God, yet it was natural they should be afraid of the darkness and gloom of the grave; and many passages in the Psalms and prophets, referring to the realm of death before the advent of Messiah, appear sad and mournful. This is natural; but when Messiah comes, they expected God would put all things under Him: joy will come in the morning, and Israel will then see the salvation of God. But the intermediate period was to them a time of great darkness. But how different is it now that the true light shineth. Jesus has *abolished* death. He has the keys of death and of hades. In His resurrection we have obtained the victory. The Christian can look death in the face, and say, "O death," and ask the question: "Where is thy sting?" We know that to depart and to be with Christ, to die, is gain. Absent from the body, present with the Lord. "Are you afraid of death?" said a friend to a German pastor. "Which death do you mean?" replied the dying man. "Jesus my Saviour saith, 'He that believeth in me hath eternal life. He that believeth in me shall not see death.' Why should I be afraid of what I shall not even *see?* The real death is past. Outward death, separation of body and soul, we have to endure, and God gives us grace and strength in this last trial; but the sting of death has been taken away."

The apostle now states the result and fruit of the Lord's condescension and work. The Son of God became man; He took hold of the seed of Abraham; He became in all things like unto us, He was tempted, He suffered, He died, He saved us; and now, by virtue of His incarnation, obedience, sufferings—through all the experiences of His earthly life, and perfected in His death—He has become "a merciful and faithful High Priest in things pertaining to God, to make reconciliation for the sins of the people." In no book of the New Testament is our Saviour called the High Priest, except in the epistle to the Hebrews; not even in the book of Revelation, where the heavenly sanctuary and its worship are disclosed to us. How precious is this epistle to us in revealing the whole rich cluster of truths and consolations which gather round this central word, High Priest.

In the 110th Psalm it is said, "Thou art a priest for ever after the order of Melchizedek;" and in the prophet Zechariah, Messiah, the Branch; that is, Jehovah's servant, who shall build the temple, is called a priest upon the throne. But the full exposition of the fulfilment of Levitical type, and of the eternal Melchizedek priesthood of the Lord Jesus, we possess only in this profound and precious portion of Scripture.

Believe then that Jesus, by His experience, by

His sufferings, and above all by His death, has become a merciful and faithful High Priest. We are now on earth, in the flesh, sin around, and alas, within us. How can the Holy God look on us, and grant us blessings? How can there be communion between heaven and earth? Jesus is ascended, and having put away sin by the sacrifice of Himself, presents us to the Father; and we are holy and unblameable before Him; and Father, Son, and Holy Ghost are able to send down the fulness of blessings, of grace and strength; to have communion with us, notwithstanding all our sin and defilement. Christ is a merciful High Priest; not merely full of pity, compassion, and grace, but full of sympathy. He knows what is in man, He understands fully all our sorrows, and is able to measure the strength of all our temptations. He is most lovingly and earnestly anxious that we should always obtain the victory and suffer no injury; for having gone through all the conflict Himself, without a single moment's wavering or surrender, He wishes us to be found continually in Him, and to conquer continually. He is faithful in bringing down to us all the gifts of God; all the counsel, will, and blessings of the Most High; faithful in taking up to God all our need and trial; all our petitions, fears, and tears; all our sufferings and all our works. What deep and infinite sympathy is in Jesus! And how much we should dwell upon it, and strengthen ourselves in the Lord. For He wishes to succour us; to take us by the hand when we are sad, weary, and exhausted; to help and encourage us; to cheer and gladden us who are still in manifold temptations and sufferings. He is Immanuel, God with us, as the *Man* Christ Jesus. We are comforted and upheld when we remember the humanity of Jesus now enthroned in glory, even as He in His dealings with us remembers what He endured upon earth. And thus we can say to Him, "O Thou, who art not ashamed to call us brethren, who Thyself didst suffer in being tempted, fulfil in us the good pleasure of Thy will, that in nothing we may yield to the adversary; however heavy our trials, however overwhelming our afflictions, and however painful our experiences in a world of sin and unbelief, O do Thou grant of Thine infinite faithfulness that through it all we may be kept looking unto Thee and following Thee, that we may always have peace and joy in Thee, and never waver in our childlike confidence in the Father!"

Now, dear friends, what else can I say in conclusion but what the apostle says, "Wherefore, holy brethren, partakers of the heavenly calling, consider the Apostle and High Priest of our profession, Christ Jesus." Think of Him; gaze stedfastly on the Lord Jesus. Consider; ponder. Let your mind be filled with Christ. Make not your sanctification the object of your contemplation, the theme of your meditation. What is it? Do you wish to ornament yourselves, and to come before God *beautiful*, or as a sinner? Do you wish to say from time to time, I have made great progress; I have advanced many steps in my heavenward journey; I have got into the higher Christian life, as people call it? Do you wish to come before God beautified? or do you wish to humble yourself, and ascribe glory unto the Lamb that was slain? . . . *Where* do we see Christ? Are we beholding the image of Christ reflected in our own hearts, in our own dispositions, states, and phases of faith? Then it will be reflected in troubled and muddy waters; and unstable and uncertain shall be the features which meet our eye there. Or shall we behold Jesus in the glory of *His* excellence, in the perfection of *His* holiness, in the beauty with which God has adorned Him? Are we not to look off unto Him in heaven, and to know that we are seated together in heavenly places, and complete in Him? Shall we say, "Oh, if I was only more holy, less selfish, more patient! if I could only see more of Jesus reflected in me!" Or shall we say, "Oh, if I could always behold the Man who died upon the cross! if I could always see Jesus, the Lamb of God that was slain! if I could always remember that I am bought with a price; and that He was wounded for my transgressions, and bruised for my iniquities!" *

I will ask you still further, Why do you wish to be holy? Is it to depend more on Christ, or to be less dependent on Christ? To think more of the sacrifice which Jesus made upon the cross, and to know and feel—

"Nothing in my hand I bring,
Simply to Thy cross I cling!"

Have you not detected it in yourself, that sometimes, when you have given way to temptation, fallen into sin you wished to avoid—when you have in the performance of duty stumbled over the same difficulty as before, that a feeling of distrust, disappointment, and despondency comes over you, a feeling of wounded pride and vanity, of impatience and irritation, and you say, "I am not making progress; it is really too bad; I am always falling into the same low state?" And then the lowest depth of self-abasement and humiliation is to go to God and to find *no change in Him;* the same Fatherly love, the same High Priestly compassion and grace, the same Comforter patient and gentle, and you discover, that in your best moments as well as in your worst, you depend exclusively and entirely on the grace

* Gossner, in Berlin, wrote a beautiful tract: *Mir ist's, als ob's Charfreitag wär*—I feel as if it was Good Friday; in which he shows that the one thing we ought to desire and aim at is, to behold constantly Christ crucified for us.

of God, which saves the chief of sinners. In fact, you have *only* stood by grace through the blood shed for vile sinners. How much we need to avoid the snare of cultivating vanity and self-seeking even in our sanctification! How apt we are to make a Saviour of self! I am anxious and troubled about the unscriptural view of the Christian life, of which we hear. Look at it. What was it in the Church of Rome that for so many centuries made the cross of Christ of none effect? They did not *wish* to ignore or reject Christ's salvation, and to make Christ of none effect. . Do not imagine that grievous errors and heresies began as it were in a bad and wicked purpose. How was it for centuries in the Church of Rome? Christ was put in the background, and the Reformers had to dig very deep, and put away a great amount of rubbish that had accumulated—the gold and silver and precious stones lay buried among wood and hay and stubble—till at last they found that Christ in whom alone we must rejoice. Look at the theology of such a book as, for instance, *Thomas à Kempis*, in which there is much that is excellent, but which suffers from the radical error of not distinguishing Christ for us, and Christ in us. These good men began to be exclusively thinking of Christ *in* them. All their attention was centred in that aspect of truth. They said, "It is true, Christ died for us;

but now we must go higher; and according as we realize Christ in us, we rest and have peace." It was by this well-meant praising of Christ *in* us that they forgot Christ *for* us. They saw that a hypocritical and superficial trust in the merits of Christ was a dead thing, which brought forth no fruit, which gained no victory over sin and the world. They therefore were anxious to see life and power. But they did not perceive clearly that our only power, peace, and life are in Christ, who died for us, and in whom we have perfection. By looking to their love to Jesus, to their imitation of His perfect example, to their resemblance to His holy image, they never could have true, perfect peace.

As a Christian never loses comfort but by breaking the order and method of the gospel, looking on his own and looking off Christ's perfect righteousness, so he that sets up his sanctification to look at, sets up the greatest idol, which will ultimately strengthen his fears and doubts, though at first it may soothe his feelings and please his imagination.

The young Christian is especially apt to fall into error. After his first zeal and love, after the spring and dawn of his spiritual life, when he is full of praise and strength, when prayer is fervent, when joy and praise abound, when love to the Saviour is ardent, when work for Christ seems refreshment, there generally succeeds a period of languor and of darkness, when he is led into the experience, painful but salutary, that even after his renewal, the old man, the flesh, is enmity against the Spirit, and that our all-sufficiency is of God. Now it is for him to enter more deeply into the valley of humiliation, to see more clearly the need and the preciousness of the blood of Christ, to ascribe more cordially and with greater contrition all glory to the God of salvation. He is, however, tempted to choose the path of what appears progress, victory, strength, and beauty; whereas God's saints say—Christ must increase; I must decrease. Christ is comely; I am black. Christ is strength; I am weakness. In Christ is all good; in me, that is, in my flesh, there is nothing good. The saints of God find, that instead of progressing from one degree of perfection to another, they discover in themselves daily more that sin which is exceeding sinful; they behold themselves vile, and cling with all intensity of faith to Jesus, who saith unto them, "My grace is sufficient for thee." They are saved by grace; they know Christ only as their righteousness and perfection; and even at the end of their earthly journey, of their labours and sufferings, they grasp "the faithful saying, worthy of all acceptation, that Christ Jesus came into the world to save sinners, of whom I am chief."

Rest in the Lord, and in Him alone. Consider the Apostle and great High Priest, Christ Jesus. Place your confidence and have your joy only in the Lamb slain. Call Jehovah, Jehovah-Tsidkenu. Day by day you are a burden to Jesus, and His grace alone upholds you, while you stand only in His perfection. You would not have it otherwise. And while you are looking off unto Him, you will run with patience the race set before you. You will fight the good, but real and painful, fight of faith; you will crucify daily the old man, who to our last breath is enmity against God; you will have no confidence in the flesh, but rejoice in Christ Jesus; and your life will be hid with Him in God. And at last Christ will present His children unblameable in body, soul, and spirit. Then shall we be like Him; then shall we have no more conflict, and no more sin. Faithful is He who hath promised, who also will perform it. Amen.

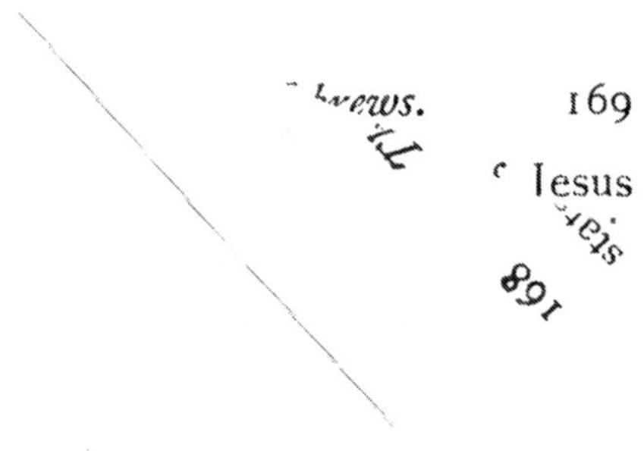

CHAPTER VII.

CHRIST THE LORD, AND MOSES THE SERVANT.

HEB. iii. 1-6.

WE commence the second section of the epistle to the Hebrews. It extends from the beginning of the third chapter to the fourteenth verse of the fourth chapter. The contents of this section may be stated briefly thus: That the Lord Jesus Christ, the mediator of the new covenant, is high above Moses, the mediator of the old dispensation, inasmuch as Jesus is the Son of God, and Lord *over* the house; whereas Moses is the servant of God, who was faithful *in* the house. And upon this doctrinal statement is based the exhortation, that we should not harden our hearts lest we fail to enter into that rest of which the possession of the promised land was only an imperfect type.

This section consists of two parts—a doctrinal

ment, which forms the basis, and an exhortation resting upon it.

The doctrinal statement, contained in the first six verses of the third chapter, is the subject of our meditation this morning.

Before the apostle advances in the argument, and shows the glory of the great High Priest by contrasting Him with the glory of Moses, the mediator of the old covenant, he recapitulates in an exhortation the teaching of the preceding chapters, and he admonishes the "holy brethren, partakers of the heavenly calling," to be continually, perseveringly, and earnestly looking unto "the Apostle and High Priest of their profession, Christ Jesus." He does not say *my* brethren, because in this epistle he keeps himself in the background; and when he speaks of them as "brethren," he evidently refers to the blessed truth just announced, that Jesus, the Son of God, is not ashamed to call us brethren. He means therefore those who by the Spirit of God have been born again, and who can call God their Father. He addresses those who of God are in Christ Jesus, who were quickened together with Him; for when He rose from the dead He was "the first-born among many brethren." He calls them "holy brethren," because upon this fact of brotherhood is based their sanctification. "He that sanctifieth and they who are sanctified are all of one." Set apart by the blood of Jesus unto the service and love of God, they are sanctified for ever by that one sacrifice which Jesus offered upon the cross. He reminds them of the "heavenly calling" which they have received now, and of which the earthly calling unto Canaan was only a type; "heavenly" because God the Father and Jesus the exalted High Priest are in heaven, and because the Holy Spirit who brought the glad tidings of salvation came down from the heavenly sanctuary to dwell among men; "heavenly" because the end of their calling is, that as the many children of God they shall be brought unto glory; "heavenly" because while waiting upon earth their citizenship is in heaven, and the whole spirit, character, and aim which characterise them is not according to this world, but according to that sanctuary and city where is their hope.

It is therefore for us to "consider" or (as the very expressive word implies), to look carefully unto "the Apostle and High Priest of our profession." This is the only Scripture in which Jesus is called the apostle, yet, though the word is not used, the thought is of frequent occurrence. Often Jesus testified that the Father *sent* Him, that He came obedient to the mission and will of His heavenly Father, that His whole life was only a fulfilment of the mission entrusted to Him; and as He was called in the Old Testament times "the Angel or

Messenger of the Covenant," so it is in accordance with the whole teaching of Scripture that He is called here by the name "apostle."* Of Christ the Head are all energies and ministrations in the body. If there are bishops, it is because Christ is *the* Bishop; if there are pastors or shepherds, it is because Christ is "the Shepherd of the flock;" if there are evangelists, it is because Christ came and brought to mankind the glad tidings; if there are apostles, it is because He is the Apostle, the head of all apostolic dignity and work. He is the Apostle sent by God to us men; the High Priest, as representing us before the Father.† Him we are to consider in *faith*; for herein is all our safety: looking unto Jesus, we have peace and joy; for this is the joy of our life, that all perfection is in Christ. And in *prayer*; for can we see Him in His holiness without the petition rising in our hearts, "O that I might be conformed unto Him!"

* Compare Heb. ii. 3, where Christ is likewise represented as the Messenger, the Proto-Apostle: ἀποστέλλειν is applied to Christ's coming in Matt. x. 40, xv. 24; Luke iv. 18; John iii. 17, iv. 9, 10. Christ is the Messenger of the Covenant, Mal. iii. 2; Exod. xxiii. 2, 3. The remark already quoted with reference to Heb. ii. 3, 4 (page 15) is applicable to this passage also. The apostle Paul, if, as we think, he is the writer, sinks his own apostleship, and points the Hebrews to the One Lord and Head.

† According to Bengel's simple distinction ἀπόστολος, qui Dei causam apud nos agit; ἀρχιερεύς, qui nostram causam apud Deum agit. But notice also the essential connection between the two ideas; He who was sent, κατ' ἐξοχήν, was sent in order by His sacrifice to become the High Priest. Lo, I come—(ἀπόστολος) to do thy will (ἀρχιερεύς).

We are to look upon Him as a painter looks upon a *model,* with the full intention and desire of imitating Him. We are to keep constantly in sight of Him, as our only infallible Guide upon earth. All this is included in that one word, that one expression, "consider." Gaze upon, meditate upon, "the Apostle and High Priest of our profession, Christ Jesus."

Let us look at the word "profession." We are very apt to undervalue things with which abuse and danger are connected, and which may be easily counterfeited. There is such a thing as a mere outward, empty, hypocritical profession; but is that a reason why we should not attach importance to confessing Christ? Jesus says, "Whosoever shall confess me before men, him will I confess before my Father, and before the angels. And whosoever shall deny me before men, him will I also deny." With the heart we are to believe unto righteousness, and with the mouth we are to confess that Jesus is the Lord. It may be merely an outward thing, a mere lip-utterance, to say, "I believe in Jesus;" it may be only a form to sit down at the Lord's table; but as the outward expression of an inward reality, it is a great and blessed fact. Let us not be secret disciples; let us not come to Jesus merely by night, ashamed to bear testimony to the gospel. Let us not despise the outward and visible church, although, alas!

there is much error and sin connected therewith. Our confession of Christ in the outward church, in the congregation of professed disciples, in the ordinances of Christ's institution, let us not undervalue it! Remember with gratitude that you have publicly professed Christ; that into the Church of Christ you have been received by baptism, and acknowledged at the Lord's Supper as a brother and partaker of the heavenly calling. Let the remembrance of this be to us continually helpful, and stimulate us to adorn the doctrine of the gospel by a Christ-like life and walk.

The Hebrews are exhorted to look unto the Apostle and High Priest Jesus, to Him of whose glory (chap. i.) and of whose sufferings and death (chap. ii.) they had been reminded; they are to look unto the Man Christ Jesus, the Son, who through His self-humiliation on earth became the merciful and faithful High Priest, having finished the work which the Father sent Him to do. And in order to show to the Hebrews the exceeding great glory of Jesus, who was faithful to Him who appointed Him * Mediator of the new covenant, he contrasts the Lord with Moses, the servant of God. †

* ποιήσαντι, literally made. But not in the sense of created, but who appointed, ordained and furnished Him with all that was necessary to carry out His great mission. "A body hast thou prepared for me." (Heb. x. 5.) Comp. also Mark iii. 14, original.

† "The servant of Jehovah, the King Messiah, will be greater

To speak of Moses to the Jews was always a very difficult and delicate matter. It is hardly possible for Gentiles to understand or realize the veneration and affection with which the Jews regard Moses, the servant of God. All their religious life, all their thoughts about God, all their practices and observances, all their hopes of the future, everything connected with God, is with them also connected with Moses. Moses was the great apostle unto them, the man sent unto them of God, the mediator of the old covenant; and we cannot wonder at this profound, reverential affection which they feel for Moses. You read in the gospels and in the book of the Acts with what joy and pride they said, "We are the disciples of Moses." It was their glory and boast; and we cannot wonder at this when we think of Moses, of his marvellous history, of his grand character, of the unique position assigned to him in the history of God's people, and the wonderful work given him to perform.

Think of the history of Moses. It was wonderful from the very commencement. Sheltered in his tender infancy from the cruelty of Pharaoh, courageously tended by his God-trusting parents, watched over by the angels and rescued from the persecution of his enemies, he was brought up at

than Abraham, more exalted than Moses, higher than all the angels of ministry."—*Ancient Synagogue's Comment on Isa.* lii. 13.

the very court of Pharaoh. Trained and educated by the Egyptian sages, he became learned in all the wisdom of the most advanced nation of the age. When he was a young man he was the only free man of his people; and of his own voluntary choice, by faith, he esteemed the reproach of Israel greater riches than the treasures of Egypt. And afterwards, when his fiery zeal, not yet chastened by the grace of God, brought him into conflict with Pharaoh, he was led into quiet and obscurity for forty years, that, leading a shepherd's life, he might learn the wisdom and patience of the saints. Then, called by the mysterious appearance of God in the burning bush, he was appointed to be Israel's deliverer, and endowed by God with power, he went forth. By faith he led his people out of Egypt, and through the Red Sea; and after ruling over the children of Israel for forty years, after a life of prayer and self-denial, of unparalleled trial and suffering, and of heroic patience and strength; after forty years of divine manifestations, blessings, and miracles, see him at last ascending mount Nebo; his eye was not yet dim, nor his natural force abated. He beheld the land, and died, and the Lord buried him, so that no man knoweth of his sepulchre. No doubt the angels who had watched him in his cradle on the waves of the Nile were there, ready to carry him into his place of rest, and with awe witnessing the conflict between Michael the archangel and the great adversary. (Jude.) What a marvellous history is the life of Moses! And look at his character. There is no man in the whole history of the Jews to compare with him, until you come to Him who is Lord of all, the Lord of glory, and to that chief of apostles, who was able to say, "Be ye followers of me, as I am of Christ." How wonderful is his faith in God! his zeal for the glory of God, and for the honour of Jehovah! his importunate prayer and wrestling with the Most High! his love for his nation, which makes him willing to die, and be blotted out of the book of life, rather than that Israel should be destroyed! his never-wearied patience and meekness! His whole life was a sacrifice of love and of obedience to the God of his fathers Abraham, and Isaac, and Jacob, who appeared to him in the burning bush; a life of self-denial and affection to the people of his choice.

Look at his peculiar position. He was mediator of the covenant, the ambassador (apostle) and plenipotentiary (as it were) of God. All God's dealings with Israel were transacted through him. He was a prophet, priest, and king in one person, and united all the great and important functions which had afterwards to be distributed among a plurality of persons. As a prophet he was different from all other prophets; for God spake to him face to face; and therefore he said, "A pro phet shall the Lord your God raise up unto you of your brethren, *like unto me.*" Jesus in His prophetic office is foreshadowed by all the prophets; but none of them except Moses could describe Jesus as a prophet like unto me. Through Moses the whole of the Levitical dispensation was instituted. The learned Bengel says—"While two chapters in Genesis are given to tell us how the world was created, there are sixteen chapters to tell us how the tabernacle was to be built. For the world was made for the sake of the Church; and the great object of all creation is to glorify God in the redemption and sanctification of His people." It is frequently and emphatically stated that Moses obeyed God fully, and made all things as he saw the pattern on the mount. As a prophet, and in the priestly spirit of love and meekness, he ruled over Israel, and showed them God's mighty wonders.

Look again at the work Moses accomplished, at the great things which the grace of God performed through him. Through him God brought Israel out of Egypt, and led them through the Red Sea; He gave the Ten Commandments and the whole law by him; by him the whole national life of Israel was organized; through him God laid the foundation of the theocracy, and all subsequent revelations of God have their root in the work which was wrought by Moses.

Even in the future, restored Israel will remember and honour him, and be guided by the law given through him. God bears witness to His servant that he was faithful in all God's house. In every department of this great and complicated building Moses obeyed the Lord implicitly and fully; according to everything that God told him, he performed it. Faithfulness is what God marks, loves, and honours; a perfect, sincere, and constant desire to obey the will of God in all that is entrusted to our care.

But after admitting fully the grandeur and excellence of Moses, the apostle proceeds to show the still greater glory of our Lord Jesus Christ. It must have struck you that in many respects Moses was a type of Jesus. Both were as infants threatened by cruel rulers, and both were marvellously sheltered by the living God. So in after life Moses was in some respects like Christ. Moses was the only freeman who espoused the cause of the nation; and Jesus was the only Free and Holy One who could take up the cause of the leper. But yet, what a difference! The zeal of Moses was not free from earth-born elements, and had to be purified. But there was nothing in Jesus that was of the earth earthy; no *sinful weakness* of the flesh was in Him who condescended to come in the *likeness* of *sinful* flesh. His love was always pure, His zeal holy, His aim single. Moses spake face to face with God, and was the mediator between God and Israel. The Lord Jesus is Prophet, Priest, and King in one person, but He is perfectly and eternally the true Revealer, Reconciler, Ruler, as the Son of God. Moses was willing to die for the nation; the Lord Jesus actually died, and not for the nation only, but to gather all the children of God into one. Moses brought the law on tables of stone; the Lord Jesus by His Spirit, even the Holy Ghost, writes the law on our hearts.

But notice the imperfection of Moses as a *servant.* The one sin of his life, which is mentioned as the cause of his not being permitted to enter the promised land, seems at first sight not to merit such a severe punishment. Moses was doubtless guilty of other sins; but why is this one sin singled out? Not merely because he was impatient, but because he did not sanctify the name of God among the people. Whereas God was willing to show pure mercy, Moses was not able to rise to the height of this great argument, and showed the vehemence of his anger and displeasure. How different was Jesus! He declared the full, perfect, and free love of God. He exclaimed on the cross: "Father, forgive them: for they know not what they do." And the message He now sends is nothing but salvation for the lost and guilty.

The house, the building, means the children of God, who by faith, as lively stones, are built upon Christ Jesus the foundation, and who are filled with the Holy Ghost; in whom God dwells, as in His temple, and in whom God is praised and manifested in glory. The illustration is very simple and instructive. We are compared unto stones, and as every simile is defective, we must add, not *dead* stones, but *lively* stones, as the apostle in his epistle to the Ephesians speaks of the building *growing*. The way in which we are brought unto the Lord Jesus Christ and united with Him is not by *building*, but by *believing*. The builders rejected the "chief corner stone" (Psalm cxviii. 22); but "coming unto Christ" (1 Peter ii.), simply believing, "ye also, as lively stones, are built up a spiritual house." When we go about the works of the law we are trying to build, and as long as we *build* we are not built. When we give up working, then by faith the Holy Ghost adds us to Christ, and grafts us into the living Vine, who is also the Foundation. We are rooted and grounded. The house is one, and all the children of God are united in the Spirit. Some are strong and are pillars, others are weak and rest upon those whom God has appointed to be strong, and to support and encourage the feeble. "None liveth unto himself;" and "if one member suffer, all the members suffer with it." If one grows and rejoices, it is for the good of the whole. The glory of the Lord is to show itself in the whole church, thus united by the indwelling Spirit. But not merely does God dwell in the church as a whole, it is the peculiarity of everything spiritual that every part of it is again a whole.* Not only is it true, that "wheresoever two or three are gathered together" in Christ's name, He is in the midst of them; but if *a single person* loves Him, the Father will love him, and will come and make His abode with him. An individual is thus also a temple, a habitation filled with the Holy Ghost. The Father and the Lord Jesus Christ dwell in him. Israel could understand this because it was symbolized by the temple, and the reality and substance of the symbol was also promised to them in the days of the Messiah. For what was the promise of the new covenant? "I will dwell in them, and they in me." What a marvellous idea is here presented to us! A Christian is like the tabernacle; he is a sanctuary. There is the holy of holies, the holy place, and the outer court. But in all the glory of God is to be revealed; the holiness of God to be shown forth. His body is the Lord's; the members of his body are Christ's members. His eyes, his lips, his feet, all the physical energies which God has given unto him, are a part of the house in which the Father and the Lord Jesus, through

* Oetinger.

the Holy Ghost, take up their abode. His reason, memory, imagination, affections, will, conscience, all that is in him, behold, it is a house where God is to dwell. God is to walk in it, to dwell in it, to rest in it. He is to be not merely a visitor, but an indwelling guest, "abiding in him." Sometimes God will convert this wonderful dwelling-place into His temple, and there will be heard the voice of prayer and praise. Sometimes He changes it into a banqueting-hall, and there will be heard the voice of rejoicing and the melody of thanksgiving, the assurance of that love which is better than wine. Sometimes it becomes a battle-field, and the Lord is a man-of-war, and conquers the enemies of the worm Jacob, and succours the saint who is tempted.

How manifold are the mansions in which He dwells! As there are many mansions in the Father's house above, as there are many mansions in His Church below, so also are there many rooms in the spiritual house of the individual believer; in various manifestations of grace, strength, and love, does God dwell in us.

You who believe in Jesus are His house, His own; for as the Father appointed Him to be Mediator, as the Father laid the foundation in Zion, so Jesus the Lord bought you with His own blood, and sent into your hearts His own Spirit. We are emphatically Christ's. This is of

God, and by the Spirit; but Christ dwelleth in us; we are His own house.

But the apostle adds—shall I call it a condition? shall I call it an encouragement? Oh, there is nothing hard in the exhortations of Scripture!—"If you hold fast the confidence and the rejoicing of your hope unto the end." I do not look upon it as a condition in the sense of contingency. If it were possible that we who have come unto the Lord Jesus Christ, and who have loved and served Him, or rather let me say, have experienced His grace and faithfulness—if it were possible that, after all, we should forsake Him, and turn away from the faith, oh, of all things this would be most fearful and of all prospects this would be the most wretched! What is the one thing which the Christian desires? What is the one great thing which he does? What is the one great secret which he is always endeavouring to find out with greater clearness, and grasp with firmer intensity? Is it not this: "My Beloved is mine, and I am His"? The inmost desire of our heart and the exhortations of the word coincide. To the end we must persevere; and it is therefore with great joy and alacrity that we receive the solemn exhortations: "He that endureth unto the end shall be saved;" "No man, having put his hand to the plough, and looking back, is fit for the kingdom of God." We desire to hear constantly the voice which saith from His heavenly throne, "To him that overcometh will I grant to sit with me in my kingdom, even as I also overcame, and am set down with my Father in His throne."

And with the exhortation is the word of promise: "Being confident of this very thing, that He which hath begun a good work in you will perform it until the day of Jesus Christ." "They that trust in the Lord shall be like mount Zion, which cannot be moved, but standeth fast for ever." "My sheep hear my voice, and I know them, and they follow me; and I give unto them eternal life, and they shall never perish, neither shall any one pluck them out of my hand. My Father, which gave them me, is greater than all; and no man is able to pluck them out of my Father's hand. I and my Father are one."

Oh, blessed word and promise of God, that He will keep us unto the end! But how is it that we are kept? Through faith, through watchfulness, through self-denial, through prayer and fasting, through our constantly taking heed unto ourselves according to His word. "Hold fast," if you desire it to be manifested in that day that you are not merely outward professors, not merely fishes existing in the net, but the true and living disciples of the One Master, "Hold fast the confidence and rejoicing of your hope firm unto the end." Faith is the mother of hope; but how often is the mother strengthened and cheered by the daughter! There is first faith—"By faith are ye saved, not of works"—then hope. "For we are saved by hope," looking forward to the recompence of the reward. Do not imagine that hope is in any way inferior to faith and love. Some seem to think hope is of nature, a feature of our natural character, an element in our natural disposition. They would not be ashamed to say they had little hope, although they would not like to confess they had little faith or little love. Why? Because they take a perfectly erroneous view of what hope is. It is a gift and fruit of the Holy Ghost just as much as faith and love. As hope is an essential feature of the Christian character, so it is of grace, and not of nature. The lively hope which God by the Spirit gives unto us, comes through the resurrection of Jesus from the dead. It has not its root in the first creation, and is not strengthened by that which is of the flesh. The same apostle who teaches us that we are saved by faith, declares that we are saved by hope. (Rom. viii. 24.) For though the grace of our Lord is exceeding abundant with faith and love which are in Christ Jesus (1 Tim. i. 14), yet we are still in conflict with sin and temptation, in a body of death and a world of evil. We *hope* for the full and perfect salvation; we shall see Christ as He is, and be like Him; we wait for the redemption of the body, and the regeneration of the world. Hence hope refers to the future, even to the coming of the Lord Jesus; and yet it possesses already the substance and earnest of the inheritance. For is not Christ, who is our hope, ours even now by faith and in love? But hope, looking to the glory of Christ and to the transfiguration of our body, is the very strength, essence, and impulse of heavenly-mindedness. In proportion as we hope, we rise above the sins and vanities of earth.*

Cherish the hope which in Christ Jesus is given unto you who believe in the Saviour. Look forward to the coming of the Lord, to the joy and glory which He will bring unto His disciples. Be not afraid, for He will sustain you during all your difficulties and trials, and you will surely be kept unto that day. And be not afraid that the glory and brightness will overwhelm you; for Christ the Lord will be glorified *in* you, and thus be your strength, and you shall shine forth as the sun in the kingdom of your Father. Hold fast the confidence and the rejoicing of your hope. In calm and humble assurance, looking only unto Christ crucified for sinners, you cannot but rejoice in hope of the glory of God. As you trust in Jehovah your righteousness, so you look forward

* Apostolic teaching on hope is both copious and unanimous. Rom. v. 1–5, viii. 15–39, xii. 12, xv. 13; Eph. i. 12–14, 18; Col. i. 5, 23, 27; 1 Thess. 1, 3; 2 Thess. ii. 16; 1 Peter 1, 3, 9–12; 1 John iii. 1 3. Beside the passages in this epistle, vi. 11, x. 23, xi. 1, &c.

to Jehovah your glory. The God of hope (the source and object of hope) fill you with joy and peace in believing, through the power of the Holy Ghost. (Rom. xv.)

What more suitable encouragement could we have at the beginning of the year than these words of the apostle? The end spoken of is nothing else but the appearing of the Lord Jesus, when hope shall be changed into sight. The day is approaching (x. 25), and with it our glory. We look back on the years through which we have been led. On a day like this we feel as if we had come to a milestone, on one side of which we can read the inscription, telling us how many years and stages of our journey have been completed. But on the other side, where curiosity expects to find the number of years yet before us, what do Faith and Love and Hope read? What else but this—"Surely goodness and mercy shall follow me all the days of my life." And again—"Unto them that love God all things work together for good." And again—"Whose house are ye, if ye hold fast the confidence and rejoicing of your hope unto the end." We know how many years have elapsed since the First Advent; but on the other side of the milestone we read, no date, but the words—"Watch, for ye know not the day nor the hour wherein the Son of man doth come." And we can also testify, "If you believe in Jesus, if you love and follow Him, if you abide in Him, then when the Lord comes again you will have confidence, and stand before Him."

Look unto Him, and be ye saved, all ye ends of the earth; and you, holy brethren, partakers of the heavenly calling, oh, *consider*, consider the Apostle and High Priest of our profession—Jesus! Amen.

CHAPTER VIII.

UNBELIEF IN THE WILDERNESS.

HEB. iii. 7 19.

THE apostle has compared and contrasted Moses, the servant of God and the mediator of the old dispensation, with the Lord Jesus, the Messiah, the Son of the Father, and the mediator of the new and everlasting covenant. Great was the glory of Moses, and whether we think of his marvellous history, of his unique position as prophet, priest, and king in Israel, of his grand and deep character, or of the fundamental and mighty work which was accomplished through him, we can easily understand why it is written, that there arose not a prophet like unto him until He came who is above all, the Lord from heaven. We judge of magnitude by comparison. It is because the Jews had some idea and appreciation of the greatness of Moses that the apostle avails himself of this, to point out to them the far higher glory of the Lord Jesus. Though in the life and character of Moses there are many striking excellencies and virtues, the faithfulness of Moses is the feature on which the apostle dwells. It is, indeed, the most important feature in our character as servants of God. This is the one thing required of us, to be faithful. And well were it for us if we laid more stress on faithfulness, and thought less of gifts and talents, or of success and results. For while it belongs to God to appoint unto each of us severally our position, to distribute gifts according to His wisdom and good pleasure, and to reward us with results and harvests, hundredfold, sixtyfold, or thirtyfold, it belongs to us to be faithful to God wherever He has placed us, and in the gift and task which His love assigns. We see the summary and result of the true disciple's life in the decisive words of the Master: "Well done, good and faithful servant; thou hast been faithful over a few things, I will make thee ruler over many things." Moses was faithful in all God's house. In every branch of the work with which he was entrusted he carried out the commandments of God. He added nothing of his own to the instructions which he received; he left out nothing, but ordered all things as he was commanded. And though sorely tried by Israel's ingratitude, rebelliousness, and stubbornness, his faithfulness never wearied nor wavered. But while Moses was faithful as a servant, Jesus was faithful as the Son. Moses, sinful and imperfect, was himself part of the house; Jesus the Holy One, the Son of God, is Lord over the house. The dispensation of which Moses was mediator was temporary, preparatory, and typical of the new covenant, in which all things are eternal, substantial, and heavenly. Moses, as the Saviour testified, wrote of Christ. The whole law pointed to the Messiah. Jesus fulfilled the law, because He was the Perfect Man, in whom alone the law in its depth and breadth was realised and manifested, and because He bore the curse and the condemnation which the law pronounces against transgressors. All the promises of salvation which the typical (or gospel) part of the Mosaic dispensation contained, all sacrifices, festivals, and priestly mediation, found its substance and fulfilment in Christ. How much greater then is He than Moses!

God spake with Moses face to face, yet is Jesus only The Prophet, for as the only begotten He declared the Father: we see the Father when we see Jesus. Moses was full of love and the priestly spirit; but Jesus was not merely willing to die for Israel, but actually laid down His life, and not for the nation only, but that He might gather in one all the children of God. Moses ruled as king in

Jeshurun; but Jesus is the true King, who by the Spirit can make His people willing in the day of His power, and renew their hearts into living obedience. Moses is the servant, but Jesus the Son is Lord.*

The glory of Christ that excelleth is described by the apostle Paul (2 Cor. iii. 6–12), a passage which should be studied in connection with our chapter.

On this contrast between the Lord Jesus and Moses the servant of God, the apostle builds his earnest exhortation. Again he interrupts the course of his massive and sublime argument by most solemn and pathetic admonition. His great aim in this epistle is to exhort. He is bent, with all intensity of purpose and of watchful love, to beseech the Hebrews to be stedfast. He is moved with fear; his heart trembles with anxiety, while he points to the glory of the great High Priest; he is continually giving vent to the pent-up feelings of affection and solicitude with which he regards the dangerous condition of the Hebrew believers. Oh, it is so like Paul, the apostle of love! He seems to me to have had a thousand

* "Moses was a type in the world. If any should say, What is the fulfilment and consummation? I answer, King Messiah: through Him such perfection will be produced as never existed hitherto throughout all generations." (Zohar.) Many passages in the Talmudic writings teach that the law shall be abolished in the days of Messiah, and that the light and wisdom of the Messianic age far exceed that of the law of Moses.

hearts. He loved each church as if it was the only one he possessed. He felt their burden, he rejoiced over their order, stedfastness, and gifts; he ceased not to give thanks for them, and to pray for the blessing and help which each of them needed; he remembered the names of their saints, he watched over them with the affectionateness of a tender mother and nurse. While he seems lost in the contemplation of divine truth, soaring like an eagle far above vale and mountain-peak, and gazing with stedfast eye into the brightness of the sun, he is always like his blessed and dear Lord, who in homely but most touching language compares Himself to a hen gathering her chickens under her wings.

In all Paul's epistles we feel the warm breath of affection; we hear the voice, tremulous with emotion, we see the earnest and loving countenance of the fatherly man. Even when he writes to the Romans, whom he had never seen, he says, "I long to see you, that I may impart unto you some spiritual gift, that ye may be established; that is, that I may be comforted together with you by the mutual faith both of you and me." What can exceed his tender love to the churches of Thessalonica and Philippi? or the soul-stirring expostulations which in anguish of mind he addresses to the Galatians, of whom he travails again in birth, that Christ may be formed in them? How fatherly, how considerate, how exquisitely delicate and sensitive is he in his treatment of the Corinthian church. In all his epistles he continually interrupts the doctrine with the expression of his love, his anxiety, his joy and sorrow; we see his heart bound up in the churches. So in this epistle he constantly exhorts and beseeches the Hebrews (and us also) to abide in Christ, to take heed unto ourselves, to be faithful unto the end.

Thus is it in all Scripture. The love of God, seeking our salvation, pervades all its teaching. Do we not throughout the whole Scripture hear God, as it were, sighing, "Oh that they were wise; that they hearkened unto my voice!" Do we not hear the tearful voice of Jesus saying, "If thou hadst known?" Do we not throughout behold the loving arms of God outstretched to receive us? May we return love with love, so that Christ's joy may be full in us.

The thought of Moses naturally suggests the Israelites in the wilderness. Faithful was the Mediator, through whom God dealt with them: but was Israel faithful? God spake: did they obey? God showed them wonderful signs: did they trust and follow in faith? And if Israel was not faithful under Moses, and their unbelief brought ruin upon them, how much more guilty shall we be, and how much greater our danger, if we are not faithful unto the Lord Jesus?

The history of the wanderings of Israel in the wilderness is most instructive. No Scripture is of private interpretation, but is catholic and eternal. Whatsoever things were written aforetime were written for our learning. Of this history especially, the apostle Paul, who dwells on it in his epistle to the Corinthians, tells us that all these things happened unto them for ensamples; and they are written for our admonition, upon whom the ends of the world are come. (1 Cor. x.) According to the solemn words addressed by the glorified Saviour to the church of Thyatira, Israel's experience is to be a warning to all the churches. The books of Moses are thus of permanent importance to God's children. Israel's history in the wilderness is typical throughout. It is a *marvellous* history from beginning to end. The exodus out of Egypt, the passage through the Red Sea, the giving of the Law at mount Sinai, the manna, the pillar of cloud and fire, the victory over Amalek, the rock that followed them, the garments that never became old; all is miracle, full of the wondrous love and power of God, who is Israel's redeemer. Consider the Messenger, the Angel of the Covenant, Christ, who led them. Their whole life and history was a life and history by the word of God. Do you know this as a present experience?

It was a history of *solemn and glorious privi-*

lege. God separated Israel unto Himself. They were shut up to God. Their daily need, their absolute dependence on divine help and bounty, the constant gift of manna, guidance and defence, which so visibly descended from the Lord, the giver of all; the daily beholding of God's mighty and gracious works—all this was a marvellous privilege, the life of faith was made near and easy. Dependence on second causes is a great snare to man; for since the fall the tendency of man is to forget the Creator. Israel in the wilderness had to live daily and exclusively by God's power and goodness. How solemn, yet how glorious, to be thus constantly depending on God and constantly beholding His omnipotent love. Is this not a picture of the Christian's life?

It is a *sad* history from beginning to end: continual murmuring, doubt, ingratitude, idolatry, sin; looking back unto Egypt and its pleasures, forgetting its degradation and bondage, doubting God's goodness and power, yielding to the temptations of lust and tempting the Lord Jehovah, the faithful and merciful Christ.*

It is a sad history, full of fearful judgments. Long, dark years, of most of which we know nothing but the ominous allusions in the prophetic books to the worship of Moloch and Remphan. And yet the Lord was with them all the days,

* Comp. 1 Cor. x., specially verse 9.

and every day, ready to bless and to gladden them. Do you understand the *parable?*

Yet was there in Israel also faith and love; and God remembers the time of their espousals, when they followed Him in a land that was not sown. There were not merely murmurings, but hymns of praise and thanksgiving; there were willing offerings unto the Lord of gold and silver, there was victory over the enemies, there were Joshua and Caleb, ho followed the Lord fully.

In the book of Psalms, which is to a certain extent a response to the five books of Moses, as well as the starting-point of the subsequent prophets, frequent reference is made to the history of the wilderness. It is remembered, first in order to ascribe glory to God, and to give thanks unto Him for His mercy and for His marvellous works. And secondly, to hold up the mirror to man, and especially Israel, that we may learn humility and faith. The apostle quotes Psalm xcv., in which the exhortation, based upon Israel's disobedience and punishment, .is peculiarly solemn and emphatic. You must have noticed how frequently the Psalms are quoted in this epistle. Our Saviour also singles them out as a special portion of Scripture. The church in all ages has honoured and loved the Psalms. David was chosen to be the sweet singer of Israel, not merely the old covenant Israel, but the whole Israel of God.

Here is perfect sympathy with all our weakness and fluctuating experience, and at the same time faithful and sure guidance; here we find a perfect expression of feeling and soul-experience; here are the deepest and truest utterances of repentance and of faith—of the soul's mournful complaints in darkness and sorrow, and of jubilant rejoicing and thanksgiving in the sunshine of divine favour; here is a true analysis of the heart; here we behold the doubts and conflicting thoughts, the fear and tumult of the soul—all that ever moves and agitates the saints of God. But the Psalter is not merely an expression of our feelings; it guides, corrects, and elevates us. David prays with us according to the mind of God. He is not merely our brother, but he is also a type of Christ. In the Psalms we learn the mind of Messiah in His union with His people. Hence the Psalter is the incomparable and comprehensive manual and hymn-book of the saints.*

* As Johann Arndt says: "The Psalter is a necklace, consisting of the gold of doctrine and salutary instruction, of heart-reviving gems of consolation, and precious stones of beautiful prayers; a theatre of the unveiled great purposes and works of God; a cheerful meadow end extensive garden of roses, in which the most beautiful and fragrant flowers delight us; an infinite ocean, in which those who experience many tempests of affliction find precious pearls; a heavenly school, where we converse with God Himself, our great Teacher; a mirror of divine mercies, in which the glorious countenance of our most compassionate Father shines forth; the most perfect anatomy of our souls, showing not merely our inmost thoughts and passions, but their corrective and medicine."

The quotation is introduced (like all Scripture quotations in this epistle) as the word of God, "as the Holy Ghost saith." Even the subjective lyrical portions of Scripture proceed out of divine depths, as well as depths of the human heart. Holy men spake and not merely spake, but sang with human, real music, in joy, in sorrow, in gladness and in tears, and yet as they were moved by the Holy Ghost. But in this quotation it is possible that the reference to the Holy Ghost has a special meaning and propriety; for it is the office of the Spirit (in the divine economy of grace) to glorify the Father and the Son, to direct us to Christ's word, to cause us to listen to the Father's voice. As the Father says of Christ, "Hear Him;" and as the Son always magnifies the Father's word, so the Holy Ghost testifies not of Himself, but of the Father and the Son.

The psalm begins with an exhortation to praise God. Joyous and festive is the tone in which it commences. It describes God in His greatness and power. It starts with the assurance that He is the Rock of our salvation. The Lord the Creator is also the Shepherd of His people. David calls on us to sing; and song is the expression of joy, peace, and love: "O come, let us sing unto the Lord: let us make a joyful noise to the Rock of our salvation. Let us kneel before the Lord our maker. For He is our God; and we are the people of His pasture, and the sheep of His hand." But with a sudden transition the psalmist, or as the apostle Paul prefers to say, the Holy Ghost, exhorts us most solemnly not to harden our hearts as Israel did in the temptation.

Notice, (1) when we hear God's voice—and, oh, how clearly and sweetly does He speak to us in the person of His Son Jesus, the Word incarnate, who died for us in Golgotha!—the *heart* must respond. The assent of the intellect, the admiration of the understanding, the fervour of the imagination, and even the conviction of the conscience, do not suffice. God speaks to the heart of Jerusalem. (Isaiah xl., original.) By this expression is meant the centre of our spiritual existence, that centre out of which thoughts and affections proceed, out of which are the issues of life, that mysterious fountain which God only can know and fathom. Oh that Christ may dwell *there!*

God's voice is to *soften* the heart. This is the purpose of the divine word—to make our hearts tender. Alas! by nature we are *hard*-hearted; and what we call good and soft-hearted is not so in reality and in God's sight. God wishes us to be delivered from hardness of heart, that is, from dulness of perception of His love and beauty, from ingratitude and lukewarmness towards Him, from pride and impenitence, from self-seeking and unrest. When we receive God's word in the heart, when we acknowledge our sin, when we adore God's mercy, when we desire God's fellowship, when we see Jesus, who came to serve us, to wash our feet, and to shed His blood for our salvation, the heart becomes soft and tender. For repentance, faith, prayer, patience, hope of heaven, all these things make the heart tender. Tender towards God, tender towards our fellow-men, tender —think it not paradoxical—towards ourselves; I mean that state of gentleness and meekness which David describes—"Lord, my heart is not haughty, nor mine eyes lofty. . . . Surely I have behaved and quieted myself as a child that is weaned of his mother." We live in the atmosphere of forgiving and merciful love, we become also tender and loving to our own true life, freed from that restless and feverish spirit of the worldly man who, indulgent to self, which is not his true and real self, rules harshly and impatiently over the desires and sorrows of the imprisoned spirit. Can we be hard —thinking much of ourselves, discontented with our lot, envious or unforgiving, worldly and restless—when we hear the voice of God: "I am the Lord thy God; I have loved thee with an everlasting love; thou art mine." "As I have loved you, love one another"? The road may be narrow, and the sun nearly set, but hearing the voice of Jesus, the heart burns within us in love and hope.

Notice, (2) all sin begins in the heart. In the epistle to the Corinthians (1 Cor. x.) the apostle describes the rivers, the corrupt branches; there he speaks of Israel's murmuring, idolatry, and lust. Here the Spirit speaks of the fountain and root: "They do err in *their hearts*." And what is the error of the heart? What else but *unbelief?* God speaks, and the heart is to believe. If the heart is hardened, it believes not; and regarding neither the threatenings nor the promises, it leans not on the strength and love of God: unbelief is the mother of all sin and sorrow.

For (3) unbelief is departure from the living God. How simple is this! As long as you trust God, you are near Him. The moment you doubt Him, your soul has departed into the strange country. Faith is the link between God's fulness and strength and our emptiness and weakness. If the soul cries out, Abide with me, or Nearer to Thee, the answer of Jesus is, Only believe!

Unbelief cannot see and understand God.* Forty years Israel had seen the works of the Most High. Every day they beheld the manna and the pillar

* To know God is the source of life and the very substance of blessedness. All the gracious purposes of God are to this end, that we may know Him. Hence when the apostle John writes to fathers in Christ, he describes them thus: "Fathers, because ye have known Him that is from the beginning." (1 John ii. 13, 14.)

of His guiding presence. How many miracles they witnessed! At the end of this long period and these daily visitations the Lord says (in sorrow and disappointment, to speak humanly), "They do always err in their heart, and they have *not known my ways.*" They do not understand me. They have no eye to see my face, no perception, no sympathy; they do not understand my meaning, my thought, my character, *myself*, though I have been constantly speaking, revealing, manifesting, yet do they not perceive; it is hidden to them.

They tempted God. By fear and murmuring, by presumption and lust, by disobedience and idolatry, ten times their evil heart of unbelief manifested itself in tempting the Lord. (Num. xiv. 22.) Although they had seen the mighty works of God, and were continually experiencing His mercy, they doubted both His power and love; they cherished bitter thoughts against Him, they challenged Him, and demanded signs, as if He had never shown unto them the wonders of His goodness.*

The Lord was grieved, and after the tenth

* The following are the ten temptations according to the Jews: (1) Exod. xiv. 11, from fear; ( ) Exod. xv. 24, murmuring; (3) Exod. xvi. 2, 3, murmuring; (4) Exod. xvi. 19, 20, disobedience; (5) Exod. xvi. 27, 28, Sabbath-breaking; (6) Num. xx. 3, chiding; (7) Exod. xxxii., idolatry; (8) Num. xi. 1–3, complaining; (9) Num. xi. 32, lust; (10) Num. xiv., unbelief. The root of all sin is unbelief, as,

temptation—so great is His patience—swore in His wrath that they should not enter into His rest. Doubtless many of those who died in the wilderness turned to God in repentance and faith. We cannot but believe that many of them joined with heartfelt contrition in the prayer of Moses: "We are consumed by thine anger, and by thy wrath are we troubled. Thou hast set our iniquities before thee, our secret sins in the light of thy countenance . . . O satisfy us early with thy mercy; that we may rejoice and be glad all our days."

But the generation as such, a warning for all ages, died in the wilderness.

Again the apostle asks emphatically, Why did they not enter into rest? And the answer is, Because they believed not. He does not single out the sin of making and worshipping the golden calf; he does not bring before us the flagrant transgressions into which they fell at Baal-peor. Many much more striking and to our mind more fearful sins could have been pointed out; but God thinks the one sin greater than all is *unbelief*. We are saved by faith; we are lost through unbelief. The heart is purified by faith; the heart is har-

beginning with Gen. iii., is taught throughout all Scripture. The two manifestations of unbelief are in opposite poles—presumption and distrust. The world is the wilderness; Israel's history a mirror of ours. The decision and victory must be in the heart. *Christ dwelling in the heart by faith*, we have peace and strength. Then can we imitate Jesus. (Matt. iv.)

dened by unbelief. Faith brings us nigh to God; unbelief is departure from God. Does it seem strange? By faith we draw near and worship God; by faith we receive God's love; through faith the Holy Ghost is given unto us; by faith we obey and follow Christ. Yet is it so natural and so like the goodness of God that all should be by faith. For the Lord is our God; He is all. He is willing to be, to give, to do all; to be God for us, to us, in us. All He asks of us is to trust Him, to receive Him; to open our empty hand to His kind and bountiful hand, and our cold and dead heart to His heart, that spared not His own Son, but gave Him up unto death. By grace are we saved through faith; and even this trust is the gift of His blessed Spirit. (Eph. ii.)

Unbelief prevented Israel's entering into the promised land. Then it follows that faith enters into rest. Believe with thy heart is the great lesson of the chapter. If we trust in God, then the wilderness will be converted into the garden of the Lord. See the true Israel, Jesus our Lord, who was tested in the wilderness. God proved and tried the Righteous One; Satan tempted Him. Then it was made manifest what was in Him, even a meek and lowly heart, strong in faith, tender and loyal towards His heavenly Father, learning obedience because He was Son. And though the wild beasts were with Him, and

His body was exhausted and weary, and the tempter's voice cunning and subtle, yet no evil came nigh unto Him; for He dwelt in the secret place of the Most High, and abode under the shadow of the Almighty. The wild beasts dare not touch Him, the exhausted frame is upheld by the indwelling spirit; the Scripture is both the weapon with which He fights and a tent in which He dwells; the very angels of God come down and minister unto Him. Thus the Son of Man by faith converted the wilderness into paradise. He entered into rest, He enjoyed peace with God; and there was given Him power to tread upon the lion and adder, and to trample the dragon under His feet. Worshipping the Father He conquered; and the angels of God refreshed and gladdened His heart with their heavenly converse.

Such is to be your life. Only believe, only worship, only harden not your heart, when in the Scripture and in the Spirit's teaching and in God's daily dealings you hear God's voice, and though wild beasts, hunger and privation, weakness and temptation beset you, you are safe, you are blessed. God is with you; who can be against you? Angels are around you, and you can give thanks; for you are more than conquerors, through Him that loved you, and gave Himself for you.

Looking unto Jesus, I return to the commencement of the psalm, and end in praise. I will listen to its solemn admonition, I will stand in awe, when I see the carcases of them that fell in the wilderness through unbelief; I will humble myself when I think how often like Israel I have murmured and doubted, how often I have grieved and tempted the Lord; but I will believe, I will cleave to Jesus, I will remember that oath which the Lord sware by Himself; As I live, saith the Lord, I have no pleasure in the death of the sinner, but rather that he should turn and live. And again, willing more abundantly to show unto the heirs of promise the immutability of His counsel, He confirmed it by an oath, saying, "Surely, blessing I will bless thee." Let us whom God hath redeemed out of Egypt, not with gold and silver, but with the precious blood of Christ as of the true Paschal Lamb without blemish and without spot; let us who have been rescued out of death and the power of Satan by the resurrection of our Lord Jesus Christ; let us who have received the law of God, not as a letter which killeth, but by the outpouring of the Spirit and in the renewal of our hearts—oh, come, let us, remembering our passover, our resurrection-day, our Pentecost, let us sing unto the Lord! Let us make a joyful noise to the rock of our salvation.

But let us listen to the solemn exhortation of the Spirit. To-day harden not your hearts. Yesterday is the past of sin and misery. To-day is the present of divine grace and man's faith. To-morrow is eternity, full of joy and glory. To-day is the turning-point, the crisis, the seed-time. To whom can we go but unto Jesus Christ, with the past of our transgression, with the yesterday of the first Adam, with the to-day of our weakness and need, with the for ever of our endless destiny? He is Jehovah, the Saviour God, the same yesterday, to-day, and for ever. Cleaving to Him we rest in mercy, which is from everlasting to everlasting.

The apostle warns us: Take heed, brethren, lest there be in any of you an evil heart of unbelief. He is anxious that not one single member of the professing Church should be lost; as he expresses it in another Scripture—he preaches Christ, warning every man, and teaching every man in all wisdom; that we may present every man perfect in Christ Jesus. (Col. i. 28.) The same spirit ought to animate the whole congregation. Each member has to take heed to himself and the whole community, to care anxiously and earnestly for each member, that *none* may be lost.

Exhort one another daily; encourage, help one another by counsel, by example, by sympathy, by brotherly aid, by united prayer and praise. Walking together in peace and harmony, keep before your eyes and hearts the end of the journey.

Let us hold the beginning of our confidence stedfast to the end, let us keep our first faith, our first love, our first hope (1 Tim. v. 12; Rev. ii. 4; Heb. iii. 6), that which was given unto us when the grace of our Lord was exceeding abundant (1 Tim. i. 14), even when we were made partakers of Christ.* In humility and fear, in self-abasement and self-distrust, let us during our wilderness journey cry out of the depths, and yet rejoice and be at peace; for we are in Christ, and the Lord for whom we wait is our light and our salvation.

* Μέτοχοι γεγόναμεν. We have become by grace, what we were not by nature, partakers of Christ; since we have part in all that Christ is and has, at present by faith, and afterwards in actual possession, as joint-heirs with the Son. ὑπόστασις, confidence means sometimes substance (i. 3); sometimes, as undoubtedly in 2 Cor. ix. 9, xi. 17, confidence and assurance. In Heb. xi. the objective and subjective aspects are combined.

CHAPTER IX.

FEAR AND REST.

HEB. iv. 1-11.

THE two words which claim our special consideration in this section are, fear and rest. I. We know only in part, in fragment. It is difficult for us to combine different aspects of truth. When doctrines apparently contradictory are presented to us, we are apt to attach importance to one, and to leave the other in the background, treating it with indifference and cold neglect. We cherish some portions of truth; we look but rarely and hastily on others. In our choice we are influenced by our natural temperament and conformation of mind, by preconceived notions, by the type of religious teaching in which we have been trained, and sometimes by our sinful tendencies, which shrink from some portions of Scripture and some aspects of divine truth, which avoid and hide themselves from the corrective and rebuking influence of some part of God's message.

It is part of our imperfection here that we cannot see the whole truth simultaneously, that we see truth in fragments, and that, while our eye rests on one phase or side of the revelation of God, the other portions are comparatively hid from our view. In eternity we shall see and know the Lord as He is. We shall behold at a glance the whole counsel of God; our light and love shall be perfect. (1 John iii. 2; 1 Cor. xiii. 12.)

It is salutary to remember our tendency to partiality and onesidedness in our spiritual life, in order that we may be on our guard, that we may carefully and anxiously consider the "Again, it is written;" that we may willingly learn from Christians who have received different gifts of grace, and whose experience varies from ours; above all, that we may seek to follow and serve the Lord Himself, to walk with God, to hear the voice of the good Shepherd. Forms of godliness, types of doctrine, are apt to become substitutes instead of channels, weights instead of wings. Here is the most subtle danger of idolatry. Doctrines and systems of doctrine are like portraits more or less faithful and vivid of a beloved and beautiful countenance. But they are necessarily imperfect. They recall some aspects, expressions, characteristics; they are helpful to recall the reality and fulness of which they are incomplete representations. But we must not substitute them in our minds and imaginations for the living face. Doctrines and circles of religious thought and experience are like channels; but we must not breathe the limited air of an enclosed space, but keep our hearts in communion with God, that out of the ocean of light and life, out of the living fountain, we may receive constant renewal and revival.

The exhortations of this epistle may appear to some difficult to reconcile with the teaching of Scripture, that the grace of God, once received through the power of the Holy Ghost by faith, can never be lost, and that they who are born again, who are once in Christ, are in Christ for ever. Let us not blunt the edge of earnest and piercing exhortations. Let us not pass them over, or treat them with inward apathy. "Again it is written." We know this does not mean that there is any real contradiction in Scripture, but that various aspects of truth are presented, each with the same fidelity, fulness and emphasis. Hence we must learn to move freely, and not to be cramped and fixed in one position. We must keep our eyes clear and open, and not look at all things through the light of a favourite doctrine. And while we receive fully and joyously the assurance of our perfect acceptance and peace, and of the unchanging love of God in Christ Jesus, let us with the apostle consider also our sins and dangers from the lower yet most real earthly and time-point of view.

The earnest counsel of the apostle in this chapter, *Let us fear*, may seem to be incompatible with his frequent and emphatic teaching that we have not received the spirit of bondage again to fear; that he is persuaded that nothing shall be able to separate us from the love of God that is in Christ Jesus; that we are to rejoice in the Lord, and that alway.

Yet a most superficial glance at the epistles, and at the Sciptures in general, will show that fear is an essential feature of the Christian.

The worldly man neither fears nor loves God. He sometimes imagines he loves God, because he is not afraid, because he is not awed by the holy majesty of God, and does not tremble at the righteous condemnation of the law. He mistakes his feeling of ease for a feeling of love to God, of whose character he has a false and shallow view. Absence of fear he mistakes for presence of love. The soul which is roused and convinced of sin fears God, His displeasure and punishment; fears the future, with its darkness and misery. This fear, created by the Spirit, has in it already elements, though concealed and feeble, of trust and affection. There is in it, as there is in repentance, a longing after the peace of God, a desire to be brought into harmony and fellowship with Him. There is in this fear, although dread and anxiety about self may predominate, reverence, conviction of sin, sorrow, prayer.

When Christ is beheld and accepted, there is peace; but is there not also fear? "With thee is forgiveness of sin, that thou mayest be feared." Where do we see God's holiness and the awful majesty of the law as in the cross of Christ? Where our own sin and unworthiness, where the depth of our guilt and misery, as in the atonement of the Lord Jesus? We rejoice with fear and trembling.

Thus the apostle Peter says, "If ye call on the Father, who without respect of persons judgeth according to every man's work, pass the time of your sojourning here in *fear*. Forasmuch as ye know that ye were not redeemed with corruptible things, as silver and gold, from your vain conversation received by tradition from your fathers; but with the precious blood of Christ, as of a lamb without blemish and without spot."

It is because we know the Father, it is because we are redeemed by the precious blood of the Saviour, it is as the children of God and as the saints of Christ, that we are to pass our earthly pilgrimage in fear. This is not the fear of bondage, but the fear of adoption;* not the fear which

* The patriarchs are often commended because they *feared* God. (Gen. xxxi. 42, 54; xxii. 12; xlii. 18.) Theirs was especially

dreads condemnation, but the fear of those who are saved, and whom Christ has made free. It is not an imperfect and temporary condition; it refers not merely to those who have begun to walk in the ways of God. Let us not imagine that this fear is to vanish at some subsequent period of our course, that it is to disappear in a so-called "higher Christian life." No; we are to pass the time of our sojourn here in fear. To the last moment of our fight of faith, to the very end of our journey, the child of God, while trusting and rejoicing, walks in godly fear.

Likewise does the apostle Paul say, "Because God worketh in you to will and to do, work out your own salvation with fear and trembling." Not the fear of the self-righteous, who are under the law, without peace and strength, but the fear of those in whom the Holy Ghost dwells with His light and energy. Fear is therefore compatible with faith and assurance. The children of God, who cry Abba, who praise the Lamb, who are sealed by the Holy Ghost, rejoice with fear and trembling.

Fear which is rooted in unbelief is evil; for it drives away from God. If we fear that God will

a dispensation of faith and love. There was as yet no law, and they walked in simplicity before God, trusting in His goodness, and depending on His guidance. It is never said in Genesis that they loved God; but their *fear of God* is mentioned, their reverential and confiding sense of the holy and loving presence of God.

not be faithful and fulfil His promises, if we doubt the efficacy of Christ's atonement, or the immovable firmness of His gracious word, we are sinning against God, and forsaking the Rock of our salvation. Looking to God, our loving Father, our gracious Saviour, our gentle and indwelling Comforter, we have no reason to be afraid. The only fear that we can cherish is that of reverence and awe, and a dread lest we displease, offend, and wound Him who is our Lord. But when we look at ourselves, our weakness, our blindness, our sinfulness; when we think of our path and our work, of our dangers and enemies, we may well *fear*, we may well feel that the time for repose and unmixed enjoyment has not come yet, and that, though sure of our ultimate triumph, we must watch anxiously and constantly; we must dread our own sinfulness and our temptations; we must fear worldly influences and estrangements; we must work out our salvation with fear and trembling.

But even this statement is not sufficient, and does not cover the Scripture teaching. It is true the Spirit witnesses with our spirits that we are God's children. It is true the Saviour assures us that His sheep shall never perish; and, as the very expression implies, they who are born of incorruptible seed possess life eternal; they abide for ever; they dwell in God, and He dwelleth in them. But why are there so many warnings and exhortations addressed to those who profess to believe in the Saviour? Why does the Lord say, "Every branch in me that beareth not fruit He taketh away"? Why does the apostle teach, "If ye live after the flesh, ye shall die"? Why does the apostle Peter say, "Give diligence to make your calling and election sure; for if ye do these things, ye shall never fall"? Some of the reasons are obvious; and if we are sincere and honest with ourselves, we must have discovered them.

The absolute safety, the fixed and unchanging position of the chosen people of God, can never be doubted. From the eternal, heavenly, divine point of view saints can never fall; they are seated in heavenly places with Christ; they are renewed by the Spirit, and sealed by Him unto everlasting glory. But who sees the saints of God from this point of view? Not the world, not our fellow-Christians. They only see our character and walk. Not we ourselves, except in the moments when the Spirit beareth witness with our spirits that we are the children of God. True, we trust in Christ, we rejoice in His love, we lean on Him; but to make our calling and election sure, to hear the voice of the Saviour, "Thou art mine;" to see the seal, "The Lord knoweth them that are His;" this is the secret, hidden, constant prayer, the concentrated work of the Christian.

From our point of view, as we live in time, from day to day, our earnest desire must be to continue stedfast, to abide in Christ, to walk with God, to bring forth fruit that will manifest the presence of true and God-given life. Hence the apostle, who says to the Philippians, "Being confident of this very thing, that He which hath begun a good work in you will perform it until the day of Jesus Christ," adds to a similar thought in another epistle, "If ye continue in the faith grounded and settled, and be not moved away from the hope of the gospel." In the one passage Paul's point of view is the heavenly, eternal one; in the other he looks from earth heavenwards, from time to eternity. And in what other way could he think, speak, exhort, and encourage both himself and his fellow-Christians but in this manner, which appears conditional, and as if it contradicted the fixed and eternal election, while to the conscience and heart of the saint there is no discord? For it is by these very exhortations and warnings that the grace of God keeps us. It is in order that the elect may not fall, it is to bring out in fact and time the (ideal and eternal) impossibility of their apostasy, that God in His wisdom and mercy has sent to us such solemn messages and such fervent entreaties, to watch, to fight, to take heed unto ourselves, to resist the adversary. The fight of faith is good; that is, beautiful (καλὸν), according to God's will, in God's strength, and of no uncertain issue: it must lead to victory. But it is a *real* fight. The enemy, the dangers, the wounds, the difficulties, the insidious and constant attacks—all are real. And can there be such a fight without fear? No: and even the fearful destruction which would follow, on our yielding to the enemy and forsaking our Lord, must be contemplated, that we may cleave to God. My soul followeth *hard* after thee; to keep within sight of my Guide, nay, leaning on my Beloved, this is my desire.

Yet the man who feareth alway is blessed; for in the *fear of the Lord*, as the wise man saith, there is *strong confidence.* Strong confidence! For if you think that the Bible doctrine of the Christian's fear favours the notion that the child of God is not to have the *knowledge* of salvation, that he is not to be filled with joy and peace through believing, you are mistaken. All Christian life starts from faith, trust, thanksgiving; not from doubt and suspense. Because Jesus the Son of God loved us and gave Himself for us, we live unto Him and serve Him. Moved with fear, like Noah, we enter into the ark, and we are safe, adoring the goodness and the holiness of our Lord and Redeemer. The fear which hath torment is that fear which turns its face from the light and love of God. And if any element of torment enters into our fear we are to turn to the Lord, and look at that perfect love which casteth out fear. Whatever time I am afraid, I will trust in the Lord, said David. When we feel our weakness, danger, and sin, we look unto the Lord Jesus, and hear His voice, "My grace is sufficient for thee."

II. But the believer has *rest*, now on earth, and hereafter in glory. Resting in Christ, he labours to enter into the perfect rest of eternity.

The apostle returns to the quotation from Psalm xcv., feeling that he has not yet exhausted the meaning of this important testimony of the Spirit.

On account of unbelief Israel entered not into rest. The promise was theirs; they heard it, but they believed not what they heard. (Isa. liii. 1.)* The word of God is addressed to the heart, and the heart receives it by faith. The understanding assents, the imagination admires, the memory retains, and yet there is no *reception* of the Word, no inward appropriation, and hence no life or growth. The rain which falls on a roof produces no real and lasting effect; but when it falls on good ground, it maketh it bring forth and bud.

Israel received the Word only superficially, and not mixing it with faith, the word did not profit them. The application is obvious. We have

* Comp. Rom. x. 16, 17. "Report," or literally that which is heard, is the same as preaching; the word of God heard is to produce faith. The prophet asks, Who hath believed that which through us was heard?

P

received the word of promise; unless by faith we appropriate and assimilate it (mark and inwardly digest it), it will be of no use to us. By faith, then, we do enter into rest.

But what did God mean by calling it *His* rest? Not they enter not into *their* rest, but His own. Oh, blessed distinction! I hasten to the ultimate and deepest solution of the question. God gives us *Himself*, and in all His gifts He gives us Himself. Here is the distinction between all religions which men invent, which have their origin in the conscience and heart of man, which spring up from earth, and the truth, the salvation, the life, revealed unto us from above, descending to us from heaven. All religions seek and promise the same things: light, righteousness, peace, strength, and joy. But human religions think only of creature-light, creature-righteousness, of a human, limited, and imperfect peace, strength, and blessedness. They start from man upwards. But God gives us Himself, and in Himself all gifts, and hence all His gifts are perfect and divine. Does God give us righteousness? He Himself is our righteousness, Jehovah-tsidkenu. Does God give us peace? Christ is our peace. Does God give us light? He is our light. Does God give us bread? He is the bread we eat; as the Son liveth by the Father, so he that eateth Me shall live by Me. (John vi.) God Himself is our strength. God is ours, and in all His gifts and blessings He gives Himself. By the Holy Ghost we are one with Christ, and Christ the Son of God is our righteousness, nay, our life. Do you want any other real presence? Are we not altogether "engodded," God dwelling and living in us, and we in Him? What more real presence, and indwelling, awful and blessed, can we have than that which the apostle described when he said: "I live; yet not I, but Christ liveth in me"? Or again, "I can do all things through Christ which strengtheneth me"? Or as the Lord Himself in His last prayer before His crucifixion said to the Father, "I in them, and thou in me"?

Thus God gives us *His* rest as our rest.

It is written in the book of Genesis that God rested on the seventh day, and that *thus* (in His rest)* all His works were finished. The rest of God is the consummation and crown of the creation. Without it the creation would not have been complete. In great condescension the loving God, by the Word and the Spirit, went out of Himself into the "all things" which He called forth. But they were created for Him and unto Him. Hence He returns unto Himself on the seventh day. Heaven and earth are to be filled with His glory.

* In considering the "rest of God" in Gen. ii., we should dismiss from our minds the questions concerning "Sabbath and Lord's-day," which are apt to narrow and cloud our view of this great subject.

The rest of the seventh day declares the sovereignty, majesty, and blessedness of God, which all things according to their capacity are to show forth and to rejoice in. Hence, if you will think of it, this Sabbath of God is the substratum and basis of all peace and rest—the pledge of an ultimate and satisfactory purpose in creation. Without this idea the world is nothing else but constant motion without progress, journey without end, toil without reward, question without answer. "Sabbathless Satan." In this word Milton expresses a great thought.

But this rest of God in creation was disturbed and marred by sin. For the rest of God means not cessation from exhausting exertion—"He fainteth not, neither is weary." It does not mean cessation from work—"My Father worketh hitherto, and I also work"—but the joy and delight of God in His good and perfect work. God's rest is no longer in the first creation. It is in redemption's new creation, of which redemption Israel's deliverance out of Egypt and entrance into Canaan was a type. God said unto Israel, "Ye are not as yet come to the rest and to the inheritance, which the Lord your God giveth you. But when ye go over Jordan, and dwell in the land which the Lord your God giveth you to inherit, and when He giveth you rest from all your enemies round about, so that you dwell in safety, &c."* And referring to this promise, Joshua said unto the two and a half tribes, "Now the Lord your God hath given rest unto your brethren, as He promised." † David said, "The Lord God of Israel hath given rest unto His people, that they may dwell in Jerusalem for ever." In this beautiful expression David refers to God's rest, as it is written: "For the Lord hath chosen Zion; He hath desired it for His habitation. This is my rest for ever: here will I dwell; for I have desired it." ‡ When David looked back upon the past history of his people, full of vicissitudes and troubles, war and conflict, bondage and chastisement, and now contemplated the prospect of peace and quiet, worship and praise, his soul was filled with gratitude and joy. Now the ark was deposited in a permanent abode. Solomon was to be a man of peace. God would rest in His people and they in Him. But these were only types. For if Joshua had given them true rest, if the rest which God gave to Israel was not a mere imperfect shadow and type of the future, why should the Holy Ghost say by David, "To-day if you hear His voice, harden not your heart"? Why should God speak of entering into His rest?

God rests in Christ as the Redeemer and Re-

* Deut. xii. 9, 10.
† Joshua xxii. 4.
‡ 1 Chron. xxiii.; Psalm cxxxii. 13, 14.

storer of fallen man. The Father was pleased in Jesus His beloved *Son*, and the Lord delighted in Him as His elect *Servant*. Jesus was the Tabernacle where God dwelt and found His rest. For our sins this Temple, holy and true, was broken; because of our justification it was built again. Now in the risen Jesus, the first-begotten from the dead, Head of the church, Heir of all things, the Father beholds His glory and the fulfilment of His counsel. In Him, as our risen Saviour, dwelleth the fulness of the Godhead bodily; and where God's rest is, there also is ours. Hence Jesus promises to give unto all who come to Him rest and peace. (Matt. xi.; John xiv.)*

Our souls long for rest. "Oh, that I had the wings of a dove! Then would I fly away and be at rest!" is the sigh of every soul. And this rest is only in God's rest. Death brings no rest to our souls. It is Jesus Christ who alone can give rest to man; for only in Him we are restored and brought into communion with God. The reason of our unrest is nothing else but our fall, our abnormal condition, our alienation from God. The centre of our life is not fixed in God, and therefore there is no harmony and no peace; there is no health in us. For rest is not in sloth

* The Hebrew word for peace (Shalom) implies restoration to perfection, to the state of normal and complete being.

or unconsciousness, or in a life of half-roused energies. When we have no light for our mind, no peace in our conscience, no love in our heart, then are we disturbed; then there is no worthy central aim and guide of life. When we are wandering in the wilderness, without knowing the end or beholding the light to direct, then are we without rest. The great promise of Christ is *rest.* For He is the Restorer. He gives us light. Men of brilliant genius, extensive information, acute and penetrating intellect, have often no rest, because they see not the Light of the world, in whom alone God, immortality, and the way of peace and holiness are revealed. Men of piety and self-denial, who possess a high standard of morality, are not at rest, because they have not Christ, and in Him, the holy and righteous, yet merciful and loving forgiveness of God. The whole spiritual nature of man is without its centre until Christ is loved, and our life is a waiting for Him, and going forth to meet the Bridegroom.

We enjoy rest in Christ by faith. But the perfect enjoyment of rest is still in the future.* There remaineth a sabbatism for the people of God.† Believers will enter into rest after their

* In like manner salvation and adoption are spoken of as future. (1 Peter i. 5; Rom. viii. 23, 24.)

† Sabbatismos (in our translation rest) is used here, and not κατάπαυσις, as in iii. 11, 18; iv. 1, 3, 5, 10, 11. Into God's rest we enter by faith when we trust in Jesus; into the Sabbatismos

earthly pilgrimage, labour and conflict, and the whole creation will share in the liberty and joy of the children of God. The substance and foretaste of this rest we have even now in Christ. In Him, as the glorified Head of the Church, the Father and the believers meet even now, and we have perfection and complete peace. But as Christ has entered into glory, we are to be glorified together with Him at His coming. Then will be perfectly satisfied the great and deep-seated desire of our heart for rest. By rest is not meant inactivity, but peace and harmony within and with all that is around us. We cannot conceive of God's children in eternity in a state of inactivity; for by reason of their union with Christ and with all angels, by reason of the central position given to the church, the glorified believers not merely behold and praise, but serve God day and night. Work is not opposed to rest. If we possessed perfect light, so that we saw clearly the end and the method of labour; if we possessed a perfect medium of work, so that mind and body were perfect and efficient tools for the directing will, so that reason, affection, and all our energies, soul and body were willing, adequate servants of the spirit; if we were endowed with sufficient

we enter when our day-work is finished and we rest from our labours (Rev. xiv. 13), and still more fully when Christ shall make all things new, and rest in the full enjoyment of His redemptive work.

and unfailing strength, so that there could be no painful exhaustion or disproportion between the design and the power of execution; and if the material to be worked upon was plastic and impressible, responsive to our thought, then work would be the greatest enjoyment, and in work would be a continued renewal of strength and an uninterrupted repose of thanksgiving. But all these conditions will be fulfilled in the renewed earth. The saints will be in light; seeing and knowing as they are known, they will possess minds and bodies, energies and powers, perfect and adequate instruments of their God-filled volitions. they will never be faint and weary, and all curse and obstructions will be removed. Thus while they praise and rejoice they will work, while they execute God's commandments they will behold His countenance. They will both reign and rest with Christ.

But the great contrast between the sabbatism we wait for and the present period is this. In the present life we are to work out according to God's energy within us; we are to sow, to lay up treasure, to grow, and make increase. We have talents entrusted, and we are to trade with them. Death stereotypes our character and ends our labours. It is here on earth that through sufferings and discipline we are conformed to the image of Christ. As we have been faithful, so shall we be rewarded.

As we have been faithful, *so are we;* whatever meekness, patience, love, humility, we have learned on earth, we shall possess throughout eternity. It is true of all God's saints, from the least to the greatest, that, delivered from the body of death, they are also freed from sin and the old man; beholding the glory of Christ, they become like Him whom they see. Yet, without contradicting this comforting truth, the Scriptures constantly connect our faithfulness, obedience, and discipline on earth with our eternal condition and blessedness, with the reward which sovereign grace will assign to the heirs of life. They who sow sparingly reap sparingly; they who sow abundantly reap abundantly. There is no sowing after death, no more laying out our talents on usury; no more development or growth. According to our life in the body is our glory; work therefore while it is day. (2 Cor. v. 10; John ix. 4.)

While this is a very solemn truth, stimulating us to diligence and watchfulness, we must ever hold fast the blessed assurance that all believers will be glorified with Christ. Believers differ in glory, and in this diversity and gradation there will be harmony and the exercise of love and enjoyment of communion. For they who are nearest Christ, and possessed of the highest glory, are most fully conformed to the image of Him who is meek and lowly in heart, and their delight is to enrich all their brethren out of the abundance of their knowledge and joy.

Have I brought before you apparently contradictory doctrines? Fear and the assurance of God's salvation, rest and labour? In Christ Jesus all contradictions are solved. Let us *learn Christ.* Look unto Him, and you will fear lest you displease and grieve Him, lest the heavenly Bridegroom should discern in you the heart of unbelief and the love of the world. And this very fear will draw you to lean on Him and to abide in Him, who is your only life and strength. Rest in Jesus, and resting in Him you will labour, you will serve Christ in the Church, you will look upon duties and trials as heavenly discipline to make you Christlike, as precious seed which will bring plentiful harvest. We can take nothing out of this world but *Christ formed in us.* And whatever may have been our calling and occupation, the only question is, Has it been made subservient to the formation of the Christ-man? Earthly things are to be viewed in their relation to spiritual and eternal realities. The sum and substance of all our experiences, actions and trials in time must needs be the character, the attitude of the heart, the strength and affection of the soul. If a Christian is in business, if he has many and complicated transactions, many difficult and important duties in which the welfare of others is concerned, large and complicated responsibilities, the question is, Has he learnt faithfulness, justice, kindness, self-restraint, generosity? has he been a steward of God's gifts? has he been heavenly-minded, fervent in spirit while not slothful in business? Then all his earthly work has been spiritual work, and his labour in time has wrought out eternal results.

Whatever our duties, trials, social position, our mental attainments may be, the Christian's one aim is, that through them all Christ should be formed in him. Thus the Christian is always feeding upon Christ, he is always eating and drinking spiritual nourishment; all things work together to promote his growth and his conformity to the Saviour. As we speak of making flesh, so we may speak of the Christian making *Spirit;* doing all things to the glory of God and in the name of Christ: he is continually labouring for the meat which endureth for ever. Though engaged in what is secular, temporal, and apparently transitory, his spiritual, eternal man is forming; he is preparing his everlasting and peculiar mansion and harvest. Christ is the Vine, and we are the branches; but the object, fruit, and glory of the vine is to produce *wine.* No emblem can set forth the truth fully; for as Christ is the Vine, so the love of Christ abiding in the heart and transforming the soul is also the ultimate blessedness and glory of believers. Even now we possess and enjoy this love; hence our labour is full of rest; and when at last we enter into the perfect rest, we shall be satisfied with His likeness when we behold His face in righteousness.

CHAPTER X.

THE WORD OF GOD, JUDGING THE CHRISTIAN BELOW; THE GREAT HIGH PRIEST'S SYMPATHY AND HELP ABOVE.

HEB. iv. 12-16.

RESTING by faith in Jesus, and labouring to enter into that perfect rest which remaineth to the people of God, the Christian, during his pilgrimage through the wilderness, is guided by the word of God, which is in his hand, and upheld and encouraged by the intercession and sympathy of the great High Priest above.

The apostle, having based his earnest exhortation on the Scripture, on what the Holy Ghost saith in Psalm xcv., naturally confirms it by reminding the Hebrews of the majesty and power of the word of God. They who are under the influence of the divine word must be decided, earnest, whole-hearted. For God's word is perfect; it enters into the inmost depths of the heart, it searches out every secret thought, and judges our life from its hidden root to all its manifestations. You who are in contact with the word of God, with the mind of Christ, with the depth-searching Spirit, are you more real and thorough than others? Does God find in you the truth He desires in the inward parts?

We are familiar with the word of God. Like Israel, we possess this treasure in our country, in our families. It is in our homes and schools. We know it from our childhood. The word is nigh thee, even in thy mouth. How often have our lips uttered the very words of the living God. But, thankful as we ought to be for this great privilege, do we know also the majesty and the power of the word of God? Do we know that, in possessing, reading, and knowing the Scripture, we are under a mighty, solemn, and decisive influence, and that this word judges us now, and will judge us at the last day? Do we tremble at the word of Jehovah? Does the word judge and decide, mould and govern, guide and comfort? What are and do ye more than others, who know only human words and opinions, to whom Scripture also is but the word of man? Is it evident, from the effects the word has produced in you, that it is the word of the living God? Oh, blessed are they who, like the author of Psalm cxix., can give to the word more than a hundredfold praise!

The expressions which are used here of the

word of God are all applicable to Christ Himself; for He is living, He is the power of God, He came for judgment into the world, He is the Searcher of hearts, His eyes are like a flame of fire. But the reference is to the spoken and written word. For in this epistle the Lord is never called the Word, as in the gospel of John and in the book of Revelation. We know how intimate and essential is the connection between the eternal, living, personal word and the Scriptures. The Son is the Word, the revealer of God, the expression of His thought, the manifestation of His light and love. Christ is the Word of God, and therefore Christ is the sum and substance of Scripture. Of Him testify Moses and the prophets. The Spirit of Christ did signify, both in the types of the law and the prophecies, of His sufferings and glory. The Scripture, as the written word, is according to Christ and of Christ; and by it Christ is heard, received, and formed in the soul.

Of this written Word, of which Christ is centre and end, as well as author and method, which is inspired by the Holy Ghost and sent by God, the gospel message is the kernel. And hence it is this gospel which especially is called the Word. "All flesh is as grass, and all the glory of man as the flower of grass. The grass withereth, and the flower thereof falleth away; but the word of the Lord endureth for ever. And this is the Word which by the gospel is preached unto you." And is not all Scripture gospel? For even the law, convincing of sin and declaring condemnation, is only sent to prepare the heart for the reception of Christ's grace and salvation. And blessed are they who are wounded by Moses, for Jesus shall heal them.

The Word is *living* (ζῶν). (Rev. i. 18, Greek. John v. 26, 21 and 24; vi. 63, 68.) God is called the Living One; and Christ the Lord calls Himself the Living One. He is the life, He has life in Himself, and He came to quicken and to give unto us life abundantly. And the Word which proceedeth out of the mouth and heart o God, the Word of which Christ is the substance, and which is given and watched over by the Spirit, is also living; for God's words are spirit and life.

The Word is the seed, which appears insignificant, but which if received in good ground shows its vitality. Hence it is by this Word that souls are born again unto eternal life. They who receive the word of God (not texts and sermons) experience that this Word does not remain within them as a dead and inert mass, a mere addition to their previous knowledge, but that it produces within them life. All words, to a certain extent, may be compared to seed; but they cannot produce new, spiritual, divine, eternal life. They may add to the knowledge, excite the emotions, stimulate the energies, rouse the conscience of *the old man; they cannot create the new life.* The word of God quickens the dead. As the Word, applied by the Spirit, produces, so it also sustains and promotes life. "As newborn babes, desire the sincere milk of the Word, that ye may grow thereby." The Saviour, who is life, calls Himself not merely bread, but living bread; so the word of God, by which our life is sustained, is a living Word.

The living Word is powerful or energetic (ἐνεργής). It is compared to the seed which possesses vitality and power. It springs up and grows while men are asleep and unconscious of its operation. First comes the blade, then the ear, after that the full corn in the ear. The word of God is continually active; it grows and energises in our thoughts and motives, it brings forth fruit in our words and actions, it impels to exertion, it sustains in trial. We can see the power or energy of the Word when it fills those that hear and receive it with strong emotions, filling them with fear and terror, with grief and contrition; we can see its power in the sudden and striking changes it produces, when the thoughtless and worldly, the selfish and depraved, are arrested and quickened by its mighty power. But while the earthquake and the fire declare the approach of the Lord, it is in the still small voice that the Lord at last appears to take up His permanent abode. There are the hidden flowers of humility, of forgiving love, of patience and meekness; there are the unseen and unknown daily conflicts and victories; there is the crucifixion of the old man, and the constant renewal of the resurrection-life; and these are especially the triumphs of the power of the Word.

The Word cannot be loving and energetic without being also a sword, dividing and separating with piercing and often painful sharpness that, which in our natural state lies together mixed and confused. The Word of God, by which all things were called forth, divided and separated darkness from light, the waters above from the waters below, the dry land from the sea. The Word of God, which came unto the fathers, tried and proved them; it was a heart-searching Word, which called forth conflict, and commanded separation from all ungodliness and all trust in the flesh. The Word of God, incarnate, was declared from His infancy set for the fall and rising again of many in Israel, that the thoughts of many hearts may be revealed. For before life enters into the soul, there is no separation, division, warfare; all things are chaotic, without form and void. The soul, or the lower intellectual and sentient life, is not distinguished from the spirit and the higher Godward and eternal life. We do not discern the inner man delighting in the law of God and the other law striving in our members. We call evil good, and do not know that there is cnly one good, even God. We savour the things that are of man and not of God; and while we think ourselves disciples, Jesus calls us Satan. We do not know nature and grace, flesh and Spirit, earth and heaven, self and Christ, Adam and the Lord, the quickening Spirit. We sing, but it is not the melody of the heart; we pray, but it is not in faith; we read the Scripture, but it is not hearing the voice of God; we preach, and visit, and work, as we call it, for Christ, and it is not as the servants who do not their own will, seek not their own glory, and rely not on their own strength. We imitate Christ, but not the real Christ, who sought only to please and honour God, who walked in love, who came not to do His own will. Oh, when the whole life of Jesus stands before the eyes of our heart, when we behold ourselves in this mirror, how deeply humbled do we feel! I think of the singleness of His aim, "I came to do not my will, but the will of Him that sent me;" I think of the uninterrupted calmness and fervour of His faith in God; I think of His absolute and inexhaustible love, which gave expecting nothing again, which was always ready to forgive and to bless; I think of Him as walking in love, love surrounding all

His footsteps, love (and that in a sinful world which hated Him) the atmosphere in which He breathed, the constant manifestation of His heart, "And when mine eye seeth Him, I abhor myself. (Job xlii. 5, 6.) The word of God comes as a sword, and separates and analyzes; it comes not to flatter and to soothe; it comes not to encourage us with half-true, half-false encomiums; it does not call the flesh Spirit, but condemns it as flesh and enmity against God. It leads you into the *lower Christian life* (John iii. 30); it discerns the thoughts and intents of the heart, the hidden self-complacency, the hidden ambition and self-will; it enters into the very joints and marrow, the energies and sentiments, the motives and springs of our actions, the true character of our rejoicing and mourning, our elevations and depressions; and then you say with the apostle: I have no confidence in the flesh, in my old nature, in *me*, body, soul, and spirit as I am of Adam. I dare not trust the sweetest frame. I cannot call my "holy things" holy, for they are full of sin. The word of God enters into my inmost soul and heart-life, and as a judge both unveils and condemns; what hitherto was hidden, is uncovered; what was disguised, unveiled; what was falsely called good and spiritual, appears now in the bright light of God's countenance; the thoughts and intents of the heart are discerned.

Thus am I brought into God's presence, as when I first was convinced of my sin and my guilt; but I feel more abased, and with a deeper knowledge and sorrow I exclaim: I am vile, and abhor myself in dust and ashes. Oh, where is Christ? I wish to be found in Him. I wish Him to live in me. What is there in me pleasing to God? Oh that Christ would sing, pray, love, live in me!

When the Word thus dwells in us, we give glory to God, and we are spiritually-minded. We live not on mere notions and impressions; we begin to apply our knowledge to our actual state and to our daily walk; we are delivered from hypocrisy, which is since the fall the great disease of mankind, especially those who enjoy the privilege of belonging to the congregation of God. What is hypocrisy but as the word signifies, living in a vain show, the semblance of things? As actors on a stage, who pretend they are kings, and possess power and large armies, who speak and demean themselves with great dignity; so men professing faith and godliness rest satisfied with a form and outline, without substance and fulness. The word of God suffers not such a semblance and shadowy deception. It brings us into the presence of Him who desireth truth in the inward part. The Christian, who is judged, chastened, and corrected, who is wounded and killed by this living and powerful Word, prays: "Search me, and try me, and see if there be any wicked thing in me, and lead me in the way everlasting."

Here alone is peace. Without this solemn awe and trembling at the word of God, there is no true rest in Christ. There may be much talk about peace and assurance, expressions which are exuberant, but proceed not out of a full heart, which sound strong and courageous, but are not of the Spirit, in whom alone is might. He who has confidence in the flesh does not rejoice in Christ Jesus. And to have no confidence in the flesh is the result of the pain-inflicting judgment of the Word. When we judge ourselves, we are not judged. When we confess our sin, He is faithful and just to forgive our sin. When we admit that we have denied Him thrice, we can say: "Lord, Thou knowest that I love Thee."*

* The expression, "two-edged sword," is used Prov. v. 4; Ps. cxlix. 6; Rev. i. 16, ii. 12. In the prophet Isaiah the Messiah saith: "He hath made my mouth like a sharp sword" (Isa. xlix. 2); and in the days of His flesh He declared, "The word that I have spoken, the same shall judge him in the last day. (John xii. 48.) They who are pierced by the word, and wounded in their inmost heart, are also healed and comforted, and shall not enter into the judgment of condemnation. The sword is bitter, but the hand that wields it is sweet and loving.

The dividing asunder of the soul and spirit, and of the joints and marrow: *μύελοι*, organs of thought and sensation; *ἁρμοί*, those of motion and activity; *ψυχή* and *πνεῦμα*, according to the Scripture, refer to the lower and higher spiritual life of man. This thought is more clearly expressed: *κριτικός*; that is, discerner and judge of the desires (soul) and thoughts (spirit) of the *heart*, in which both soul and spirit centre. Thus the heart by the word is brought into the presence of God, with whom we have to do, and before whom all things are open (*τραχηλίζειν* means here, expose to view).

The Word judges us on earth, and we are humbled; the Lord Jesus represents us in heaven; He intercedes for us, He sympathises with us. We look from earth and self to the sanctuary

The intimate relation between the personal word of God and the written word is evident. Now what is said of the latter always points to its source and fountain, the Lord Himself.

The following remarks of Ötinger are practical: "The word of God in the Spirit separates soul and spirit out of a state of confusion; as often as I conquer myself by recollection of Scripture passages, by spiritual thoughts, which lie already prepared in my mind, this separation takes place; the affections, prejudices, and complicated departures from the truth, which arise from below, are corrected and judged by the spirit above. Our lower mind has many preconceived ideas, which are full of distrust, doubt, and hypocrisy, as regards the gospel. To distinguish these from the enlightened thoughts of the heart is the redemption through *faith*. Spiritual we call the mind, which is planted in us through the heavenly doctrine of the gospel; when this mind is established in us and confirmed, the apostle Peter calls it the incorruptible essence of a meek and quiet spirit. It expresses itself in thoughts which are true, and which continue solid and stedfast, and in a wisdom which pervades all our actions, not in optical, unsubstantial thoughts (that is, mere theoretical, shadowy notions and images). As soon as by grace this mind is planted in us, the separation spoken of in Hebrews iv. commences. To know this is a matter of experience. If we find that we ourselves experience the effects of the word which we expect it to exercise on others; if I know from Rom. vii. that there are two wills in me, the one out of the truth, the other out of the imagination (God-estranged), the one of God, the other of self, the Holy Ghost assists me in an indescribable manner to discern what is in me, to distinguish between the spiritual inner man and the lower carnal. Thus the Spirit leads me into truth. To be spiritually-minded is life eternal and liberty. If I allow the word of God to exercise its separating power (according to the true method of the Scripture and the sacraments), I am brought into the true spiritual condition and understanding; the more faithful and patient I am in my reception of the most delicate words and operations of the Spirit, of all the sayings and commands of Jesus, the clearer and freer becomes my mind, and flesh and spirit are separated, so that I am no longer in the flesh (Rom. vii.), but in the Spirit (Rom. viii.; Gal. ii.), although I still live in the flesh. (2. Cor. x.)"

above, and find there nothing but love, grace, sympathy, and the fulness of blessings. He is our great High Priest. Israel in the wilderness, though full of sin, was brought nigh to God through the priesthood, and especially through the High Priest. We have the substance, of which tabernacle and priests were types. Christ is our great, eternal and all-sufficient High Priest in heaven. We must lift up our eyes and hearts to *heaven* in order to find peace and consolation. Jesus the Son of God (Heb. i. 2), who by His sufferings and death became a merciful and faithful High Priest (ii. 17), has, according to the will and word of the Father (i. 3, 13), passed through the created heavens, and sat down at the right hand of the Majesty on high. He, as our Lord and High Priest, is in heaven itself (αὔτος ὁ οὐρανός Heb. x. 24); He is called great, for Aaron and Melchisedek are but types, while He is the true and eternal Priest. The throne on which He is seated is the same throne which is called the throne of the majesty. But unto us it is now a throne of grace. The Father, the Lamb, and the Spirit, are One, the God of salvation. We who are justified by the blood of Christ are now in the presence of the Father. All divine attributes and perfections are now full of peace and consolation; we behold the throne of God as a throne of grace. As forgiven, accepted, nay, as the righteousness of God in Christ, we are before God. Beholding Jesus as our great High Priest, we shall have strength to hold fast our profession, notwithstanding all our difficulties and sins, and we shall have boldness to go to the throne of grace, to obtain mercy and help in the time of need.

Judged and humbled by the word on earth, we are strengthened and comforted by the great High Priest in heaven. Through suffering and temptation, through infirmity and conflict, the Son of man ascended high above all principalities and powers, thrones and dominions; high above all heavens, into the very presence and glory of God. He has entered into the holy of holies; He possesses now, as the Son of man, the glory which He had with the Father from all eternity. Far above all created heavens, far above all created angels, we behold now Him who first descended into the lower parts of the earth. Our Lord Jesus, who hungered and thirsted, who lived in the weakness and infirmity of the flesh, who sighed and wept, who prayed and agonized, who was tempted of the devil, who died on the cross, who was buried and descended into Hades, He is now in the most excellent glory, and He is there as our High Priest, Representative, and Head. "Glory to God in the highest," sang the angels; and in that highest region—if we may so call that which is above space as eternity is above time—lives now our Lord, with whom we are one.

Think not of the quiet resting-place of the saints who, free from sin and toil, are asleep in Jesus—think not of the heavens of angels, who in strength and love execute God's commandment—but high above them, in the sanctuary, in the palace, in the very throne of the glorious and ever-blessed Godhead, is the Man Christ Jesus. And we who were co-crucified with Him are there in Him. The Father beholds us in Christ; we are whiter than snow, and the beauty of the Lord shines on us.

In that sanctuary of blessedness and glory Jesus, who was tempted in all things as we are, apart from sin, is touched with the feeling of our infirmities. He remembers His earthly experience. He knows our frailty, the painfulness of the conflict, the weakness of the flesh.

"Where high the heavenly temple stands,
The house of God not made with hands,
A great High Priest our nature wears,
The Guardian of mankind appears.

"He who for men their surety stood,
And poured on earth His precious blood,
Pursues in heaven His mighty plan,
The Saviour and the Friend of man.

"Though now ascended up on high,
He bends on earth a brother's eye;
Partaker of the human name,
He knows the frailty of our frame.

"Our fellow-sufferer yet retains
A fellow-feeling of our pains;
And still remembers in the skies,
His tears, His agonies, and cries."

He knows our danger, and that Satan hath desired to have us, that he may sift us as wheat. While the Saviour thus regards us with compassion and with sympathy, He has no lower standard for us, no lower aim, than He had for Himself. We are to be in the world as He was, to overcome as He overcame, and to end even where the Lord is; it is Christ's will, that where He is we who believe in Him should be likewise. As He was in heaven, even while He lived on earth, so He desires that, even while in the wilderness, we should have our citizenship in heaven. And as He overcame, and is set down on His Father's throne, so He desires that we should overcome and share His throne and dominion.

Remember both the tenderness of the High Priest's heart, and the comprehensive scope of His intercession. This indeed is true sympathy, not with the sin, but with the sinner. The perfectly holy and victorious One alone can give true sympathy, seeking our real, our highest good. Sympathy comes to us from the "very highest" heaven.

His intercession is perpetual, unceasing; it is sovereign, and part of the divine covenant-gifts. Even as He died for us, and rose again, and ascended into heaven for our salvation, so He ever liveth to intercede. It is not in answer to our prayer, it is not according to our works and merits, that He died for us. Even so is His intercession His own divine, gracious, sovereign gift. As His infinite and inexhaustible love brought Him from the throne of His glory to live and die upon earth, so the same love is now the source of His constant care and faithfulness, and of His never-ceasing intercession. We are upheld according to His lovingkindness, according to the multitude of His tender mercies. Justified by His blood, we are now much more abundantly saved by His life.

And having such a High Priest in heaven, can we lose courage? can we draw back in cowardice, impatience, and faint-heartedness? can we give up our profession, our allegiance, our obedience to Christ? Or shall we not be like Joshua and Caleb, who followed the Lord fully? Let us hold fast our profession; let us persevere and fight the good fight on earth. Our great High Priest in the highest glory is our righteousness and strength; He loves, He watches, He prays, He holds us fast, and we shall never perish. Jesus is our Moses, who in the height above prays for us Jesus our true Joshua, who gains the victory over our enemies. Only be strong, and of a good courage; be not afraid, neither be thou dismayed. In that mirror of the Word in which we behold our sin and weakness we behold also the image of that perfect One who has passed through the conflict and temptation, who as the High Priest bears us on His loving heart, and as the Shepherd of the flock holds us in safety for evermore. Boldly we come to the throne of grace. In Jesus we draw near to the Father. The throne of majesty and righteousness is unto us a throne of grace. The Lord is our God. In one aspect Christ tells us that He does not pray to the Father for us, because the Father Himself loveth us. We behold in Christ's intercession the Father's love, even as in the death of Christ we recognise the love of God. Our *God* then is enthroned in grace. There is not merely grace on the throne, but the throne is altogether the throne of grace. It is *grace* which disciplines us by the sharp and piercing Word; it is grace which looks on us when we have denied Him, and makes us weep bitterly. Jesus always intercedes; the throne is always a throne of grace. The Lamb is in the midst of the throne. Hence we come boldly.

Boldly is not contrasted with reverently and tremblingly; boldness is not contrasted with awe and godly fear. It means literally "saying all," with that confidence which begets thorough honesty, frankness, full and open speech. "Pour out your heart before Him." Come as you are, say what you feel, ask what you need. Confess your sins, your fears, your wandering thoughts and affections.

Jesus the Lord went through all sorrows and trials the heart of man can go through, and as He felt all affliction and temptation most keenly, so in all these difficulties and trials He had communion with the Father. He knows, therefore, how to succour them that are tempted. How fully and unreservedly may we speak to God in the presence and by the mediation of the man Christ Jesus.

The Lord Jesus is filled with tender compassion, and the most profound, lively, and comprehensive sympathy. This belongs to the perfection of His high-priesthood. For this very purpose He was tempted, He suffered.—Our infirmities, it is true, are intimately connected with our sinfulness; the weakness of our flesh is never free from a sinful concurrence of the will; and the Saviour knows from His experience on earth how ignorant, poor, weak, sinful, and corrupt His disciples are. He loved them, watched over them with unwearied patience; prayed for them that their faith fail not; and reminded them the spirit is willing, but the flesh is weak. He remembers also His own sinless weakness; He knows what constant thought, meditation, and prayer are needed to overcome Satan, and to be faithful to God. He knows what it is for the soul to be sorrowful and overwhelmed, and what it is to be refreshed by the sunshine of divine favour, and to rejoice in the

Spirit. We may come to Him expecting full, tender, deep sympathy, and compassion. He is ever ready to strengthen and comfort, to heal and to restore. He is prepared to receive the poor, wounded, sin-stained believer; to dry the tears of Peter weeping bitterly; to say to Paul, oppressed with the thorn in the flesh, "My grace is sufficient for thee."

We need only understand that we are sinners and that He is High Priest. The law was given that every mouth may be shut, for we are guilty. The High Priest is given that every mouth may be open, for Jesus receives sinners. He saves and upholds all who put their trust in Him. It is by reason of that secret pride and self-righteousness, which Satan as a subtle poison infuses into the human heart, that when we feel our sinfulness and transgression we do not go boldly to the loving and compassionate High Priest, to the throne of grace. And this latent self-righteousness often expresses itself in such regretful phrases as, Well, I must just depend on the mercy of God; as if the mercy of our God and Saviour was a last resource when other and better things have failed, as if it was not our only peace, joy, and glory, as if it was not the best robe and the unspeakable gift, as if Jesus was not all in all, as if our song in time and eternity were not—"Worthy is the Lamb that was slain. He loved us, and washed us from our sins in His own blood."

We come in faith as sinners. Then shall we obtain mercy; and we always need mercy. As pilgrims on earth we always need mercy, to wash our feet, to restore to us the joy of salvation, to heal our backslidings, and bind up our wounds. We shall obtain help in every time of need. For God may suffer Satan and the world, want and suffering, to go against us; but He always causes all things to work together for our good. He permits the time of need, that we may call upon Him, and, being delivered by Him, may glorify His name. He will send timely (εὔκαιρον βοήθειαν) help before we succumb to the infirmities and temptations which beset us. For He, who will not suffer us to be tempted above that we are able, will send deliverance at the right moment, when all the purposes of grace and chastening discipline have been secured. All the help we need—wisdom, patience, strength, daily bread, all is treasured up for us in the heavenly places; the sanctuary is also the treasury; the High Priest is also King. From the throne of grace God will send it. Come boldly.

Jesus belongs to the sinner. From His infancy in Bethlehem's manger to the garden of Gethsemane, and from His agony on the cross to His ascension high above all heavens, He belongs to us, poor, guilty and helpless sinners, who trust in Him. He is altogether ours. He came to seek and to save us who were lost. His obedience, His life of sorrow and love, His prayers and tears, His sacrifice on the cross, His resurrection, all is ours, because we are the wayward and helpless sheep who went astray, and whom He found.

And in the heavenly glory He is ours, and His love, sympathy, faithfulness and power, give unto us in our need and misery, all things which pertain unto life and godliness. It is with us sinners that the glorified Saviour is now constantly occupied. We are His thought, His care, His work, and—oh that it were so more abundantly!—His joy, His garden, His reward. In Jesus God is ours. In the ocean of His love, in the fulness of infinite covenant-grace, we can rejoice. The God with whom we have to do seeth and knoweth all things; He is a consuming fire—and yet is He our God, Father, Saviour, indwelling Spirit; His throne is the throne of grace; nay, our very life is hid with Christ in God; we are in the bosom of Jesus, who is in the bosom of the Father. Hold fast, brother, and come boldly. Amen.

CHAPTER XI.

CHRIST, AS SON OF MAN, CALLED AND PERFECTED TO BE OUR HIGH PRIEST.

HEB. V. 1–10.

WE enter now on the third section of our epistle, which extends from chapter v. to chapter x. 39, and which sets before us the Lord Jesus Christ, the High Priest of the everlasting covenant, greater than the Aaronic priesthood. Twice already the apostle has referred to Christ as our High Priest, and he now enters on the development of the central theme of his epistle, Christ a priest for ever after the order of Melchizedek. But in order to explain the priesthood on which Christ entered after His death and resurrection, and of which not Aaron but Melchizedek was the type, it is necessary for him to show how the Lord Jesus fulfilled all that was typified of Him in the Levitical dispensation, and possessed in perfection all the requirements which, according to divine appointment, were needed in the high priest, and which could not be possessed in perfection by sinful men like the Aaronic priests.

The High Priest in Israel possessed these two qualifications: First, He was one of the people, taken from among men for men. Secondly, He was appointed expressly by God Himself. The Lord Jesus was accordingly man, and appointed by the Father to be High Priest. But in His case a third element is added. As our Lord is not only the High Priest, but the sacrifice, on the foundation of which He exercises in heaven the functions of the High Priest, it was necessary for Him to suffer and to enter into the lowest depth of agony and death. And after having in perfect obedience and faith endured all, He entered into heaven, to be the High Priest for ever after the order of Melchizedek.

Before Israel was redeemed out of Egypt, sacrifices and offerings were brought unto God by the fathers of families, and the paschal lamb was offered in every household. The whole nation, redeemed by the blood of the lamb, was called to be a nation of priests; that is, they were separated unto God, and called to worship Him, and to offer unto Him sacrifice. It was only when the people became deeply conscious of their sins, guilt, and pollution, when the law revealed to them more fully the awful majesty and holiness of God, that the priesthood was appointed, typical of the true mediation between God and man. The priests were appointed by God, separated unto Him, or holy, to bring the people's sacrifices and offerings before God; they were permitted to draw near to God, and this as representatives and mediators. And they brought to the people God's gifts, viz., reconciliation and blessing.

Now it is evident that the priesthood suffered from two essential defects, and that it was only a shadow and type of our Lord.

In the first place, the priests were as sinful as the people whom they represented. It was on account of sin that Israel felt the need of a mediator. But Aaron and the priests were only officially holy, they were not in reality spotless and pure. Hence they had to offer sacrifices for their own sins and infirmities, as well as for those of the people.

Secondly, the mediator ought not merely to be perfect and sinless man, he ought also to be divine, in perfect and full communion with God, so that he can impart divine forgiveness and blessing. Only in the Lord Jesus therefore is the true mediation. And now that He has come and entered into the heavenly sanctuary as our High Priest, the word priest in the sense of sacerdotal mediator dare never be used any more. Through Jesus the whole congregations of believers have boldness to enter into the holy of holies. He who loved us, and washed us from our sins in His own blood, hath made us kings and priests unto God.

The two qualifications of the Aaronic high priest, that he was from among men and that he was appointed by God, were fulfilled in a perfect manner in the Lord Jesus. But in considering these two points, we are struck not merely by the resemblance between the type and the fulfilment, but also by the contrast.

First, Aaron was chosen from among men to offer gifts and sacrifices for sins. Jesus was true man, born of a woman and made under the law; He became in all things like unto His brethren. But whereas the Jewish high priest had to offer for himself, as he was a sinner, the Lord was harmless and undefiled, pure and spotless. His mediation was therefore perfect.—The Aaronic high priest was able to have compassion on the ignorant and on them that were out of the way. The expression 'ignorance' refers here to the great distinction which was made in Israel between sins for which there were sacrifices, and the sin of determined and presumptuous defiance of God's authority for which there was no sacrifice but judgment: "That soul shall utterly be cut off; his iniquity shall be upon him." (Num. xv. 22-31.) The Aaronic high priest could have compassion*

* The expression μετριοπαθεῖν (translated in the margin can

on fellow-sinners, knowing and feeling his own infirmities and transgressions, and knowing also the love of God, who desireth not the death of the sinner, but that he should turn and live.

But this compassionate, loving, gentle, all-considerate, and tender regard for the sinner can exist in perfection only in a sinless one. This appears at first sight paradoxical; for we expect the perfect man to be the severest judge. And with regard to sin, this is doubtless true. God chargeth even His angels with folly. He beholds sin where we do not discover it. He setteth our secret sins in the light of His countenance. And Jesus, the Holy One of Israel, like the Father, has eyes like a flame of fire, and discerns everything that is contrary to God's mind and will. But with regard to the sinner, Jesus, by virtue of His perfect holiness, is the most merciful, compassionate, and considerate Judge. For we, not taking a deep and keen view of sin, that central essential evil which exists in all men, and manifests itself in various ways and degrees, are not able to form a just estimate of men's comparative guilt and blameworthiness. Nay, our very sins make us more impatient and severe with regard to the sins of others. Our vanity finds the

bear with) seems to have originated in Greek literature as the contrast to the apathy of the stoic, and apparently means that feeling of kindness and tenderness towards the sufferer, in which due regard to justice and rectitude is not forgotten.

vanity of others intolerable; our pride finds the pride of others excessive.* And again, blind to the guilt of our own peculiar sins, we are shocked with another's sin, different indeed from ours, but not less offensive to God, or pernicious in its tendencies. Again, the purer and higher the character, the quicker its penetration and the livelier its sympathy, discovering and loving any element and tendency heavenward and godward. Again, the greater the knowledge of divine love and pardon, the stronger faith in the divine mercy and renewing grace, the more hopeful and the more lenient will be our view of sinners. And finally, the more we possess of the spirit and heart of the Shepherd, the Physician, the Father, the Brother, the deeper will be our compassion on the ignorant and wayward.

The Lord Jesus was therefore most compassionate, considerate, lenient, hopeful in His feelings toward sinners and in His dealings with them. He was infinitely holy and perfectly clear in His hatred and judgment of sin; but He was tender and gracious to the sinner. Beholding the sinful heart in all, estimating sin according to the divine standard, according to its real inward character, and not the human, conventional, and outward measure, Jesus, infinitely holy and sensitive as He was, saw often less to shock and

* Fenelon.

pain Him in the drunkard and profligate than in the respectable, selfish, and ungodly religionists. Again, He had come to heal the sick, to restore the erring, to bring the sinner to repentance. He looked upon sin as the greatest and most fearful evil, but on the sinner as poor, suffering, lost, and helpless. He felt as the Shepherd towards the ignorant and erring, the wayward and foolish, the helpless and perishing; He felt as the Physician towards the guilty and sin-stricken; He felt the yearning of parental love and pity toward the children of Jerusalem; and even on the cross, when their sin appeared in its most fearful intensity, the Lord prayed—"Father, forgive them; for they know not what they do!" Again, He fastened in a moment on any indications of the Father's drawing the heart, of the Spirit's work. He loved the rich young man; for, though his words sounded most self-righteous, Jesus beheld Him, and saw he was not peaceful and calm in his soul. He knew how to stir up the hidden remnant, however small it was, of religious knowledge in the woman of Samaria, so that she asked Him about worship, and said, "I know that Messiah cometh!" He rebuked Peter as Satan, and yet He knew and loved him as a true and sincere disciple. And thus, while Jesus, in His perfect holiness, judges most truly, lovingly, and tenderly of us, He knows by experience the weakness of the flesh, and the difficulty and soreness of the struggle. What a marvellous fulfilment of the Priest's requisite, that he should be taken from men! one to whom we can look with full and calm trust, our Representative, the man Christ Jesus, possessed of perfect, divine love and compassion.

Secondly, the High Priest is appointed by God. No man taketh this honour unto himself, but he that is called of God, as was Aaron. The High Priesthood of Christ is identified here with His glory. Christ glorified not Himself to be made a High Priest. Blessed truth, that the glory of Christ and our salvation are so intimately connected, that Christ regards it as His glory to be our Mediator and Intercessor! This is Christ's glory, even as it is the reward of His suffering, that in Him we draw near to the Father, and that from Him we receive the blessings of the everlasting covenant. He rejoices to be our High Priest.

God called Him to the Priesthood. In Psalm cx. it is written: "Thou art a priest for ever after the order of Melchizedek." When Jesus entered into the Holy of Holies, when He sat down at the right hand of God, then He actually entered on the exercise of His priesthood. But the calling of Jesus to the High Priestly dignity is based on His Sonship. For, as we have already seen, the true Priest or Mediator must be divine as well as human. Because Jesus is Son, He is the Prophet, perfectly revealing God; because He is Son, He is the true Sacrifice and Priest; for only the blood of the Son of God can cleanse from all sin, and bring us nigh unto God; and only through Christ crucified and exalted can the Father's love and the Spirit's power descend into our hearts.

Here the comparison and contrast between the Lord and Aaron ends. The apostle now enters on that which is peculiar to our Saviour Jesus. The types and figures of the old covenant could not be perfect and adequate; for that which is united in Christ had necessarily to be severed and set forth by a variety of figures. The priests offered not themselves, but animals. Now the obedience, the conflict, the faith, the offering of the will in the true, real, and effective Sacrifice could not possibly be symbolised. Nor could any single symbol represent how Jesus, by being *first* the Sacrifice, became thereby the perfect, compassionate, and merciful High Priest. Christ was the victim on the cross. His whole previous life of obedience was the necessary preparation for His ultimate obedience unto death. And because He was the true sacrifice, and had learned obedience, He became the compassionate and faithful High Priest in the heavenly sanctuary. Hence we must combine the Levitical types (regarding sacrifice, and the entrance of Aaron into the holy of holies) and the Melchizedek type (regarding priesthood), in order to obtain a true view of the work and person of our Lord. We must read Leviticus in the light of the gospels and epistles, rather than explain the fulfilment by the necessarily imperfect and fragmentary types; and in doing so we shall see as much contrast between the type and the reality as resemblance between the shadow and the substance.

Called of God to be a High Priest for ever, the Lord Jesus, though He was the eternal Son of the Father, and though He was returning to glory, even to the right hand of the Majesty on high, learned obedience by the things which He suffered. He knows the path of temptation, sorrow, and conflict. The following verses unfold to us that the Lord descended into the lowest depth of human weakness, anguish, and death, and that only through this dark path He entered into His heavenly priesthood. It is in like manner that in the epistle to the Philippians the mind which was in Christ Jesus is described. He who was in the form of God emptied Himself, and was obedient unto death, even the death of the cross; and it is for this reason that the Father hath highly exalted Him. In one passage the emphasis is laid on His priesthood, in the other on His royal supremacy. In both the voluntary and perfect obedience of Jesus as the eternal Son of God is presented to us.

The Son of God, according to the eternal counsel, came into the world to be obedient even unto death. "Lo, I come to do Thy will." His obedience was characterized throughout by such continuity, liberty, and inward delight, that we are apt to forget that aspect of His life on which the apostle dwells when he says, that though Christ was a Son, yet learned He obedience by the things which He suffered. The Lord Jesus was always doing the things which pleased the Father. There was no break or hesitation, no pause or retrogression in His path: it was the path of the just man, which is as the shining light, which shineth more and more unto the perfect day. And as it was continuous, so it seemed without an effort, flowing forth abundantly and spontaneously out of the full well-spring of His heart. He seems refreshed and not exhausted by doing the will of the Father that sent Him.

And yet Jesus learned obedience, as He Himself said, He came not to do His own will. He who is Lord, eternal, infinite in power and glory, was made flesh, and with a human will, amid the toil and temptation incident to humanity, He continually submitted Himself to God His Father. Real and great were His difficulties, temptations, and sorrows; and from the prayers and complaints ascribed to Messiah in the psalms and prophets, we can understand somewhat of the burden which weighed on His loving and sensitive heart, and the constant dependence with which He leaned on the Father, and obtained from Him light and strength. Jesus believed; He lived not merely before, but by the Father.

Thus is Jesus the author and finisher of faith. He went before the sheep He is the forerunner. He has experienced every difficulty, and tasted every sorrow. He knows the path in all its narrowness. Was Abraham a sojourner in the land of promise as in a strange land? Jesus, who was appointed heir of all things, had not where to lay His head. Did Moses refuse the treasures in Egypt? Jesus was offered the whole world, with all its kingdoms and glory. Did David, anointed by the Lord, experience what it is to be rejected, hated, and persecuted by the proud and ungodly? What enmity, contradiction, ingratitude had our Lord to bear! Did Jeremiah weep tears of bitter sorrow on account of Jerusalem's impenitence and the false security of Judah, misguided by false prophets? Jesus, foreseeing still greater judgment on Israel's apostasy, wept over the city, and loved the nation with a sorrowing and faithful heart. Jesus felt all our infirmities and sorrows, He bore our sicknesses, He sighed over the misery that is in the world through sin culminating in death, the great and last enemy; and while acknowledging divine justice His compassionate love rested on the sufferer. Jesus was all the days of His flesh* a man of sorrows, and acquainted with grief; but in the garden of Gethsemane He entered into an experience different from His previous suffering and conflict. He saw the cross from the beginning; He had set His face stedfastly towards Jerusalem, to go up and suffer there, and the anticipation of that awful cup sometimes filled His soul with fear; His soul was straitened until His baptism was fulfilled. (Luke xii. 50.) When the Greeks came to the feast His soul was troubled; the earnest of the harvest, represented by the inquiring Gentiles, reminded Him that the corn of wheat must die first, and He cried to the Father, "Father, save me from this hour: but for this cause came I unto this hour."

The apostles had seen Jesus weep over Jeru-

* The days of His flesh are in contrast to the state of exaltation after He was perfected. The apostle Peter also uses the expression Christ "suffered in the flesh" (1 Peter iv. 2); and the apostle Paul speaks of our present earthly existence as life in the flesh. (Phil. i. 22; Gal. ii. 20.) The reference is to the life of Christ before His resurrection, where He, God's "own Son," was "in the likeness of sinful flesh" (Rom. viii. 3) a partaker of flesh and blood, that He might suffer death. (Heb. ii. 14.) Of the risen Saviour we read that He had flesh and bones (Luke xxiv. 39, notice, not flesh and blood); that He possesses now σῶμα δόξης—a body of glory.

salem; they had seen His tears and heard His groans at the grave of Lazarus. But there was something so overwhelming in the agony of Gethsemane, that the evangelists evidently struggle with the inadequacy of language to describe the impression left on the minds of the apostles who were witnesses of that awful hour. So heavy was this weight on His soul, that in most touching words He seeks the sympathy of His disciples' presence. "My soul is exceeding sorrowful, even unto death: tarry ye here, and watch with me." He knelt down; He fell on His face; so great was His conflict that, as Luke the beloved physician notices, His sweat was as it were great drops of blood falling to the ground.

What a contrast to the calm strength and peaceful joy with which immediately before He had comforted His sorrowing disciples, whose hearts were troubled and full of fear and sadness! (John xiv.–xvii.) He had spoken to them of His glory, of His going to the Father and sending to them the Spirit, of His joy being perfected in them, and of their abiding with Him for evermore. He had sung a hymn of praise with them. In the prayer which He had offered before them unto the Father there was no tone of sadness, there was nothing but peace and the calm assurance of victory.

But now, though never swerving from implicit

submission to His Father, He is well-nigh overwhelmed by the prospect of death before Him. We know the reason. It was not the prospect of physical pain, excruciating as it was, and sensitive as was His pure and sinless body. It was not the anticipation of the external manifestations of Israel's ingratitude and hatred, deep as was His love to Jerusalem. It was not the shadow of the valley of death; for David and many saints are able to say, "Then I will fear no evil." No: Jesus, who is the adoration and strength of rejoicing martyrs, died not the martyr's death, He died the just for the unjust. That which men ordinarily mean when they speak of death had no terror for the Lord Jesus. "Our friend Lazarus sleepeth," He said to His disciples, and, comforting them on that last evening, He spoke of His death as simply going to the Father, and exhorted them to rejoice because He went to His Father's house and throne. And with perfect calmness He finally committed His Spirit into the Father's hand. The enmity and opposition, the malice and contempt of His nation with their rulers, keenly as His loving heart felt it, had been known by Him for years, and He had borne it patiently and calmly, and with undisturbed hope and courage, knowing that by meekness He would conquer, and that the Father would cause His work to prosper. Fearlessness, such as must accompany perfect faith in God, had always characterized Him. He never feared man. As He exhorted His disciples not to fear them that can only kill the body, so He Himself met all danger and opposition with the most peaceful calmness and collectedness of implicit and uninterrupted faith in God. Whence the sorrow, the anguish, the overwhelming agony in the garden of Gethsemane?

He knew that on the cross, as our substitute, He would be left to suffer in connection with the judgment of sin; that His soul would be left without the light of the Father's countenance; and that which was His sole joy and strength, the very life of His life, would be taken from Him.

He tasted that death of which sin is the sting and the law the strength. When He saw what was before Him—*death in its organic connection with divine wrath*—He trembled, and was in agony.

Here we see, as nowhere else, how abhorrent He was of the iniquity which was about to be laid on Him, and how wonderful was His love to God and to us. The Lord Jesus, because He was the Son of God, and perfect, holy man, could not but shrink from that cup, the Father hiding His face from Him. He prayed with strong crying and tears. We behold Him as the Son of man. He felt that this was the hour and power of darkness. Satan doubtless used the fear of death, and presented it to the Lord's mind to throw anguish into His heart. The anticipation of His agony on the cross overwhelms Him. Yet He remains faithful. He cries unto God. His tears betoken the earnestness of His prayer; His prayer reveals the holy, submissive character of His tears.

Who can fathom the depth of Christ's prayer, or understand the full import of His tears and cries? Even in our infirmities the Spirit helpeth us, making intercession for us with groans which cannot be uttered. What must have been the petitions and the cries of the Lord Jesus when He offered Himself unto the Father! He sanctified the Lord His God in His heart, He hallowed His name, He magnified His holy justice, while He beheld His infinite love! He submitted Himself to His counsel, He surrendered Himself to suffer the most agonizing pain, and yet He trusted in His almighty and faithful deliverance! Here was the most wonderful combination in the human soul and spirit of Christ, that He most fully acknowledged and adored the holiness and the justice of God, while with perfect love He continued to identify Himself with guilty and lost sinners, and with unshaken confidence He trusted in the faithfulness of God, who would crown Him with glory, and give Him an innumerable multitude for His reward. And in this agony He learned to know fully what is the weakness of the flesh, and what is the real difficulty and painfulness of the struggle, even to surrender our own will, and to say, "Thy will be done." Thus He entered into our lowest depth, and for this reason is He able now to have perfect sympathy with us.

He cried unto God, and because of his filial devotedness, which made the Father's will His own, He was heard.* The Father sent an angel to strengthen Him. The anguish that well-nigh overcame Him was conquered. He rose, and set His face stedfastly to the work before Him. With meekness He bore the kiss of Judas; He went forth with calm majesty to meet the soldiers who were sent to take Him captive; He restrained the false zeal of Peter, as afterwards He remembered him, and looked upon him with forgiving and tender love; He witnessed a good confession before Pilate and the high priest; He called Jerusalem's daughters to repentance; He prayed for Israel's forgiveness; He heard the petition of the dying thief, commended Mary His mother to the care of the beloved disciple, and then entered into the mysterious darkness of His expiatory suffering.

* Some expositors explain, "He was delivered from the fear of death." This is indeed true; but it seems more in accordance with the meaning of the word εὐλάβεια to translate it "on account of His fear" of God. And, as Delitzsch says, no more suitable expression could be found to denote the Saviour's attitude of filial, reverential submission to God's will.

With strong crying and tears* the Son of God offered up prayers and supplications unto Him that was able to save Him from death. In the depth of His weakness and anguish He looked unto the Father's power. He poured out all His heart before Him. He prayed not to be spared the suffering of death; He asked not for twelve legions of angels to deliver Him. He had made the will of God His own, and because of this perfect surrender of Himself to that death, which appeared to Him so awful, He was heard. The answer to Christ's prayer was fully given when God brought again from His grave that great Shepherd of the sheep through the blood of the everlasting covenant. "Thou hast heard me" is in the twenty-second Psalm, the connecting link between the Beloved One forsaken and the Beloved One exalted, declaring the name of God to His brethren. Thus He learned the obedience

* The expressions of this verse recall the remarkable passage in the prophet Hosea respecting the patriarch Jacob: "He had power with God (or was a prince): yea, he had power over the angel, and prevailed: he wept, and made supplication unto him." Israel was an image of the Lord. Moses relates the words of earnest supplication, but does not mention Jacob's weeping. But the earnest and intense petition naturally issues in tears. ("Implorare est fletu rogare." Compare the French *implorer* and our word *cry.* —PUSEY, on *Minor Proph.* 76.)

Bengel says, in reference to this passage, "Awful cup! Reasonable fear! Unviolated obedience! Mighty prayer! Speedy answer!" The expressions in our passage evidently harmonize especially with the account of the evangelist Luke. (xxii. 39-46.)

through the things which He suffered.* The mind which was in Christ from the beginning was the mind of perfect filial submission and obedience. He brought this mind with Him into the world, into His prophetic ministry, into the garden of Gethsemane, and to the cross of Golgotha. But in His sufferings this mind was tested, manifested, perfected. And now that He has offered *the* obedience, by which many are made righteous, and the Father, in answer to His prayer, has raised and exalted Him, He is fully fitted for and consecrated unto His High Priestly life.† The Father now addresses Him as High Priest after the order of Melchizedek.‡ (Verse 10.)

The man Christ Jesus enthroned in heaven is now our perfect High Priest. He who endured all temptations, who glorified God in the midst of sin and suffering, who became acquainted with all sorrow and grief, who tasted the bitterness of death, who offered Himself by the most perfect surrender of His own will to the Father as our substitute, He by His obedience unto death has become the author of eternal salvation to all them

* Notice the force and beauty of the original, ἔμαθεν ἀφ' ὧν ἔπαθεν.

† Hebrews ii. 10: God made Him perfect through sufferings with reference to His future compassion and sympathy, through His exaltation with reference to His power and position as High Priest.

‡ The term προσαγορευθείς, which occurs only in this place, means *addressed*.

that obey Him;* and unto all whom He has saved by His blood He is the Priest after the order of Melchizedek.

What marvellous insight does Jesus possess into all that is human! What tender sympathy is His, and how high and perfect is His aim, that God's will should be done by us, even while we are in the body and in a world of sin and trial!

With what power do the words come from His lips, "Only believe! Follow me!"

Thus the glory of His exaltation is full of consolation and peace for us. Because He was faithful, because He was obedient unto the death, because His love conquered every enemy and overcame every darkness, He is enthroned by the Father as the Lamb, He is solemnly addressed by Him as the High Priest, who is the perfect and eternal Mediator, by whom everlasting salvation is given to all who obey Him. The glory of Christ is the result of His obedience, and the fruit of the experience of earth, through which He went, is His perfect sympathy with us, and His all-sufficient grace, which is able to uphold us in every trial, and to carry us safely through all our conflicts, and present us unblameable in body, soul, and spirit before the Father. And herein

* Kurtz points out that the reason why believers are here described as those who obey Him is because, as Christ was perfected through His obedience to the Father, so we can only be perfected by our obedience to Christ.

we adore the love of God, who gave up His Son, who sent Him, who spared Him not, in order that He might become a perfect High Priest, merciful and compassionate. Herein is the marvellous love of the Father, that He gave His own Son to be not merely the Saviour, but the Brother, the Head, the source of strength, light, and consolation to those who believe in His name.

Let us therefore dwell on the perfection of our great High Priest; for, as throughout Scripture, so here, the glory of Christ is unfolded in order that we may have perfect peace, and that we may take out of His fulness, and grace upon grace. Our sorrows and our temptations, our weakness and our danger, are fully known and constantly remembered by Jesus, who most tenderly sympathizes with us. Our sins have not merely been pardoned, but our daily trespasses and infirmities, our constant sinfulness, the sins which we commit without being conscious of them, need not keep us at a distance from God, or take from us our confidence and peace. Let us confess our sins, let us in humility acknowledge the sinfulness within us, and the defilement which clings to all our actions, even our holy things, and Jesus will be to us a merciful, considerate High Priest, by whom we are not only forgiven, but healed, corrected, and chastened; so that while we are judged in the flesh, we are quickened in the Spirit. We are before the Father in Christ the High Priest. While our prayers and thoughts, the words of our mouth, and the meditation of our heart, and the work of our hands, are acceptable, because the Lord Jesus presents them to the Father; all blessings of the covenant, all needful light and strength, grace and consolation, are bestowed on us by our omnipotent Melchizedek from the heavenly Jerusalem.

Remember who He is—the High Priest, the God-man—what He suffered, how in our nature He ascended, and then give thanks, and be of good cheer, and whatever clouds and difficulties may arise, however painful and heavy the burden of sin, of weakness, of work, never for a moment forget that nothing shall be able to separate you from the love of the Father, which is in Christ Jesus the Son of God, the Brother and High Priest of all who put their trust in Him.

We never know the strength and the love of Jesus until we lean on Him with the heavy burden of our sins, temptations, doubts, and sorrows; until in confiding trust and humble candour we speak to Him of all that oppresses and perplexes us. Then we experience that Jesus is the Man, who is God's equal, the Man of God's right hand, whom He hath made strong, mighty to save; that He is the Messenger of the covenant, the true Presence and Light, who guides us through the wilderness, while he sends down all blessings from the heavenly sanctuary. And then we experience the wonderful tenderness, the compassionate love, the perfect sympathy of Him who is not ashamed to call us brethren, who is afflicted in all our afflictions, who is constantly interceding for us in heaven, while He is constantly sustaining our inner life by His Spirit.

> "The love of Jesus, what it is
> None but His loved ones know!"

He alone knows what is in man; the sorrow which lies too deep for human ministry He is able to understand and heal.

When there is such a High Priest in heaven, when such a Man is seated at the right hand of God—almighty, omniscient, all-loving; glorious in His holiness, power, and truth; unspeakably merciful, compassionate, brotherly; Son of God, and Son of Man; bringing the ocean of divine love through the channel of human brotherhood and sympathy, and the fulness of life and glory through the agony and the death He suffered on the cross; when such a Saviour of sinners, Friend and Guide, nay, Lover and Bridegroom of the soul, is revealed unto us, will any one of us continue to go through life alone, alone with sin and guilt, with the accusations of the past, the burden of the present, and the awful gloom of the future; alone with the thirst of the soul, and the sorrow of the heart, and the afflictions, trials, and dangers of our path; alone with the guilt and power of sin, and the darkness of the grave and eternity? Oh for one simple look to Jesus, and He is yours, with His plentiful redemption, His peace, His life, His love! And you who believe in Him, and are in manifold afflictions and trials, lean on His grace and rest in His love.

"Thy risen life but fits Thee more
  For kindly ministry;
Thy love unhindered rests upon
  Each bruised branch in Thee."

CHAPTER XII.

GROWTH IN GRACE AND KNOWLEDGE.

HEB. V. 11-VI 3.

THE apostle has scarcely entered on the central and most important part of his epistle, when he feels painfully the difficulty of explaining the doctrine of the heavenly and eternal priesthood of the Son, and this not merely on account of the grandeur and depth of the subject, but on account of the spiritual condition of the Hebrews, whom he is addressing. He had presented to their view the Lord Jesus, who after His sufferings was made perfect in His exaltation to be the High Priest in heaven. When he quotes again the 110th Psalm, "Thou art a priest for ever after the order of Melchizedek," the solemn and comprehensive words which are addressed by the Father to the Son, he has such a vivid and profound sense of the exceeding riches of this heavenly knowledge, of the treasures of wisdom and consolation which are hidden in the heavenly priesthood of our ascended Lord, that he longs to unf ld to the Hebrews his knowledge of the glorious mystery; especially as this was the truth which they most urgently needed. Here and here alone could they see their true position as worshippers in the true tabernacle, the heavenly sanctuary. Here and here alone was consolation for them in the trial which they felt on account of their exclusion from the temple and the earthly service in Jerusalem; while from the knowledge of Christ's heavenly priesthood they would also derive light to avoid the insidious errors, and strength to overcome the difficulties which were besetting their path.

The subject being so central and glorious, and its practical bearing on the Hebrews so direct and important, the apostle, in his eagerness to develop the truth which he has only stated, feels himself checked by the spiritual condition of the Hebrews. He had many things to say concerning the Melchizedek priest; many things important, useful, nay, necessary; many things full of consolation and joy; but he felt that they were hard to be uttered, because the Hebrews were dull of hearing. They had fallen into a state of spiritual inertness. Their perception had become blunted, their vision dim. It seemed almost necessary to teach them the first principles of the oracles of God; not that they had lost the knowledge of them, but they had failed to lay to heart their solemnity, and to live in the power of the saving truth.* In times past they had known clearly, confessed joyfully, and suffered with great willingness. But instead of progressing they had retrograded. And with this retrogression they had lost their spiritual insight and vigour; they had become earthly-minded and unskilful in the word of righteousness. In this feeble state into which they had fallen, they were exposed to great danger. When heavenly realities became dim and vague to their hearts, the visible form and power of Judaism became both a difficulty to the mind and a temptation to the soul. The peril in which the apostle beholds them is the awful one of apostasy. He sees them on the brink of a precipice, and therefore he addresses them in the words of keen but affectionate expostulation.

But while he is filled with anxiety, he still cherishes hope. Remembering their former faith and patience, remembering, above all, the mercy and love of God, who had enlightened them and counted them worthy to suffer for the gospel's sake, the apostle enters with earnestness and

* τὰ στοιχεῖα Pauline expression. Comp. Gal. iv. 3 and 9. The expression λόγια τοῦ Θεοῦ occurs also, Acts vii. 38; Rom. iii. 2; 1 Peter iv. 2.

trustful expectancy on his difficult task. He does not allow himself to be deterred or diverted from his purpose by the difficulty of the subject and the low condition of the people. Here is not a case where the wisdom of educating love is justified in withholding deep truths which the disciples are not yet able to bear. It is only by the exposition of deep truths, by the full manifestation of the glory of Christ as our exalted High Priest, of the glory of the heavenly sanctuary, into which the believer has access, that the imminent danger of apostasy can be averted, and the dim spark of light and joy be sustained and revived. The Hebrews, we are told, were dull of hearing: "For when for the time ye ought to be teachers, ye have need that one teach you again which be the first principles of the oracles of God; and are become such as have need of milk, and not of strong meat." They are blamed for being babes, and not "of full age," or perfect.* In the Church of Christ there are little children, there are men, there are fathers. It is evident that the apostle refers in our passage to the wisdom of the heart and of life. There is a distinction between "little ones" and young men and fathers. In one sense the Saviour calls us all children. We remain always learners, and blessed are we if we belong to the "babes" unto whom the Father reveals the

* *νήπιοι*, babes, here opposed to *τέλειοις*. Compare 1 Cor. ii. 6.

mysteries of the kingdom. We are exhorted by the apostle Peter, as new-born babes, to desire the sincere milk of the Word, that we may grow thereby; and the apostle John describes the various stages of Christian experience when he writes to little children, because their sins are forgiven for His name's sake; to young men, because they are strong, and have overcome the wicked one; to fathers, because they have known Him that is from the beginning.* What can be more lovely than the Christian in his infancy, in the springtime of his spiritual life, when the flowers appear and the voice of gladness is heard, when in his first love he rejoices in the Saviour? Such babes are to be cherished with great affection and tenderness. Christians differ in their measure of understanding and strength, as well as in the gifts of grace, which by the Spirit and according to their natural endowments and providential position are bestowed on them. Those who have only recently been brought into the fold cannot possess the experience and the wisdom of the elder. The Lord, who is the head of the church, distributes also gifts and talents according to His good and

* 1 John ii. Notice here, as in other Scriptures, indications that in spiritual things the last and the first go together. The beginning contains the germ of the whole. Children also are described as knowing the Father. (*v.* 13.) Thus in the Beatitudes the poor in spirit (*v.* 3), and the persecuted for righteousness' sake (*v.* 10), have the same promise.

wise will. Some members of the church are called to be teachers, appointed to be pillars, lights, and guides, sons of consolation and fathers in the gospel; whereas others will, perhaps, always remain weak, and in need of constant help and guidance. Now the Lord, who Himself is full of love and tenderness, exhorts the church to be gentle, considerate, patient toward the young and the inexperienced; to comfort the feeble-minded, to support the weak. They that are strong ought not merely to bear the infirmities of the weak, but exercise self-denial in accommodating themselves to their less enlightened brethren; even as Christ pleased not Himself, we ought to please our neighbour for his good to edification. We must exercise a wise and patient discretion, even as Jesus had many things to say to His disciples, but remembered that they could not bear them.

Having stated this principle in defence of the weak and the babes in Christ, we may safely proceed to remind you of the Scripture's uniform declaration, that the Spirit is given and the church instituted for the very purpose that we should not remain children, but grow unto the measure of the stature of the fulness of Christ; that in understanding, in stedfastness, in courage, we must become men; that after awhile they who at first could not bear strong meat ought to advance in knowledge and wisdom, and ultimately to become teachers. This view is expressed often directly, and still more frequently indirectly. And of all the ways in which it is stated, none to my mind is so impressive as the prayers of the apostle Paul for his congregations, in which he beseeches God to give unto them the Spirit of wisdom and revelation in the knowledge of Him. Paul was anxious that Christians should comprehend the length and breadth, and height and depth. For this he laboured, he wrote his epistles, he bowed his knees before God. This was his constant prayer, and he felt it necessary to tell the churches that his soul's desire was their growth. All the children of God, from the least to the greatest, are to progress in the knowledge of God in Christ Jesus, and thus they grow in grace. According to the new covenant, and by the indwelling of the Holy Ghost, they are all called to know the things which are freely given unto us of God. For since they are Christ's, and Christ is God's, all things are theirs. (1 Cor. iii. 21, 23.) They are to know the mystery of the Father and the Son, the mystery of Christ and the church, the mystery of Israel, the mystery of the apostasy. The little children are to become men, able to teach others; and if they do not grow, it is either because that which is their nourishment is not the sincere milk of the word, or because they do not really, by faith in prayer, meditation, and obedience, live on the truths of the gospel. This subject is important, and is frequently neglected or misunderstood. Starting, then, from the admission, that according to the divine word and God's will all Christians are called to grow and to become fully instructed and established, let us inquire into the nature and method of this growth.

1. The comparison between a newly-converted man and a babe is, like all comparisons, imperfect. For in one sense a Christian is born by the Holy Ghost full-grown; as Adam came into the world a perfect man, full of light and insight, who gave names to all the living creatures, who understood and spake. The newly-converted man is born into the spiritual world, and from the first moment he sees and knows Christ, and has the mind of Christ, the Spirit, so that he can immediately understand all spiritual things. The milk of the word, as contrasted with strong meat, does not refer to any real and inherent difference between the gospel first preached and afterwards taught. From first to last we present the same truth, the same circle of truths, the whole truth. The apostles preached the first and second advent, the person and work of Christ, the gift and indwelling of the Holy Ghost; they preached the whole counsel of God to all men. They preached Jesus as the centre; but in their preaching they presented the whole circumference of truth. Do not

allow modern practice to cramp your ideas of what is meant by "preaching the gospel" even to unbelievers. Experience will decide whether the apostolic method is not the safer and better.

Hence we find that congregations after a very short time were fully indoctrinated, and that such epistles as those to the Ephesians and Thessalonians could be addressed to men who a few months ago worshipped idols, and did not know the name of Jesus. The most comprehensive and profound view of the whole plan of redemption was given unto them by the apostle Paul. He explained to them the great mystery of Christ and the church, and the position of believers in the heavenlies.

For the understanding and reception of truth depend chiefly, if not exclusively, on the *heart;* as Paul says, "the eyes of your *heart* being opened." The babe in Christ (I mean he who is a babe naturally, and not unnaturally through his own worldliness and indolence), full of love to Jesus, and impressed with the importance and blessedness of heavenly things, learns very easily and very rapidly. He delights in the word; he is humble and tender; he does not resist truths which condemn the flesh and correct our waywardness; he is unworldly, heavenly-minded, and nine-tenths of the Bible becomes clear, when we are willing to deny ourselves, and take our cross and follow Jesus. Yes, we run well at the commencement. It is apathy, worldliness, sluggishness, conceit, which afterwards render Christians slow of heart to understand all that is written. The lukewarm church must needs be an ignorant church. The divided heart must needs be confused and dim-sighted.

It is for this reason that the apostle blames the Hebrews for not having progressed in knowledge. If it was an intellectual effort, if the progress meant a mere matter of thought, research, and study, would such importance be attached to the slowness of their progress? But it implies the growth of faith and of love; their retrogression was based upon a moral and spiritual retrogression and decay. Their senses had not been exercised; that is, they had not walked closely with God, they had not followed the Master, listening earnestly to His voice, and proving what is that good, and acceptable, and perfect will of God. They had not conscientiously applied the knowledge which they had, but allowed it to remain dead and unused. If they had really and truly partaken of the milk, they would not have remained babes. If people really loved and cherished what they so fondly call "the simple gospel," their knowledge and Christian character* would deepen, and all

* "The word of righteousness" is the gospel, for therein is the righteousness of God revealed from faith to faith. (Romans i. 17.)

the truths which are centred in Christ crucified would become the object of their investigation and delight, and enrich and elevate their experience. For

2. It is not that there is a higher truth or life for the older Christians. The apostle in writing to the Corinthians blames them that they were still carnal, that they were still babes, and that therefore he was to feed them with milk and not with meat. And yet in this very epistle he states most emphatically that he knew nothing among them but Christ and Him crucified, and that this is the wisdom of God, wisdom among them that are perfect.

There are no doctrines more profound than those which are preached when Christ's salvation is declared, and to which they who are more advanced are admitted, as to an esoteric wisdom. All our progress consists in learning more fully the doctrine which at first is preached unto us.

Let us beware of entertaining erroneous views as to what is meant by milk and meat. "Milk" designates gospel truth preached simply, so that thereby true nourishment is given, and faith is both called forth, and the new spiritual life

When we abide in Christ, we add to faith knowledge; we learn to distinguish spiritual things; we do not dwell exclusively and morbidly on consolatory aspects of truth, but seek to be conformed to Christ, and to profit by the whole Scripture.

strengthened and increased. Hence, there is nothing in the term meant to depreciate, but, on the contrary, to exalt the first declaration of saving truth in Christ. The strong meat, the doctrine of Christ's high priesthood in heaven, is also milk, pure and nourishing, simple, and only received by the child like heart; whereas pride and ambition often call speculative and unprofitable discussions strong meat, though they are of no use to the spiritual man, but minister only unto strife and the exaltation of the flesh.

The Colossians dreamt of a higher and deeper wisdom than the gospel of grace. They wished to speculate about the nature of angels; they wished to ascend to a higher platform, a so-called higher Christian life of worship, devotedness, and obedience. But the apostle corrects them. He shows them that Christ is all; that in Him are hid all treasures of knowledge and understanding; that we are to learn *Him*, and to abide in the simplicity of the inexhaustible gospel. While they fancied they were advancing, they were falling back into the elements of the world.

It is the fleshly mind that is puffed up with dreamy speculations and self-invented gradations of worship. The spiritual mind knows that to know Christ, to know more and more what we saw and believed at first, is the whole progress of the Christian in time and eternity.

Connected with this is also the Corinthian error. It seems at first contradictory that the apostle calls them babes, and at the same time speaks of them as enriched in all utterance and in all knowledge. The church at Corinth was gifted in a remarkable degree. Very manifold were the manifestations of the Holy Ghost among them. But their knowledge became a snare to them, and ceased to be true knowledge. False knowledge puffeth up; it is unsubstantial, and without value. A man may possess much knowledge of Scripture truth; he may possess intellectually a vigorous and comprehensive grasp of doctrine; he may see the relation of various aspects of truth, and the application of truth to human character; he may be able to express doctrine and experience in lucid and glowing language, to detect error, subtle and false teaching, in a keen and masterly way, and yet he may be a *babe* in Christ; that is, in true spiritual knowledge of Jesus, in the tone of his mind, in the character of his daily walk, in his knowledge of his own heart, and his skill and wisdom in the conflict with sin, the world, and Satan. True knowledge is of the heart, and in love. Hence the apostle explains, in the epistle to the gifted Corinthians, so fully and with such earnestness and beauty, the pre-eminence of love. When love is perfect, knowledge is perfect. The child of God grows, obeying and honouring God, meditating on the word of God, applying it to himself, and moulding his life according to the mind of Christ, he becomes strong, his vision clear, his perceptions sensitive, his heart established. The secret of the Lord is with them that fear Him. They that follow on to know shall know. The fear of the Lord is the beginning of wisdom. Beginning means not merely the temporal commencement, but the very root and life of wisdom.

Returning to our passage, let us notice that the apostle refers to the wisdom of the heart and of life. The Hebrews had become as babes. Hence the word, which elsewhere is the sweetest expression of divine love and favour, is a term of reproach when it indicates an unnatural and dangerous condition of spiritual weakness, the result of a culpable and habitual inertness. It had not always been thus with the Hebrew Christians. For we read that when they were first enlightened they endured a great fight of affliction. Then, although they had many and grievous sufferings, they were strong, and rejoiced in Christ; and why? Because they were heavenly-minded. They believed and knew that they had in heaven a better and an enduring substance. Then, though young in the faith, they were more fervent, and therefore more spiritual, possessed of clearer knowledge and perception. And therefore the apostle is so anxious to lead them on to perfection, that is, to fix their thoughts on Christ in heaven. Their earthly-mindedness constitutes both the necessity and the difficulty of his task.

For the perfection unto which the apostle desires to go is not an esoteric doctrine or method of holiness peculiar to an imaginary second stage of faith. It has nothing to do directly with any thing in our heart and conduct. It refers, on the contrary, to heaven, to the High Priest above, to our position in Him who is seated at the right hand of God. The perfection the apostle speaks of is the beholding Christ by faith, our righteousness, strength, and life, in the heavenly sanctuary. It is to know that we are priests, worshippers in Spirit and truth, that, being reconciled to God by the death of Christ, we have now been brought nigh to the Father; and our citizenship, the source of our life and strength, the things which we seek, the blessings with which we are enriched, are no longer on earth, but in heaven. Here is perfection; for here and nowhere else is the Christ who was crucified. Christ was made perfect. The law made nothing perfect. But in the incarnate Son of God, in heaven, after His death and exaltation, there is now perfection for all who believe in Him. This is the strong meat, the same as the milk, viz., Christ is here, who was crucified, yea, rather that is risen, sitteth at the right hand of God, making intercession for us. And here alone is the power and safety of the Christian during his earthly life. Looking unto heaven, he keeps himself unspotted from the world; he is delivered from this present evil age, and he is able to follow the Lord, and to go outside the camp bearing His reproach.

The apostle exhorts the Hebrews to go on unto perfection, to become men in understanding, to fix their thoughts on Christ ascended into heaven, and representing them inside the veil. For this reason he wishes to leave aside the elementary and fundamental doctrines through which they were initiated as disciples. He enumerates six doctrines, and in a form with which the Jews were familiar. As Bengel says: "The six particulars here specified had been, as it were, *the Christian Catechism* of the Old Testament; and such Jews, who had begun to recognise Jesus as the Christ immediately on the new light being shed on these fundamental particulars, were accounted as having the elementary *principles* of the doctrine of Christ." To turn from dead works, a life without God, in which there was no true life, and to turn by faith unto God, this is the very commencement of all discipleship. They who had thus repented and believed, received, in baptism and by the laying on of hands, the sign and seal of covenant gifts, and the power of the Holy Ghost to labour in the work of the church; and, sealed with the earnest of the inheritance, they looked forward unto the resurrection of the just, and the final separation unto the kingdom of glory.*

1. Repentance from dead works and faith toward God.

The divine message to sinners has always been to turn from sin and ungodliness to the mercy and power of God, who is willing to forgive sin and able to renew the heart. Repentance and faith are inseparably connected. All true repentance has its source in the declaration of God's holiness and grace. He who turns unto God believes both the justice and the mercy of the Lord. Repentance was never preached except in connection with redemption: the kingdom of God is at hand; the loving arms of God are open; turn unto Him before the great day of His wrath. The whole message of the old covenant prophets is the solemn and yet sweet message of repentance; and this also was the preaching of John the Baptist, and the Lord Jesus Himself, during His prophetic ministry.

* This is another illustration of the fact, that the most elementary instruction of apostolic days was more comprehensive than what is now called the 'simple gospel.' It embraced not merely teaching concerning the holiness of God and the guilt and depravity of man (repentance), but also the doctrine of the gift of the Holy Ghost and the work of the church, as well as the doctrine of the second coming and kingdom of Christ, of which all Scripture testifies.

Repentance is unto life. The deepest explanation, and the most lovely illustration of the true nature of repentance, is in the gospel of Luke (chap. xv.); the publicans and sinners drawing near to Jesus to hear Him. To draw near to the Saviour, and to trust, is to repent.

Again, faith cannot be without repentance. When Cornelius and his friends believed the gospel preached unto them by the apostle Peter, their conversion is described by these words: God has given repentance unto the Gentiles. (Acts x.)

But while repentance and faith are thus inseparably connected, in repentance the negative element preponderates, in faith the positive. In the one, because of God's holiness and grace, we turn from sin and ungodliness; in the other, because of our sin and misery, we look unto the holy and merciful Lord. Hence sorrow and fear are prominent features of repentance; hopeful trust and loving joy characterize faith.

The expression "repentance from dead works" refers to the truth that, apart from God and from the life which His grace implants, even our good works are without life; possessing no vitality, they are unfruitful; that is, they do not glorify the Father (John xv. 8), and they do not issue in the reward and blessedness which Scripture connects with good works wrought in God.

As long as man is alienated from God, he, though living, is dead in trespasses and sins; and while he is apart from the true Vine he can do nothing. The works of the law performed in the spirit of bondage have no inward truth and substance. The good works of a godly man reveal his inner life; they exert a life-influence on those that see them (Matt. v. 16), and they react on the character and spirit of him who performs them. But our old life, before the grace of God renews us, is a life of "dead works."

Opposed to the life of dead works is faith; that is, the positive aspect of conversion; the soul turning in confidence and appropriating trust to the grace of God as revealed in redemption. Faith in God the Redeemer, the covenant God, who will abundantly pardon, and with whom is plenteous redemption, was the life of God's saints, from Abel to John the Baptist. The just always lived by *faith* (Hab. ii.), and by faith they possessed that life which is of God and eternal. And since God has now fully revealed Himself in Christ Jesus, and given us in Him the true and perfect redemption, it is evident that the object of our faith is now specially the Lord Jesus Himself, and yet the same Holy One of Israel, in whom the fathers trusted.

2. The doctrine of baptisms and the laying on of hands.

The Jews were familiar with baptism as a rite of initiation, by which Gentiles were separated from the unholy and idolatrous communion to which they belonged, and admitted into the commonwealth of Israel. The baptism of John required for this reason no explanation as to the act itself; the only thing remarkable about it was, that it was applied to the children of the kingdom, and not to those who stood without. The baptism which our Lord instituted differed again from that of the Jews and of John the Baptist, in that it was a sign and seal of the covenant of grace, and in the name of Father, Son, and Holy Ghost, signifying and sealing the gift of a new life, through the redemption which is in Christ Jesus and the renewal by the Holy Ghost. Those who had been baptized were viewed as having put on Christ, as being washed from their sins, and as having received the Holy Ghost. The laying on of hands was a symbolic act which from time immemorial, and with divine sanction, had been connected with prayer, invoking the divine benediction. And they who had been admitted into the church, and recognised as believing and renewed members, were viewed as priests, and each one was called to exercise the gift which the Spirit had bestowed on him for the good and edification of the whole; while some, called to special work of evangelisation or other ministry, were set apart for the work, after fasting and prayer, by the laying on of hands.*

3. Intimately connected with the doctrine of the Holy Ghost, as set forth in baptism and the laying on of hands, is the doctrine of resurrection and eternal judgment. In the Creed (commonly called the Apostles') we find this connection illustrated; believing in the Holy Ghost, we see His

* The Synagogue calls the laying on of hands סמיכה, and connects it with the setting apart to the office of teacher in sacred things. The hand is viewed in Scripture as the organ by which gifts are imparted and transferred. The Israelite laid his hand on the sacrifice, on the burnt-offering (Lev. i. 4), on the peace-offering (iii. 2); Aaron and his sons, upon the sin-offering (viii. 14) and on the scapegoat, as we read xvi. 21, thereby symbolically putting all their transgressions upon the head of this goat. In the case of the sacrifices for sin, the laying on of hands symbolises the transference of guilt and transgression; in the thank-offering, the transference of gratitude and self-surrender. We find the laying on of hands among the patriarchs connected with benediction on the seed of promise. (Gen. xlviii. 14.) This custom still continues among the Jews—the father blesses thus his children on the Sabbath day. Under the law we find it connected with setting apart to special ministry. (Num. xxvii. 18.) In the New Testament we read of our divine Lord laying His hands on the sick, and healing them. (Luke iv. 41; Mark vi. 5.) We then read of the apostles laying on hands on disciples (Acts viii. 17); and Ananias (not an apostle notice, but simply a member of the church) laid his hands on Saul, and immediately his eyes were opened. Thus the laying on of hands was a symbolic action accompanying the communication of divine gifts. Lastly, in connection with special work and ministry. (Acts xiii. 3; 1 Tim. iv. 14.)

The laying on of hands has justly been retained by the churches of the Reformation in the setting apart of men to the ministry into which they are called of God. But perhaps we have not used this symbol, sanctioned of God, sufficiently in the admission to the Lord's table and in praying with the sick.

creation in the Catholic Church, His power and indwelling in the communion of saints, His consolation in the renewed assurance of forgiveness of sin, His ultimate and crowning work in the resurrection of the body and the life of glory, which is eternal. By the spirit that dwells in us God shall quicken our mortal bodies. (Rom. viii. 11; compare also 2 Cor. v. 5; Ephes. i. 14.) The doctrine of resurrection, which was strenuously held by the Pharisees, is so intimately connected with the Messianic hope that the apostle Paul could say truthfully: "Men and brethren, I am a Pharisee, the son of a Pharisee: of the hope and resurrection of the dead I am called in question." (Acts xxiii. 6; compare xxv. 6.) As this fundamental doctrine was held by the Jews, so in its full and deepest sense the resurrection was the crowning and ultimate object of the apostles' hope, the goal to which they constantly looked. "If by any means I might attain unto the resurrection from among the dead." (Phil. iii. 11.) This is the resurrection of the just, of which our Lord speaks; this is the first resurrection, in which the blessed and holy have part. (Rev. xx. 6.)

The judgment is called eternal; for the word judgment (κρῖμα) means not the act or process of judgment (which is κρίσις ix. 18 and x. 27), but its result or judicial sentence, which is final and irrevocable. For nowhere does Scripture hold out the prospect of that sentence "Depart from me" being changed. It is the uniform doctrine of Scripture, that the gulf between the saved, the "blessed of my Father," and the lost, is fixed, and that the life of glory as well as the death of anguish is everlasting.

Such was the elementary Christian instruction, summed up in the form of sound words, with which the Jews were familiar. The germ of all truths is contained in them; they present an outline and sketch of the whole building. And yet these fundamental doctrines did not set before the Hebrews with sufficient fulness and clearness the truth of which they stood in need to keep them from apostasy, and to strengthen and comfort them in their sore trial and temptation. It was necessary for them now to fix their thoughts on the "heavenly things" to which our Saviour alludes in His conversation with Nicodemus, to the perfection of the High Priest and the heavenly sanctuary.

John the Baptist preached repentance and faith; he baptized with water, and spoke of the baptism with the Holy Ghost; he testified of the approach of judgment, of the wheat gathered, and the chaff burned up. And yet John the Baptist stood not in the full light of Pentecostal fulfilment. It behoved the Hebrews to go on in their knowledge unto perfect manhood, till the measure of the stature of Christ's fulness be attained. And it not merely behoved them, but it was absolutely necessary. For, notwithstanding their dulness of hearing, the apostle, deeply impressed with a sense of their danger, and hoping in the never-failing mercy of our compassionate Lord, takes courage to unfold to them the deep things of God.

Here is a very important lesson for our times. When we think of the state of the church and of Christendom, we naturally ask what is the best method of rousing and strengthening that which is languid and feeble, of bringing back those who have strayed, and of fortifying the tempted against the errors and the God-opposing spirit of the age. This is specially a solemn question for those who are teachers, stewards of the mystery of God, under-shepherds of the flock. Is it sufficient to preach the simple doctrine of the gospel, to declare the fundamental truths of repentance and faith, limiting ourselves to what is absolutely essential to the commencement of Christian life, and simply reminding our people of the great salvation, that Jesus died because of our offences, and was raised again because of our justification? Is such a method scriptural? and, viewing it from the lower point of expediency and experience, is it safe and effectual? Does not Scripture teach us that we should keep back nothing that is profitable, that we should not shun to declare the whole counsel of God, that the children of God should comprehend with all saints what is the breadth, and length, and depth, and height? Do we not continually notice that scanty, elementary, and one-sided teaching does not even secure the true, living, and healthy knowledge of simple and fundamental truths? And with regard to those who are still strangers to the grace of God, is it not our duty to lay before them the divine message in all its fulness and beauty, in its comprehensiveness and depth, and by unfolding to them as far as man is able the Scripture, teaching to counteract the unscriptural opinions which refer not merely to the central questions of personal salvation, but to the character of God, the origin of the world and man, the nature of sin, the history and the ultimate destiny of our race? Above all, is it not for us to preach Jesus Christ; Jesus, the Messiah promised to Israel, the Saviour of sinners and head of the church; Jesus, the Son of God and Son of man; Jesus, the High Priest in heaven and the coming Lord, who will be King over the whole earth?

Perhaps no church had fallen into so low and dangerous a condition as the Hebrews. The remedy which apostolic wisdom and love applied was (contrary to what most of us would have suggested) a profound exposition of the glory of the exalted Saviour as the royal High Priest. He endeavours to bring before them the wonderful perfections of the Lord Jesus as their all-sufficient Mediator, that thus their hearts may be drawn from earth and filled with the peace and joy of God. Thus nothing is more needed in our days, both for the church and the world, than a faithful and deep exposition of Scripture, of the whole Scripture, of Scripture in its organic unity and comprehensive fulness, in order that by grace mind, conscience, and heart may be convinced that here are revealed unto us thoughts higher than our thoughts, divine realities and blessings, things which eye hath not seen, nor ear heard, neither have entered into the heart of man. And thus, while they who believe not will acknowledge that God is in us of a truth, the children of God will be kept stedfast and faithful; they will be furnished unto every good work, and, forgetting the things that are behind, will press toward the mark for the prize of the high calling of God in Christ Jesus.*

* The want of docility and of active inquiry into divine truth manifests itself in various ways. Sometimes in ignoring prophecy, as if prophecy was isolated and not essentially and inseparably connected with the other portions and aspects of truth, as if the whole word was not the sure word of prophecy, the word of Him who was, and is, and is to come. Sometimes in a shrinking from the deeper meaning of the types, such as the sacrifices and festivals, or those of David and Solomon. Sometimes in neglect of the Jewish Scriptures, and in forgetfulness of the mystery of Israel, and the relation between the church and the kingdom. Again there is the morbid and exclusive repetition of the blessed truth, "peace

Going on unto perfection, beholding Christ in heaven, we continue in the simplicity which is in Christ Jesus. When by the grace of God we were converted, we became as little children; we were made humble, docile, cheerfully dependent on God's mercy, and joyfully accepting His gift. Having no wisdom, righteousness, or strength of our own, we were made willing to receive Christ Jesus. By Him are we continually brought as little children to the Father. When we abide in faith and love, though in understanding we become men, yet we continue childlike, we are children in malice. Thus only do we retain the humble, trustful, joyous, obedient, and plastic character of childhood, the dew of our youth. In one sense we always sing—

> "Sweet the moments, rich in blessing,
> Which before the cross we spend."

Christ crucified is the sum of our knowledge. For here is not merely the foundation on which our faith rests, the source of our love and obedience, of our strength and hope; but here we behold the eternal coûnsel of God, and the glory which shall hereafter be revealed. But it is the living Christ, the Lord Himself, who is the object of our faith

in believing," apart from the new life, the conflict of faith, the service of love, and the crucifixion of the flesh. What we need is not (so-called) intellectual or æsthetic or eloquent preaching, but pneumatic (spiritual) preaching of the "whole counsel of God" as unfolded in Scripture.

and contemplation. We behold Him who was dead but is now living; it is in Him that we now see and learn God. He who became man that we might be made partakers of the divine nature, who died that by His blood we might be brought near unto God, who ascended and sa down at the right hand of God to send unto us the Spirit, and to present us perfect before the Father, is the true Mediator, in whom divine light, life, and love are given unto us. Thus is fulfilled the saying of Israel's great King, "The way of life is above to the wise, that he may depart from hell beneath." In Christ ascended is our only safety. To look unto Him is the only way in which our feet can be kept from falling, in which we can worship in the presence of God, and, beholding the countenance of our Father, serve Him on earth.

There is a simplicity which is the result of full and profound knowledge, of varied experience and conflict; a simplicity which is the indication of abundance and depth, which is the result of meditation, prayerfulness, and a humble walk with God. They who are fathers in the church, who, like the apostle John, lean on the bosom of Jesus, who behold the glory of the only-begotten, and in singleness of heart rest in His love, reach a lofty and calm mountain height, and they express their knowledge and experience with great simplicity and brevity. We often fancy we understand their quiet and axiomatic words, or that we have fathomed their meaning, and yet we may only have come into contact with the surface. The apostle John is thus the simplest and deepest teacher in the church. Like the Sabbath-day, he appears among the disciples; a solemn, yet childlike quiet and simplicity characterize his words; we meet with no complicated arguments, no noise and struggle, no upward steep ascent from earth to heaven, law to grace, Levitical type to Melchizedek perfection; we are transplanted at once into the high region of God's light, love, life. These simple yet inexhaustible words are the constantly recurring realities of which he testifies. To reach this simplicity is the object of the Christian individual and of the Christian church.

While we are serving the Lord amid trials and sorrows, and waiting for His second coming, let us behold, as we are taught in the epistle to the Hebrews, the High Priest in heaven—let us see, as the apostle John testifies in the Apocalypse, "the Lamb in the midst of the throne." This is the simplest and most comprehensive word of Scripture. "The Lamb on the throne." This sums up all Scripture history and prophecy, all Scripture doctrine and consolation; this fulfils all Scripture types; for here is the sacrifice, the sanctuary, and the royal High Priest. He who was slain for us is the Divine King; He unto whom all power is given in heaven and in earth is the Lamb, full of love and tenderness. We are at peace; we learn the patience and wisdom of the saints as followers of the Lamb. Called to suffer in fellowship with Him, we look forward with hope to His return; for the Church is the bride, the Lamb's wife. To behold the Lamb in the midst of the throne, this is "going on unto perfection."

CHAPTER XIII.

THE DANGER OF APOSTASY; THE PATIENCE OF FAITH AND THE ANCHOR OF HOPE.

HEB. vi. 4-20.

THE danger of retrogression is, perhaps, nowhere in Scripture placed before us in such a forcible and alarming manner as in this solemn chapter. One of the promises which occurs very frequently with regard to Israel after their conversion and restoration, is their stedfastness; they shall never turn back, but love and serve the Lord for ever. The prophetic word represents to us the picture of Israel continuing faithful during all the centuries that may be before them in the promised land. They shall never lapse. After, by the grace of God, and the appearing of the Lord Jesus, and the outpouring of the Holy Ghost, they are brought to repentance and faith, they shall continue for ever walking in the light of His countenance, and rejoicing in the rock of their salvation, serving and glorifying God their Redeemer.

The apostle Paul may be regarded as a striking and eminent type of Israel. Converted on his way to Damascus by the appearing of the Lord of glory, he typifies the sudden and direct manner in which the Jews, who, ignorant of God's righteousness, reject the gospel, shall be turned from darkness unto light, and experience the forgiving love of Joseph their brother, whom they hated and sold into Egypt.* And the subsequent life of the apostle seems a type of the subsequent uninter-

* "For my part," says Mede, "I incline to think the Jewish nation shall be called by *vision* and *voice from heaven,* as St. Paul was; and that that place of Zech. xii. 10, 'They shall see Him whom they have pierced,' and that of Matt. xxiii. 39, 'Ye shall not see me henceforth, till ye shall say, Blessed is He that cometh in the name of the Lord,' seems to imply some such matter. They will never believe that Christ reigns at the right hand of God until they see Him. It must be an invincible evidence which must convert them after so many hundred years' settled obstinacy. But this I speak of the body of the nation; there may be some *Praeludia* of some particulars converted upon other motives, as a forerunner of the great and main conversion.

"The Jews will not be converted unto Christ by such means as were the rest of the nations, by the ministry of preachers sent unto them; but by the revelation of Christ Jesus in His glory from heaven, when they shall not say, as when they saw Him in His humiliation, 'Crucify Him,' but, 'Blessed is He that cometh in the name of the Lord.' Whose coming then shall be as lightning out of the east, shining unto the west; and the sign of the Son of man shall appear in the clouds of heaven, and every eye shall see Him, even those which pierced Him, and shall lament with the spirit of grace and supplication for their so long and so shameful unbelief of their so merciful Redeemer."

rupted faithfulness and service of renewed and restored Israel. Think of the career of the great apostle. When it pleased God to reveal His Son in him, obedient to the heavenly vision, and without conferring with flesh and blood, he became the servant of the Lord, whom before he had persecuted. From that day on he continued stedfast, and through a life full of danger and suffering, of incessant toil and sacrifice, he went on with increasing ardour, vigour, and alacrity, never pausing, never relaxing his effort, or diminishing zeal, until at last, facing death, he was able to say, "I have fought the good fight, I have finished my course, I have kept the faith." He never for a moment relaxed in his intense energy, in his fervent devotion, in his arduous labours. He went on with a steady step and a loving heart. His affection, his faith, his self-forgetfulness, his courage, seem to increase and shine with a brighter and stronger light. He never seems to rest satisfied with his past attainments, or to be content with the measure of suffering and reproach endured for Christ's sake, or with the measure of victory gained in the beloved Master's cause. He is always, as he himself describes it, doing one thing, forgetting the things that are behind, and reaching forth unto those things which are before, he pressed toward the mark of the high calling of God in Christ Jesus. Many and painful were the disappointments which met him in his work. He had constantly to bear the enmity of the Jews, the opposition of the Greeks, the suspicion with which many Jewish Christians regarded him, the interference of false teachers, the ingratitude and the unfaithfulness of many of his own converts; but his zeal remained unaltered, he continued in faith, in patience, in that love which endureth all things and hopeth all things. No stripes or imprisonment, no perils by land or sea, among robbers or false brethren, no sufferings or hardships, were able to cloud his confidence in the grace and power of the Lord Jesus who had sent him, or to lessen that ardent affection which he felt for unbelieving Israel, and that tender and fatherly love with which he regarded all the faithful. He continued bearing the churches on his heart, praying for them, and writing to them words of heavenly wisdom and fervent affection. The ingratitude of men seemed only to deepen his love and stimulate his zeal. Forgetful of self, he addressed words of encouragement and rejoicing from his prison and in the prospect of death. With ever-increasing brightness of knowledge, faith, love, hope, he patiently *ran* the race set before him, though none of God's servants had such a rough and thorny path. Jesus, who said of him that he was a chosen vessel unto Him, also declared, I will show him how great things he must suffer for my name's sake. As the Lord Jesus showed forth all long-suffering in him *for a pattern*, so by the grace of God the apostle Paul is an illustration of perseverance and faithful service.

I am not idealising the apostle. I am not guilty of hero or saint-worship. He was a chosen vessel, appointed to be a pattern, both of converting grace and of the power and stedfastness of the new life, bestowed by the Holy Ghost. He was able to say to the churches, "Be ye followers of me, even as I am of Christ."

With what force and significance do exhortations to perseverance come from him. How willing ought we to be to listen to him when he exhorts us to work out our own salvation with fear and trembling. He was always giving diligence to make his calling and election sure. His constant aim was, to know Jesus, and the power of His resurrection, and the fellowship of His sufferings, being made conformable unto His death, if by any means he might attain unto the (first) resurrection from among the dead. Filled with love to the saints, he is anxious to see them all strong and joyous in the faith, that God may be glorified.

When he thinks of the Hebrews, who through lukewarmness and culpable inertness had become again like babes, unable to receive the doctrine of the glorified Saviour and of His perfect priesthood, he is filled with sorrow and great anxiety. Although new-born babes are weak, yet the apostle, like his divine Lord, rejoiced over them, and gave thanks unto the Father for their faith and love. The life of the newly-converted souls is full of promise. With eagerness they listen to the doctrine of apostles, and in their first love they are swift to hear and to understand. But when old Christians become again like babes, their state is dangerous. The apostle regards the retrogression of the Hebrews with dismay. He sees in it the danger of an entire, continued, wilful, and irrecoverable apostasy from the truth. He beholds them on the brink of a precipice, and he therefore lifts up his voice, and with vehement, yet loving earnestness, he warns them against so fearful an evil.

"It is impossible for those who were once enlightened, and have tasted of the heavenly gift, and were made partakers of the Holy Ghost, and have tasted the good word of God, and the powers of the world to come, if they shall fall away, to renew them again unto repentance." These solemn and awful words have occasioned much controversy, and caused much alarm to anxious and sensitive hearts; but let us also hope that, blessed by the Spirit, they have achieved the purpose for which they were written; viz., to rouse the careless and indolent, who have fallen asleep on the enchanted ground; to show unto the backslider and unto the unfaithful and slothful servant the evil and danger of his way; to cause earnest heart-searching before God, and to encourage the humbled soul to return to the love of the Father and the grace of the Lord Jesus; for it is evident that the apostle's great aim in this chapter is to *encourage* the Hebrews to persevere and to stand fast in the grace of God, that returning unto the Lord they may have full assurance of hope.

The Hebrews had become lukewarm, negligent, and inert; the gospel, once clearly seen and dearly loved by them, had become to them dim and vague; the persecution and contempt of their countrymen a grievous burden under which they groaned, and in which they did not enjoy fellowship with the Lord Jesus. Darkness, doubt, gloom, indecision, and consequently a walk in which the power of Christ's love was not manifest, characterised them. Now if they continued in this state, what else could be the result but apostasy? Forgetfulness must end in rejection, apathy in antipathy, unfaithfulness in infidelity.

Such was their danger. And if they succumbed to it their state was hopeless. No other gospel remains to be preached, no other power to rescue and raise them. They had heard and known the voice which saith, "Come unto me, and I will give you rest." They had professed to believe in the Lord, who died for sinners, and to have chosen Him as their Saviour and Master. And now they were forgetting and forsaking the Rock of their salvation. If they deliberately and wilfully continued in this state, they were in danger of final impenitence and hardness of heart.

The exhortation must be viewed in connection with the special circumstances of the Hebrews. After the rejection of the Messiah by Israel, the gospel had been preached unto the Jews by the apostles, and the gifts and power of the Holy Ghost had been manifested among them. The Hebrews had accepted the gospel of the once crucified and now glorified Redeemer, who sent down from heaven the Spirit, a sign of His exaltation, and a pledge of the future inheritance. Having thus entered *into the sphere of new covenant manifestation*, any one who wilfully abandoned it could only relapse into that phase of Judaism which crucified the Lord Jesus. There was no other alternative for them, but either to go on to the full knowledge of the heavenly priesthood of Christ, and to the believer's acceptance and worship through the Mediator in the sanctuary above, or to fall back into the attitude, not of the godly Israelites before Pentecost, such as John the Baptist and those who waited for the promised redemption, nor even into the condition of those for whom the Saviour prayed, "for they know not what they do;" but into a state of wilful and conscious enmity against Christ, and the sin of rejecting Him, and putting Him to an open shame.

Though the apostle hopes better things of the Hebrews, as we shall see immediately, yet he cannot in faithfulness and love but present this solemn warning to them, and as this warning, like all Scripture teaching and exhortation, applies not merely to the people to whom it was primarily addressed, but is written also for us, it becomes us more fully to consider and weigh its meaning.

It has been asked whether the description here given is the description of a truly converted and renewed soul. While some, remembering the Scriptural truth, that the sheep of Christ can never perish, and that the children of God are born of incorruptible seed, have attempted to explain the terms used, as not reaching fully the description of regeneration by the Spirit; others have insisted on the expressions denoting unmistakeably the renewal of the heart by the grace of God.

The true explanation seems to be, that the apostle uses expressions to describe what the Hebrews were in profession and outward appearance. He describes them as we describe our fellow-Christians—as they appear to us, as they themselves profess to be, and as we think of them from their words and actions. Hence the apostle would doubtless use different expressions if he wished to describe (objectively) the believer. From the eternal, heavenly, and divine point of view, a believer is one who is born of God, who has been quickened together with Christ, who is accepted in the Beloved—who was chosen before the foundations of the world were laid—who has received the Holy Ghost as an earnest of the inheritance: he is of God, and the seed of God abideth in him; he is one of Christ's sheep, and can never perish. The new life which is given by the Spirit is an eternal life. The union between Jesus and the believer is an indissoluble one. The apostle therefore could never join the description of a true believer with the description of final apostasy. But he does join (and so does all Scripture) the description of the *apparent* and *professing* believer, and that taking him at his highest and best, with the consequence of retrogression, and lukewarmness, and sin. The Hebrews professed, and to all appearance had been enlightened. They had tasted of the heavenly gift, for they expressed their joy in believing the glad tidings; they seemed to have been made partakers of the Holy Ghost, for they called Jesus Lord; they seemed to have tasted the good word of God and the powers of the world to come, for they were willing to suffer and to lose their worldly goods for the sake of the eternal reward. But now, unless they gird up the loins of their mind and rouse themselves from their slumber, unless by repentance and faith they collect and concentrate their energy, and ascend the steep and rugged height as Jesus commands us to follow Him, their path is downward and unto eternal ruin.*

In no other form could this most necessary exhortation have been given. And it is equally unscriptural to blunt the edge of this severe warning as it is to deduce from it the doctrine that the truly-renewed soul can finally fall away from God. While the apostle entertains the hope that the Hebrews are true and sincere, and that

* This warning does not refer to isolated sins, but to a protracted and habitual condition of mind; to neglect and disbelief of truths once recognised and confessed; and it places before us the result of a series of unfaithful and wilful rejections of spiritual influences and privileges. Many humble and timid Christians have misunderstood the whole scope and purport of this passage. He who judges himself is not judged. The man who fears always is safe, because he trusts in the living God and Saviour. But, as we know from Scripture, and, alas! also from experience, there are some who appear to the church to be zealous and true Christians, and who yet have not received the word in a good heart, and by and by fall away. Such men are in a most deplorable condition. Their antipathy to truths, once known and professed, is very great, and different from the apathy of the worldly; theirs is a bitter and subtle hostility. Yet even their case should not be received by us as hopeless; but we should pray for them, that God may give unto them true repentance and living faith. The wilful and conscious rejection of the testimony of the Holy Ghost is another subject, and not spoken of in this passage.

by the grace of God their faith will be revived, he feels that this can be effected in no other way than by showing them their present actual condition, and the inevitable results which must follow their continuance in it. If they continue in their downward career, it will then become manifest that they received the good seed only superficially, that they had no depth, and therefore after a short season of joy fell away. Land which drinks in the rain that comes down from heaven shows that it is good land, because it brings forth fruit, and the blessing of God is visibly and evidently resting upon it. Land which, though visited by the same benign influences, and watered by the same rain, brings forth nothing but briers and thorns, shows that it is reprobate, and well-nigh unto destruction and cursing. Think it, then, no slight or unimportant matter whether you are bringing forth fruit or not. Delay not, but retrace your steps; return to the Lord; go forth and weep bitterly, and then hear the Lord's question, "Lovest thou me?" Choose between ignorance, apathy, gloom, and the favour and blessing and service of the Lord.

It is strange that some have failed to perceive that all Scripture warnings are given according to the same method; and it is difficult to see how they could possibly be framed differently. For instance, the apostle says to believers, "If ye live after the flesh, ye shall die." (Rom. viii. 13.) Does he teach that they unto whom there is no condemnation, who are in Christ Jesus, shall die? No; but he wishes to show that the consequence of living after the flesh would necessarily be death. "If a man abide not in me, he is cast forth as a branch, and is withered." If one who appears to be a member of Christ does not continue in the communion of faith and obedience, the inevitable result is that, having no vital union with the source of life, he must perish. Again, if ye forgive not men their trespasses, neither will your Father forgive your trespasses. And still more clear is the parable of the unmerciful servant who, having received his Lord's forgiveness, would not forgive his fellow-servant who owed him a debt. Here the hypothesis is converted into a narrative. The point to be illustrated is this, forgiveness which is not accompanied by a renewal of the heart, inclining it to be merciful, compassionate, and forgiving, is only apparent and superficial, and on the day of decision it will be made manifest that it was not genuine and God-given. Now, in what other way could this thought be illustrated than by representing the hypothesis as an actual fact? The servant's debt is remitted; he meets his fellow-servant; he shows no pity, but is unrelenting; the Lord finally pronounces judgment, and cancels his pardon. Does this parable then contradict the truth that the gifts and calling of God are without repentance, that being justified by faith we have peace, and stand in grace, that once in Christ, we are in Christ for ever? Take again the parable of the servants, and the picture given of the unprofitable servant who brought the one talent hid in a napkin. What is the truth taught here, but that most solemn one, that there is a semblance of conversion, of faith, of preaching, of works, in which there is no truth, substance, and life; that there is a counterfeit of conversion and renovation; that many profess and think they have been pardoned and accepted, of whom yet Jesus says, "I know you not"? The Lord Jesus represents this in a history. The question is not, Has this servant (who afterwards is manifested to have been unprofitable) received true grace? But the conduct of one, who appeared and professed to be a servant of Christ, is described, and the result is declared for our instruction and warning. Our election of God is a secret, and to make our election sure is the constant desire, aim, and prayer of the godly. The Lord's people are known only unto Him; there is no outward, unmistakeable sign or seal given to any individual or to any community, whereby they stand out as the chosen saints of God, who shall be with Him in glory everlasting. Tares are among the wheat. Think of the twelve apostles, chosen and called by the Lord Himself. What higher position could be assigned to men? What greater dignity could be bestowed, or what surer indication given of divine favour and of future glory? And when Jesus said to the twelve, "Ye shall sit upon twelve thrones, judging the tribes of Israel," did it not seem as if the throne had been already prepared for Judas Iscariot? And so it must have appeared—from our human point of view—to the twelve disciples, and to him also who afterwards betrayed the Lord. Yet the divine Master, while He thus spake, warned all the apostles, (and it is beautiful to hear them ask, in true humility, "Lord, is it I?") and with faithfulness and solemnity He warned Judas especially. Every individual must see to it that he builds upon a sure foundation, that he possesses not merely the form, but the power of godliness. The whole Church of God, as an actual, outward, and visible community, even the innermost circle of apostles, and still more the innermost sanctuary—the heart of the chosen believer—must be constantly kept in the attitude of humble watchfulness; and we must continually remember that faith is in *life*, that there is a necessary connection between self-denial, obedience, stedfastness to the end, and the final manifestation of the elect of God, chosen from all eternity in Christ Jesus to be His for evermore. "He that endureth to the end shall be saved."*

Yet, dear friends, all these warnings and exhortations do not for a single instant militate against the truth of electing love and the grace of God sustaining the believer unto the end. There is a higher region of truth and of doctrine revealed unto us in Scripture. If we look at the disciples of the Lord Jesus Christ from the earthly, or time-point of view, as I have said already, then all these exhortations are in full force, and who can doubt their necessity? The Lord Jesus said, "If the light that is in thee be darkness, how great is that darkness!" He warned us that if the salt lose its savour it is good for nothing, but must be cast out and trodden under foot. And did it not happen that whole congregations, whole churches, whole regions, who had the gospel of the Lord Jesus Christ, but who through unfaithfulness lapsed, have become entirely forsaken by the light and by the grace of God? Thus we read warnings in the seven epistles which Jesus sent from heaven. He threatens that the candlestick shall be removed, and the candlestick was removed, and many of those churches in the East

* The most popular and graphic illustration of these remarks is BUNYAN'S *Pilgrim's Progress*, in which we see that Christian meets many, who, though apparently they have left the city of Destruction, and are on their way to the heavenly Jerusalem, yet have not the love of God in them, and never reach the pearly gates.

lost their savour, and became almost worse than the people that were around them. The condition of churches who once possessed the knowledge of God became so low—Christians, so-called, fell into such superstition, deadness, and idolatrous practices, that even Mahometanism, notwithstanding its imposture, and with all its grievous errors, was to a certain extent an improvement on the fearful hypocrisy and ungodliness of those who were called by the holy name of Messiah.

But let us consider now the other and the higher aspect of truth. The children of God are born again of incorruptible seed, and they can never die. They that believe in Jesus, who really, and not in word only, trust in the Saviour, are born of God, and they cannot sin, because the seed of God abideth in them. They who belong to the flock of Christ can never perish. Have you noticed the use of the word "sheep" in Scripture? We read of true disciples and of false disciples, of wise virgins and of foolish virgins, of faithful stewards and of unfaithful stewards; but we never read of sheep in any other sense than as the elect who are saved with an everlasting salvation. "For my sheep hear my voice, and I know them, and they follow me: and I give unto them eternal life; and they shall never perish, and none shall pluck them out of my hand. My Father, who gave them me, is greater than all." The sheep of the Lord

Jesus Christ are saved by the blood of Jesus, chosen by the Father from all eternity, and quickened by the Holy Ghost; in vital union with Him who is the resurrection and the life, they shall receive that blessedness which is eternal and full of glory. In like manner, the Lord Jesus Christ says, that in the latter days there shall be many false Christs, many false teachers, so that they shall lead astray many, and, "if it were possible," even the elect. What is the meaning of that "if it were possible"? The meaning of it is simply, that it is not possible; that the elect of God are perfectly safe; that if it were not for the power of God that keeps them, the sophistry and the fascination of false teachers would certainly lead them astray; but because God holds them, and Jesus prays for them, and the Holy Ghost seals them, therefore they cannot fall away.

These abundant assurances of the word of God are illustrated by every aspect of the work of salvation, by the election of the Father, by the sacrifice of the Son, and by the work of the Holy Ghost. They are confirmed by our own experience; for every Christian can sing:

"'Twas thy love, O God, that knew us
Earth's foundation long before;
That same love to Jesus drew us,
By its sweet constraining power,
And will keep us
Safely, now and evermore."

While we have these abundant assurances of the position of safety that all the chosen of God have in Christ Jesus, it is by these very warnings and exhortations that we are kept humble, vigilant, clinging unto Jesus.*

But the apostle hastens to comfort and encourage, lest the Hebrews should be overwhelmed with fear and sorrow, or lest they should think that their condition was regarded by him as hopeless. The affection of the writer is now eager to inspire hope, and to draw them with the cords of love. The word "beloved" is introduced here most appositely, a term of endearment which occurs frequently in other epistles, but only once in ours; not that the apostle was not filled with true and fervent love to the Hebrew Christians, but that he felt obliged to restrain as it were his feeling by reason of their prejudices against him. But here the expression bursts forth, as in a moment of great danger or of anxious suspense the heart *will* speak out in tender language. He assures them that, although he thus speaks, he is persuaded better things concerning them, and things which are connected with, which grasp and accompany,

* Thus in a large crowd a father might exhort his child to keep close to his side, and not to lose hold of his hand, representing how helpless and perilous the child's condition would be if left to himself. While the father's love is ever watchful, the child's attitude ought to be obedient and humble, yet confiding dependence on his care and affection.

salvation. This thought is eminently Pauline, and a comment on the words, Love thinketh no evil, and hopeth all things. So he says to the Romans, "I myself am persuaded of you, my brethren, that ye are full of goodness" (Rom. xv. 14); and to the Philippians, "Being confident of this very thing, that He which hath begun a good work in you will perform it until the day of Jesus Christ: even as it *is meet for me to think this of you all, because I have you in my heart.*" The things which accompany salvation, or are linked to it, are humility, faith, patience, diligence, prayer, stedfastness. His confidence is, that as true children of God they will persevere unto the end. For he recalls the days of their first faith and love, when they willingly suffered for Christ's sake, and when they ministered unto the saints. God also remembers it; and as in His grace He has connected reward with our good works, wrought by faith in Jesus, so it would be unrighteous in Him to forget what they had done and suffered for the gospel. He will reward them, and what better, higher, and sweeter reward can God give us than to keep us faithful, to sustain us to the end, to shed abroad His love in our hearts; for God Himself is our sure portion, and our exceeding great reward.

Having this encouragement and hope, his heart's desire is that every one of them should show the same diligence to the full assurance of hope unto the end. He reminds them of their father Abraham. In faith and patience he continued stedfast, though his hope was not accomplished. How long had Abraham to wait for the fulfilment of the promise! How severely was his faith tested! If the Hebrews were sorely tried, if they felt it a great hardship to be excluded from the temple, to be regarded as strangers from the commonwealth of Israel; if they felt it difficult to look by faith unto Jesus and unto His return, waiting for the possession of the promised inheritance, let them remember the patriarchs, who likewise lived by faith, who not having received the promises, but having seen them afar off were persuaded of their substance and certainty, and embraced them; who made pilgrimage their willing choice, and, though dwelling in tents in a land which was not theirs, rejoiced in hope of the glory of God.

Abraham believed the word of God. He hoped against hope. He staggered not at the promise of God through unbelief, but was strong in faith, giving glory to God. The birth of Isaac fulfilled his hope, but did not terminate the trial and conflict of faith. But when the decisive trial was past, and Abraham by faith had offered up Isaac, then God gave unto him the reward in a final confirmation of the promise by His oath. The promise which was thus renewed and confirmed to Abraham, after the patience and wonderful endurance of faith, was most comprehensive and emphatic: "Blessing I will bless thee . . . . and in thy seed shall all the nations of the earth be blessed." The words "blessing I will bless thee," express that this blessing is not an outward and transient act of God, but the manifestation of His cherished purpose and of His inmost love. It expresses the truth which runs through the whole Scripture, that God has chosen His people, that His delight is in them, and that He Himself is their glory and blessedness. And knowing our weakness to grasp such infinite blessings and to rely on promises so exceeding great, knowing our difficulties and temptations, God confirmed the word with an oath. Among men an oath is an end of all strife. It is the ultimate and highest confirmation of statement and promise. God in His wonderful condescension and considerate remembrance of our weak hearts, which are slow to believe the exceeding riches of His grace, confirms the promise with an oath, and since there is none greater than Himself, the Lord by an oath mediated (ἐμεσίτευσεν ὅρκῳ) between Himself and the heirs of promise.

Jesus is the Mediator, the seal as well as the fulfilment of God's promise. He is as it were the Oath of God. "Verily, verily, I say unto you" is the majestic commencement of the Saviour's declarations and blessings. In Him all the promises of God are yea and Amen; in Him all covenant blessings are made sure. How much more abundant ought the faith of those to be, who in the resurrection of Jesus and in His exaltation behold the confirmation of God's counsel. Abraham possessed the promise, and in the oath of God the assurance of the immutability of His counsel. We possess a more abundant confirmation in fuller manifestation of the oath. The eternal blessings and the future glory of the covenant are sealed to all who believe by the resurrection of Jesus, by the outpouring and indwelling of the Holy Ghost, by Baptism and by the Lord's Supper.

So abundant is the encouragement which God gives to all faithful though tried disciples. The apostle therefore expresses his eager desire that every* member of the congregation show the same diligence and zeal in regard to the full assurance of hope. In this chapter his object is to rouse the lukewarm and inert, to lift them out of their apathy and gloom, and to raise them to the sunny and joyous height of faith and hope. Assurance, or fulness of hope (Comp. Col. ii. 2; 1 Thess. i. 5; Heb. x. 22), means a living, constant, and firm expectation of the coming of our Lord Jesus, who will give rest and glory unto all who wait for Him.

* Heb. iv. 1; vii. 11; Col. i. 28.

We rejoice in hope of the glory of God. By hope we anticipate the future blessedness, and thus live in the power of heavenly realities, influenced by the promised reward. Thus the apostle, who so clearly teaches us that we have been saved by grace through faith, also teaches that we are saved by hope; we wait for the adoption, that is the redemption of the body. In this patient waiting we are the followers of the Old Testament saints. They also, from Abraham, to whom God confirmed the promise by oath, looked unto the same advent of Messiah which we are awaiting. The fathers, who pertained specially to the Hebrews (Rom. ix.), cherished the same hope, which was more fully revealed by the gospel, and which therefore we should hold fast with greater stedfastness and joy.

The severe rebuke of the apostle thus ends in words of strong encouragement. Fulness of hope is to characterise the believer. In like manner, Scripture speaks of the assurance or fulness of faith. The kingdom of God is not in word, but in power. To say that we are sure of our salvation, to force ourselves as it were into expressions of certainty and peace, without possessing that inward and true calmness which flows from communion with God, is of no avail. It is dangerous to anticipate by imagination an experience which we have not reached, and to adopt the expression of feelings which we covet, but do not actually possess. It is unwise of teachers to urge people to use words of assurance and triumph. The true assurance of faith is given unto those who in humility look unto Jesus; for assurance of faith means not a peculiar kind of faith, but simply faith in full, healthy, vigorous exercise*—the singleness and sincerity of trust which looks only to the promise, which leans only on the perfection of the Saviour's grace. To look unto Jesus only, to see Him as our light and life, our righteousness and strength, is the fulness of faith; and to wait for the fulfilment of the promises at the coming of our Lord Jesus, is the fulness of hope.

We wait for the Son of God from heaven; and in the fact that the Son of God is in heaven we possess the substance as well as the pledge of our future inheritance. Jesus Himself is our hope. The soul is like a ship, tossed to and fro by the tumultuous waves of the sea, exposed to the temptations of Satan, the afflictions and sufferings of this present life, the difficulties and dangers of our earthly course, to doubts within and storms without. But we have an anchor, even hope; and this anchor is fixed, not in the depth below, but in the height above, even in the heavenly sanctuary, the everlasting and immovable throne of the Most

* πληροφόρια πίστεως—"In the full sail of faith, bearing right on with the wind, all canvass up."—J. DUNCAN.

High. Where but in heaven, in eternity, in that which is infinite, can we find rest, can we find the object of faith, love, and hope? Only He who from everlasting to everlasting is God, can be the dwelling-place of His people in all generations; only God the Father in Christ Jesus can be the object of our faith, our soul's trust and stay; only infinite love can kindle in us love, and be the love of our love. Thus only God Himself is our hope. And as God in Christ is the sinner's faith and love, so it is the Lord Jesus, once crucified and now enthroned, who is our hope; and while earthly joys and encouragements vary and vanish, the Spirit commands the troubled and disquieted soul to hope in God.* (Ps. xliii.) And this suggests to the apostle another illustration.† For

* Anchor is never mentioned in the Old Testament, either in the literal or figurative sense; in the New Testament only here, and in its literal sense, Acts xxvii. 29, 30, 40. It occurs as the emblem of hope in Greek and Roman authors.

† Dr. Brown remarks: "Two images beautifully combined: I. The *soul* is *the ship;* the *world*, the *sea;* the *bliss beyond* the world (ch. xi. 13), *the distant coast;* the *hope* resting on faith, the *anchor* which prevents the vessel being tossed to and fro (Eph. iv. 14); the *encouraging consolation* through the *promise* and *oath* of God, the cable connecting the ship and anchor. II. The world is the fore-court; heaven, the holy of holies; Christ, the High Priest going before us, so as to enable us, after Him and through Him, to enter within the veil (Lev. xvi. 2, 12, 15; Num. xviii. 7; cf. below, ch. ix. 3, 12, x. 19, 20)." Estius explains, "As the anchor does not stay in the waters, but enters the ground hidden beneath the waters, and fastens itself in it, so hope, our anchor of the soul, is not satisfied with merely coming to the vestibule; *i.e.* is not content with

when the mind beholds vividly spiritual truths, when the heart is filled with the fervid vision of heavenly realities, the fulness of glorious blessings can only be expressed by combining the scattered and imperfect rays in which, through symbols, the light shines unto us. The believer on earth is, as it were, in the outer court of the Tabernacle. In the holy of holies is Christ the Lord. The veil that separated the holy place from the most holy was the body of Christ. When He died the veil was rent, sin was put away, transgression was finished, the curse was removed, Satan and death were conquered, and an everlasting righteousness was brought in. We who believe in Jesus, by faith and prayer enter now into that which is within the veil; we who trust in Jesus, who died for us, are now, as it were, on the other side of the cross. Sin, condemnation, death, have been put away, and within the veil is the region of resurrection life, peace and glory, the eternal election, love, and favour of God. It is only through the death of the Lord, through the rent veil of His flesh, that we are saved; but having been recon-

merely earthly and visible goods, but penetrates even to those which are within the veil; viz., to the holy of holies, where it lays hold on God Himself, and heavenly goods, and fastens on them. 'Hope, entering within heaven, hath made us already to be in the things promised to us, even whilst we are still below, and have not yet received them; such strength hope has, as to make those that are earthly to become heavenly.'"—THEOPHYL.

ciled to God by the death of His Son, much more, being reconciled, we shall be saved by His life. "Within the veil,' Jesus, in the prayer which He offered before His death unto the Father, reveals unto us this highest region when He says, "I have declared unto them thy name, and will declare it: that the love wherewith thou hast loved me may be in them, and I in them." The eternal and infinite love of the Father, who has loved us as He loved Jesus (John xvii. 23), this is "within the veil." This anchor is sure, it never yields even to the strongest pressure; it is stedfast, it never moves from its place, it never varies with the changing condition of our feelings. Many are they that rise up against us, and often are our foes increased; but when hope enters into that within the veil, we can say, "Who shall lay anything to the charge of God's elect? It is God that justifieth. Who is he that condemneth? It is Christ that died, yea rather, that is risen again, who is even at the right hand of God, who also maketh intercession for us."

Jesus Himself is our hope; for He (and not merely His work and death) is for us entered, the forerunner. And by this thought and expression the apostle returns to the theme of the epistle, which he never forgets; viz., the Melchizedek Priesthood of the Lord Jesus. Aaron went into the holy of holies only once a year, and then it was not to abide there. Moreover, only the high priest was allowed to enter; and not even the priests, still less the people, were permitted to follow him. But here is one, Jesus (for the apostle dwells emphatically on the human nature of our Lord), the Man who is God's equal, and who died on the cross, who enters the holy of holies, to abide there in royal dignity, and to prepare a place for us—the Forerunner, by whom all believers are brought into the very presence of God. He is therefore a priest, not after the order of Aaron, but after the order of Melchizedek, the eternal High Priest, in whom is perfect mediation.

Let faith only behold Jesus on the right hand of God, let hope only enter as an anchor into that within the veil, the eternal Father-love in the glorified Son who died for us, and we have reached perfection. Amid all dangers and temptations, amid all struggles and conflicts, though sin is still present with us, though we have no confidence in the flesh, and with increasing sorrow and contrition judge ourselves, we are persuaded that nothing shall be able to separate us from the love of God which is in Christ Jesus. We are in Christ; "old things have passed away; behold, all things have become new." Christ is in heaven, and His prayer is, "Father, I will that they also, whom thou hast given me, be with me where I am."

Read again this solemn and severe chapter, and

say, "Let the righteous smite me; it shall be a kindness: and let him reprove me; it shall be an excellent oil, which shall not break my head." All God's words are in love, the thoughts of His heart are peace. Blessed are they who listen to the voice of heavenly wisdom, who love instruction, and turn not from correction; for the bitter arrows of reproof are sent by the sweet hand of a Father, and the earnest words of warning come from the home of everlasting truth and peace. There is a sweetness which is not wholesome, and a calmness which is treacherous; there is the voice of the flattering woman, there are the enchanting words of a spurious gospel, which bids us not go outside the camp bearing the reproach with Jesus, which tells us not of our heavenly citizenship, and of our having been crucified by the cross of Christ to the world. But let us who are risen with Christ *seek* those things which are above, where Christ sitteth on the right hand of God. Faith and hope rejoice; for of God is our righteousness and our glory, even Christ.

CHAPTER XIV.

MELCHIZEDEK A TYPE; AND THE CHARACTER OF THE INSPIRED SCRIPTURE.

HEB. vii. 1-5.

THE apostle now enters upon the main argument of the epistle. The High Priestly dignity of the Lord Jesus Christ, upon which He entered after His death and ascension, is infinitely higher than that of Aaron; and as the Levitical priesthood was imperfect and only the shadow and type of the substance, so the Lord is the true Priest of the heavenly and eternal sanctuary. (vii. 1-9, 18.)

We are first reminded of the absolute perfection of the High Priest Himself, and for this purpose Christ is compared with Melchizedek and contrasted with Aaron.

The incident recorded in the book of Genesis is in itself very remarkable and instructive. But the comment which David five centuries after gives in the psalm, of which the Lord Himself testifies that in it David spoke by the Spirit, and the exposition of the psalm which after a thousand years is given here, unfold unto us depths which our own investigation, be it ever so minute and careful, would never have brought to light. May not, therefore, this exposition of Scripture by Scripture be useful to us in giving us a fuller and deeper view of the character of the history of Israel, and of the record of this supernatural history?

The victory which Abram the servant and friend of God had gained over the kings was a remarkable and significant event. It was before Isaac was born and the sign of the covenant was given unto our father, whose faith was counted to him for righteousness. Obedient to the call of the God of glory, Abram left his father's house and country. He believed in God and in the promise which God gave unto him to make him a great nation, and to bless all the families of the earth in his seed. The character of Abram appears from the beginning one of singular beauty and greatness. The sincerity as well as the strength of his faith manifested itself in sacrifice and self-denying obedience. The treasure which he had found in the love of God made him willing to be a stranger on earth. Seeking a better country, that is a heavenly, and believing Him faithful who promised, Abram left all and followed the Lord. Full of the generosity and the meekness of true love, he allows his nephew Lot to choose the land where he wished to dwell; and after Lot, who had chosen what appeared good and fertile, had separated from him, the Lord renewed and confirmed the promise to Abram, giving unto him the length and breadth of the land which he should afterwards receive for an inheritance, and in the plain of Mamre the God-fearing man built an altar unto Jehovah. Love is always the companion of faith, and self-denial the daughter of love. And God always sustains and rewards those who for His sake love and serve the brethren. Lot's righteous soul was vexed with the iniquity of the people among whom he dwelt, and the place chosen for its prosperity soon proves a place of trial and danger. When Abram heard that Lot had been taken captive, with that love which, forgetting injuries and remembering kindness, is eager to help the needy, he armed his trained servants, and with a small band of three hundred and eighteen men, who were doubtless filled with the same spirit of faith as himself, and united with him in the bond of affection, he completely conquered the kings, and regained the captives, and all the goods which had been taken. While no doubt love to his kinsman, unclouded by any reminiscence of his somewhat selfish conduct, was his chief motive, he was actuated by the justice of the cause, and he showed the purity and disinterested motive of his enterprize by his refusal to receive any reward from the liberated kings; and in this he appealed unto the Lord, the most high God, the possessor of heaven and earth; as if the servant of such a Master must needs represent in all things the honour and dignity of the almighty and bountiful Lord.

So great and lovely was our father Abraham from the very first days of his faith, so simple and earnest was his trust in God, implicitly believing and immediately obeying the call from above; so meek and lowly, and yet so heroic, valiant and courageous; so affectionate and tender-hearted towards his kinsmen, so generous and royal towards all men. Blessed is the memory of the just; their very name is full of fragrance, and we delight to recall the features of their spiritual countenance.

Returning from the victory, he was met by Melchizedek, king of Salem. Let us view this incident first in the light of the statement in Genesis. Let us limit ourselves to the facts there stated by the historian.

This king, whose name was King of Righteousness, was also a priest of the most high God. He lived at Salem; he brought forth bread and wine; and he blessed Abram, and said, "Blessed be Abram of the most high God, possessor of heaven and earth: and blessed be the most high God, which hath delivered thine enemies into thy hand." And Abram gave him tithes of all.

This priestly king was a worshipper of the true God. Idolatry was then predominant. Even Abram's father was a worshipper of idols; yet, as this instance shows, the primeval revelation was not entirely forgotten, and there were still cities and tribes in which God was adored and served. Melchizedek calls God the most high God. This expression implies that he knew and worshipped the only true and living God, who is above all. Though there are many that are called gods and lords, there is only one God, high above all gods. The expression also means that God is above creation, high above heaven and earth; the Lord whose throne and sanctuary are now no longer on earth, as they were once at the entrance of the garden of Eden, but high above.

He was king and priest, and, it seems to me, because of the priesthood, a king. It was his peculiar position in relation to God which invested him with authority over men. Because he knew God, and in the name of God pronounced blessings, was he king, and, as his name expresses it, the prophet and dispenser of righteousness. Salem, or peace, was the name of the city where he reigned and exercised his priesthood.

This venerable man, in whom we behold as it were the glorious sunset of the primeval dispensation, met Abram and brought unto him bread and wine, evidently as symbols of the gifts of God in creation, to sustain and gladden fallen man; and he blessed Abram, as belonging by faith to the same God; and he blessed God, as having given through Abram and his victory a new manifestation of Himself. Abram received the blessing, and gave tithes of all unto him, thereby recognizing Melchizedek's superiority.

What did Melchizedek see in Abram? Evidently the future—a new dispensation of divine grace and truth. What did Abram see in Melchizedek? The past, in its universal character embracing all tribes and families of the earth; in its character of simplicity and fulness, the blessing of God in the reign of righteousness, priestly intercession, and peace—type of the ultimate future, which shall terminate the period of Israel and the church. Melchizedek is thus greater than Abram, because the past dispensation, which he represents, is a type of that future dispensation of which the Abrahamic is only preparatory. As the last chapters of the Apocalypse correspond with the first chapters of Genesis, as the garden of Eden was a type and earnest of the ultimate reign of blessedness, which the last pages of the book of Revelation describe, so the Melchizedek reign and priesthood prefigure the glory of the Christocracy, which we await, and which is the consummation of the period commencing with Abram, and including the history of Israel and the times of the Gentiles. In the bread and wine Abram saw the pledge of God's abundant grace. After the expulsion from Paradise, and the judgment of the flood, bread and wine are the gifts by which man's life is nourished and invigorated, and which, though, like all good gifts, coming primarily from God, are yet obtained through processes symbolic of suffering.

Abraham is blessed of the most high God, possessor of heaven and earth. The expression "possessor" is significant. The patriarch "possessed" nothing actually; but by faith he possessed all things promised unto him. Abraham had to buy even the burying-place for Sarah of the sons of Ephron. But He in whom he trusted was the possessor of heaven and earth, and the promised inheritance was therefore sure. Abraham, like all the faithful, was blessed of God. In Him he was rich; by Him he was strong and victorious. All things are ours, if we are God's—if His blessing rests on us.

Such are the main features of this remarkable incident, as recorded in the Book of Genesis, and viewed apart from the inspired exposition of its deeper meaning, as given in subsequent portions of Scripture. Before entering on the consideration of the Davidic and Pauline exposition, it may be useful to recall the peculiar character of the history and of the record of revelation.

We must always view Scripture in its connection with Israel and with Christ. The Lord Jesus is of Israel, and therefore to Abraham's seed were given the oracles of God. While we believe that God is not the God of the Jews only, but also of the Gentiles, that in all history His wisdom, power, and grace are to be recognised, and that all history is typical, illustrating spiritual principles, a mirror of things invisible and future, we believe that the history of Israel is in a special sense miraculous and supernatural and in immediate connection with the great plan of redemption. Israel is the nation; chosen for the sake of all nations, separated unto God, and for the good of the whole world, that through them the glory and salvation of God might be made manifest. God has connected from all eternity, and in a necessary and inseparable manner, the Word, who is the brightness of His glory, and the express image of His person; Israel, His chosen nation; the oracles or Scripture; and Jesus, the Son of God and man. As the Word was with God, and the centre of the divine counsel, as the Word became the centre and medium of creation, so the Word was set apart to be the centre of redemption, and the centre of the future glory and inheritance.

This great plan of God, while it had the Son of God for its centre, had Israel, as it were, for its immediate and primary circumference. God selected Israel as the garden in which the blessed Branch should appear. From all nations he separated Israel, that out of them should come the Redeemer and Saviour of mankind. And as Israel was chosen in Christ, and for Christ's sake, so their whole history and education were according to that great object.

The Scripture, which is the testimony of God's dealings in mercy as Jehovah, could therefore not originate anywhere else than among the Jews. It was according to the divine plan that Jesus should be of Israel, and likewise the Scripture must needs be Jewish. Israel's history is therefore central in importance and symbolical in character. It is for the sake of the Redeemer, chosen in the counsel of God, that fallen and sinful humanity is allowed to continue; it is for the sake of the final restoration that there is a history of nations: in Israel's Messiah shall all nations of the earth be blessed. And since God chose Israel, and revealed Himself and His grace unto them in word, act, and type, it cannot be otherwise than that the whole history of this nation should be a grand series of symbols of spiritual and eternal truths, and that the Scriptures recording the history should possess a vitality and depth of meaning which can never be exhausted.

The history of the chosen people of redemption was supernatural, and all events and institutions connected with it under the immediate guidance of God and under the immediate influence of the Holy Ghost.

The supernatural character of Israel's history must be obvious to every one who believes the miraculous birth of the Lord Jesus. As He was conceived of the Holy Ghost, and born of the God-chosen Virgin Mary, so His birth was the last link of a chain, the consummation of a long series of miraculous revelations and acts of the Redeemer-God. The offspring of David is also the root of David; the seed of Abraham is before Abraham was; and the whole history of Israel is the going forth of Him who is eternal.

Thus we understand the great and outstanding events of this history, such as the birth of Isaac, the sufferings and exaltation of Joseph, the Exodus, the fall of Jericho, the reign of David. Thus we understand the types, the sacrifices and festivals. Thus we perceive that the tabernacle was not framed by human wisdom, but that the Holy Ghost symbolized through this mysterious sanctuary the eternal truth as it is in Jesus. Nor can we be astonished that this supernatural, symbolic, and eternal character of Israel's history should manifest itself not merely in central events and persons, but that it should pervade the whole, and enter into every detail. The very names Abraham, Joshua, David, the very sequence of events and promises, the colours and numbers in the arrangements of the tabernacle, were ordered of God, and are full of deep meaning. And as the history of Israel by reason of its central character is symbolic, mirroring the experience of the individual soul and of the congregation in every possible circumstance, in patriarchal infancy, in the house of bondage, in the wilderness journey, in Canaan's warfare and temptation, in Davidic and Solomonic rule, in Babylonian exile, so is it also typical and prophetic, and stands related to that ultimate development of the divine kingdom, towards which tend all God's dealings, and of which all the prophets of the eternal witnessed from the beginning.

The whole history of Israel is a golden history, if we may so say—a Holy Ghost history. It differs from every other history. This nation God formed for Himself; and in all the events, institutions, and great men of this people God in a special manner revealed Himself and the truths of His kingdom. And this because the eternal Word, the Saviour of sinners, the King of the Jews, the Head of the Church, the Heir of all things, who is the upholder and end of all ages, Jesus Himself, is organically and inseparably connected with this chosen nation; He is of the seed of David, of the seed of Abraham.

Now such being the character of the history, was the record of this history (or the Scripture) the work of man, depending on the capacity and grasp of human intellect, the faithfulness of human memory, on man's wisdom and design? Is not the casket also golden which contains the invaluable jewel? If the spirit and substance were God-given, has He not also clothed it with a body prepared and perfected by His own omnipotent and all-wise hand? We believe that Scripture is given by inspiration of God. We do not believe it possible that this book, world-wide and eternal in its character, could have been written by holy men, unless they were moved by the Spirit, who searcheth the deep things of God, and guided by Him who was, and is, and is to come. We *believe* Scripture to be inspired. And our faith in the inspiration of Scripture has its basis and root in our faith in God Himself. It is because we have experienced the divine power of the truth Scripture contains, and because in the reading of Scripture we have heard the voice of God; it is because God speaks to us in this written word that we believe it is God's. This faith is a conviction, an inward beholding and seeing, a knowledge which far transcends in light and strength, in certainty and firmness, all human evidence and argument. We cannot communicate this faith to our neighbour; for faith is the gift of God, and "they shall be all (and each) taught of God;" we can only testify of it and give a reason, a connected statement of the knowledge that is in us. But on no lower ground can we build our assertion, that Scripture is God-inspired; not on the testimony of the Church, not on the evidences (valuable as they are) of the historic faithfulness of the record, the fulfilment of prophecy, the effects of the sublime teaching on human minds, &c. The inspiration of Scripture is an object of faith; and faith can only rest on the word of God, the testimony of the Spirit to the soul.

When we are asked: Is this inspiration verbal? or does it refer only to the divinely-revealed truths and promises? it is not necessary fo us to enter into distinctions which Scripture itself does not make. We need no adjective to qualify the substantive, inspiration. It is impossible for us to form a theory of inspiration. Even of that influence of the Spirit of which we possess personal experience in our own conversion and daily renewal, it would be impossible for us to frame a theory; for the work of the Spirit is mysterious. We cannot trace the beginning or end of His path (John iii. 8); His "intercession is with groanings which cannot be uttered" (Rom. viii. 26); we cannot explain His indwelling in the heart; and as His love is infinitely tender, entering into our deepest and most individual peculiarity and need, so is it impossible for us to analyze His constant vivifying influence, guidance, and rule. If it is thus with the work of the Spirit, of which we have experience, why should we attempt to form a theory of inspiration of which none of us have experience? Most probably the prophets themselves could not explain and analyze the operation of the holy and infinite Spirit upon and within their spirits, and could give no other reply to our enquiry than the statement which Scripture contains: the Spirit of the Lord came upon them; they spake not of themselves, but as they were moved by the Holy Ghost.

The inseparable connection between thought and word, between the substance and spirit and the form and expression, is obvious. The Holy Spirit, who reveals truth and spiritual reality to holy men, moves them also in speaking; influencing also the words, so that they are correct and adequate expressions: the spoken and written word is an adequate manifestation of the word* inwardly

* The Hebrew דבר means thing and word. "The word of God is more exact than is generally thought in its expressions; because the expression has its origin in the thing itself."

revealed. To separate thought and word, spirit and embodiment, matter and manner, is at all times a very difficult and perilous thing; for not merely is the boundary line between the idea and the expression almost impossible to find, but the Spirit who animates the body which it has formed can only be retained by us *in the word.* Hence, as Martin Luther said against the rationalists of his day, "Christ did not say of His Spirit, but of His words, *they* are spirit and life." Scripture is *God's* word; it is His gift, and a revelation of Himself. It is God's *word*, the revelation of eternal and spiritual truth in a written record.

The language of Scripture accordingly is perfectly unique; it possesses an indescribable something which is not found in any (merely) human writings; the Spirit, who seeth all things in their depth and reality, and who knoweth the end from the beginning, speaks here in a way so profound and comprehensive, that the wisdom and experience of all ages cannot exhaust His meaning, and yet with such simplicity and definiteness, that all childlike hearts find guidance and consolation in their daily path of duty and trial. The style of Scripture betokens its inspiration. Here is a depth, a solemnity, a heart-winning sweetness and familiarity, which we meet nowhere else. Here is the voice of One who speaketh with authority, and communicates to us out of an inexhaustible fulness what is profitable for us in our present condition. The Scripture is to other books as Nature is to the works of art, as the ocean is to a lake; the Scripture sees all things from a great height, and breathes the atmosphere of eternity. In the best human books, in the loftiest poetry, in the most fervent and devout utterances of man, there is always something unreal, artificial, self-conscious; something morbid and necessarily ephemeral. Scripture is the only true, real, eternal book.

The apostles and the Lord Himself teach us that not merely was Israel's history, if we may so say, inspired, under the special influence of God; but they teach us also that the *record* of this history is inspired, that the Scripture which narrates God's dealings with Israel is also under the special and infallible guidance of the Holy Ghost. It must be evident, from the preaching of the apostles to Jews and Gentiles, from the manner in which they decide difficult questions of doctrine and practice, from the epistles they addressed to the churches, that they believed Scripture inspired in the fullest sense, and regarded the men by whom the word was written as the instruments, but the Lord, and more especially the Holy Ghost, as the true author of the whole organism of the Jewish record.

It appears from this very chapter (and from

the whole epistle) that its author regarded the Scripture as inspired in the most absolute sense of the word; for his whole argument here is based upon the manner in which the Holy Ghost narrated the incident of Melchizedek's appearing and blessing. Because there is no statement given of his descent, of his beginning and end, the apostle sees in this omission the indication of a very important and fundamental truth. Genesis is the book of genealogies. Most carefully and minutely the descent of men is traced; their age is stated, and the fact of their death chronicled. In a human work no further inference could be drawn from an omission of this kind. It is otherwise, however, in Scripture. As in music, not only the notes, but also the pauses are according to the plan and mind of the composer, and instinct with the life and spirit which breathe through the whole; so the very omissions of Scripture are not the result of chance, or of the accidental ignorance of the writer, but according to and in harmony with the wisdom of the eternal Spirit, who is the true author of the record. The apostle evidently thinks that the Holy Ghost teaches by not stating these points. In like manner he attaches importance to the names of Melchizedek and Salem.

When he writes to the Galatians he bases a very important argument on the word seed—not many, but one—showing that Christ is the promised seed and heir. He represents Sara and Hagar as typical of the two covenants—of Jerusalem and of Sinai—gospel and law, liberty and bondage; and, in a manner quite analogous to our chapter, he points out that the promise given to Abraham four hundred years before the giving of the law could not be disannulled by it. He affirms that the Scripture, foreseeing that God would justify the heathen by faith, preached before the gospel unto Abraham, saying, "In thy seed shall all nations be blessed." And again, The Scripture hath concluded all under sin, that the promise of faith might be given to them that believe. He personifies the Scripture as omniscient, foreseeing all things, and speaking in harmony with the whole counsel of God.

The apostolic "as it is written" is rooted in a very deep conviction of the divine perfection of the written Word. The whole Scripture is one organic structure; and in its minute and subsidiary portions, as well as in the more prominent and fundamental parts, the Scripture is inspired of God (θεόπνευστος): the infinite and eternal Spirit reveals through the Scripture the truths and realities of God's salvation.

Hence the names of persons and places, the omissions of circumstances, the use of the singular or plural number, the application of a title,—all things are under the control of the all-wise and gracious Spirit of God.*

I may also add a word on the manner of quotation. Scripture passages are quoted by the Lord in the gospels and by the apostles not always with verbal accuracy, giving an exact repetition of the expressions used by Moses or the prophets. This appears at first sight a difficulty, and not in harmony with the doctrine of inspiration. But on investigation it will be found to confirm this truth; for here also the Spirit is revealed as the Spirit of truth and liberty. The original meaning of the Spirit is developed with increasing clearness and fulness; the Lord and His apostles quote the Scripture according to the deepest and truest meaning of the inspired Word, and according to the new requirements of the dispensation and the condition of their hearers. The prophets themselves knew that their prophecy was above them; they therefore searched with diligent zeal what Messiah's Spirit which was in them did signify. In the fulness of the Spirit the Messiah Himself quotes Scripture; in the fulness of the Spirit, re-

* Compare Paul's commentary on the word "all" in Psalm viii. 7, and the important deductions from it in Heb. ii. 8, and 1 Cor. xv. 27; on the word "new," Jer. xxxi., Heb. viii. 13; the singular "seed," Gal. iii. 16. What a wonderful superstructure is built on Ps. cx. 4! Each word is full of most important and blessed meaning. In Ps. xxxii. 1, 2, no mention is made of works; hence Rom. iv. 6. Many other instances might be quoted.

ceived on the day of Pentecost, the apostles quote and apply the Scripture to confirm and illustrate the truth as it is in Jesus, to guide and to exhort the church in her present course. This refers also to interpretation. The allegorical interpretation, if applied by man, is dangerous; because he may either be without the mind of Christ, and then he will certainly *introduce* thoughts contrary to and apart from Scripture, and his interpretation will not be the *unfolding* of the divine truth; or he may possess the Spirit, yet by reason of imperfection and sin fail to see the true and real meaning of the Word. But when the Lord Jesus and the inspired apostles interpret Scripture, it is as if the author of a book himself explains his true, real, and full meaning to those who have read it. It is authentic exposition of the original Word; an exposition which, on account of the further development of God's counsel, is more profound and luminous than could have been given at the time of its first utterance.

It seems as if in the outward form of Scripture, in the quotations and comments, there is such apparent imperfection in order that faith may be tested. Outwardly, there seems no difference between Paul's allegorising and that of the Rabbis or of Philo. It was said of Jesus, "Is not this Jesus, the Son of Joseph, the carpenter?" So it may be thought that Scripture is merely human.

The Word (that is Christ, and also the Scripture) came, as Luther says, "in unser armes Fleish und Blut"—in our poor flesh and blood.

Above all, remember that the Lord Jesus, our one and only Master, the Son of God, who is the Truth, honoured, confirmed, and fulfilled the Scripture, and led His apostles into a deeper, because more loving, reverence for the inspired word, and into the true and full understanding of its mysteries. Remember how Jesus referred to Scripture when He was teaching the people, or refuting gainsayers, or resisting and conquering Satan, or instructing and comforting His disciples. Remember how He appeals to Scripture as the ultimate judge, declaring as an axiom that the Scripture cannot be broken, and that not one jot or tittle of the law can pass away. Remember His questions: How does David in the Spirit call Him Lord? How readest thou? Have ye not read? Remember His references to the whole scope of prophetic teaching (it is written in the prophets, They shall be taught of God); to Moses, who wrote of Him; to the prophets and psalms; to the whole Scripture (the things written concerning me); and to single words and expressions, incidents and institutions, contained in the Scripture. Remember Christ's references to Scripture on the cross, how the whole prophetic word passed before His mind; and in the conviction of His having fulfilled all that by the Holy Ghost was written concerning Him, after He had said, "I thirst," He uttered that great and blessed word, "It is finished." And after His resurrection, appearing unto His chosen disciples and witnesses, He opened unto them the Scriptures, beginning with Moses, unfolding unto them His suffering, and giving and commanding them to preach, *because* they understood now the word. "Thus it is written, and thus it behoved Christ to suffer, and to rise from the dead the third day, and thus preach repentance and remission of sins in His name."

It is impossible to separate the Lord Jesus either from Israel or from the Scripture. Faith in Jesus, the true and real Jesus, who died and rose again according to Scripture, must lead to childlike and reverential faith in the Scripture as the word of God, inspired and perfect.

On the testimony of the Lord Jesus and the apostles I receive the Scripture as God's word. Like David, I pray that God may open mine eyes to see wonders hidden in God's law, in the history and ordinances, recorded in the Scripture; like the psalmist, I view the history of Israel as a parable, a symbol of spiritual and eternal truth. (Psalm cxix. 18, lxxviii. 2, &c.) Not as a critic dare I approach this book as if it were an ordinary book, which I may hope to master and fathom. It is above me, and I cannot exhaust its fulness; it knows me, even the hidden things of the heart, and judges me, bringing me into contact with the all-seeing God. I enter with reverence into the temple of Scripture, which, from the height of God's eternal counsel and out of the depth of God's infinite love, beholds and comprehends all ages, and is sufficient for the guidance and perfecting of souls in all generations—praying with trustful hope that out of Christ's fulness the Spirit will minister unto me also grace upon grace.

But while I thus stand in awe, beholding the grandeur and infinite depth of the Scripture as one organic spirit-built temple, and the beauty, perfection, and exquisite skill which characterize the most minute portion of this structure, I feel at home and as in a peaceful and fragrant garden. For our admonition was the Scripture written; for us upon whom the ends of the world are come. Moses and the prophets minister unto us, to whom the fulness of salvation is revealed. Through comfort of the Scriptures we have hope. I am not paralyzed by the divine perfection and the infinite depth of the Word; for such is the love, such is the perfection of God, that even from a child I may know the Scriptures, and be made wise by them unto salvation. And while it may be given to me in some favoured moment to take a comprehensive view, and to behold somewhat of the length, and breadth, and height, and depth,

I know that every word of God is pure, every name which He has revealed, every promise which He has given, every word He has uttered, is perfect; and in it He is a shield unto them that put their trust in Him. Thus I possess the whole in every little fragment; though weak, ignorant, and limited, I have perfect peace and the light of life. And often I find the truth of that saying, so characteristic of that great lover of the word,* "In Scripture every little daisy is a meadow."

Is not this the experience of the Christian? We are at home in the Scriptures, because we have found the Messiah, of whom the Scriptures testify. Once we are in possession of this central truth, we see unity, order, light, and beauty throughout. Though many things seem dark, wonderful, and beyond our comprehension, it is the mystery of love. It does not alarm our heart, or contract our affection, joy, and courage. The whole Scripture is full of the goodness, the sweetness, and the beauty of the Lord. Yea, in one sense we know all things; for we have received the anointing of Christ; the Spirit Himself is our teacher and guide. Everywhere in Scripture we behold Jesus, the Lord; our great High Priest, enthroned in heaven; King of righteousness and Prince of peace, who brings unto us the blessing

* Luther.

of God; who sustains our inner life, and who gladdens and strengthens our hearts by giving us continually bread to eat and wine to drink. Do you know the Bread? He came down from heaven; He suffered and died; He was buried and rose again. This is the bread—the body that was broken, the flesh that He gave for the life of the world. Do you know the Wine? He is the true Vine, and the wine which He gives to us is the fruit of the suffering of bitter agony, when He was crushed under the weight of transgressions not His own; it is the blood which was shed for the remission of sins. Are you a child of Abraham? Is yours the righteousness which is of faith? Are you waiting for the inheritance? Then in the reading of Scripture Jesus will bless you, and give you the bread and wine which the world knoweth not, because it seeth no longer Him who is now in heaven.

CHAPTER XV.

MELCHIZEDEK A TYPE.

HEB. vii. 1–17.

THE High Priesthood upon which our Lord entered after His sufferings, death, and ascension (Heb. vi. 20), is infinitely higher than the Aaronic. It possesses perfection; it is heavenly and eternal. Hence it is impossible that it should be prefigured by the Aaronic priesthood;* and therefore the apostle illustrates it by the type of Melchizedek, in accordance with the interpretation given centuries before by David, when in the Spirit he declared the divine decree—"Thou art a priest for ever after the order of Melchizedek."

It was difficult, though absolutely necessary, to explain to the Hebrews the imperfect, shadowy,

* Christ *is* at present a Priest after the order of Melchizedek, and not after the order of Aaron, though the *exercise* of His priesthood at present is according to the type of Aaron, as within the veil on the great day of atonement.

and temporary character of the Levitical priesthood, and to show unto them that with the change of priesthood there must needs be also a change of dispensation. The Aaronic priesthood and the Levitical dispensation were indeed of God, and possessed glory. And our Lord, who on the cross was the Sacrifice, and who by His own blood entered into the holy of holies, fulfilled all that was typified by these divine ordinances. Hence the apostle neither makes void the Aaronic institutions, nor does he depreciate their importance, value, and power. But Jesus, the Messiah, having come and fulfilled that which was written of Him, and being the substance of the shadow, there has begun now the exercise of a real, living, continuous, and perfect High Priesthood, of which a type is found in the pre- and super-Aaronic priesthood of Melchizedek. Jesus is in heaven, dispensing the blessings which He purchased with His blood, and in perfect mediation bringing us to God, and the favour and life of God to us.

The argument of the apostle, deducing and illustrating the superiority of Christ's priesthood over the Aaronic, from and by the relation of Melchizedek to the Levitical priesthood, is in some respects analogous to the argument of the apostle with regard to the law, and its parenthetical and inferior position, as compared with the gospel. You must have noticed the sluggish tendency in man which renders him unwilling, and to a certain extent unable, to understand quickly, and to accept readily any change and development in the manifestation of God's purpose; so that when that which has been preparatory, and which from the very outset was given only for a time, and with indications of its imperfect and intermediate character, is removed, he feels, so to say, to a certain extent disappointed, and as if some injustice had been done unto him, or as if God was changeable, and the revelations of God not consistent. It was in this way that the Jews were shocked when the apostle Paul taught that it was not necessary for the Gentiles to observe the law; that for the new covenant church the law of Moses was no longer the rule and form of life. And therefore the apostle, in his epistle to the Galatians, tells them that the law was given four hundred years after the promise had been made unto Abraham, and that therefore there was no injustice, and no inconsistency, in the bringing in of a new dispensation, which was in fact only a return in a fuller and more perfect manner to that which was from the beginning in the mind of God. There was in it nothing that was derogatory to the majesty and holiness of the law.

The original promise which through Abraham was given both to Jews and Gentiles was brought prominently into the foreground, and the law set aside, which had come in as an intermediate dispensation, a schoolmaster to bring men unto Christ, a guardian to keep the appointed heir during the years of his minority. The twofold object of the law was now fulfilled. The law was to convince man of sin, and to declare God's condemnation. Christ was made a curse for us; He is the end of the law unto righteousness. The law was also to teach us our deadness; for it could not give life; it could not minister the Spirit; but the Spirit of Christ, as the Spirit of the Son, is now sent into our hearts. Hence, the law being fulfilled, we enter fully and substantially into the covenant which was made before law.

It is in like manner that he argues in the epistle to the Romans with regard to our father Abraham. Abraham was justified by faith; he received the promises; the covenant was made with him. He believed God, and his faith was counted to him for righteousness. But when was this? Was it not before circumcision was instituted? And is it not clear from this that God may again return unto His original, primary, and more comprehensive idea, and bring in that righteousness which is by faith, irrespective of all ordinances and of all temporary and intermediate institutions? Thus in the present day some regard the doctrine of the ushering in of a new dispensation—the advent of the Lord Jesus Christ with His glorified Church, and His reign in the age to come, as something disturbing. They feel unwilling to enter as it were upon a new phase; it seems troublesome to have to understand and to comprehend new developments. Remember that God, who is the eternal, is the Lord of all times and of all dispensations. And although the ages change, His truth remains for ever the same. Time only brings out more fully that eternal and immutable counsel which He purposed in Himself when He appointed Christ, the incarnate Son, to be Lord and Heir of all. And yet no portion of Scripture can ever become antiquated, losing its instructiveness, significance, and value. No period of the history of God's people, no type, no institution, no event of any dispensation, can be forgotten; nothing that God has said, given, or done, will be lost. For the eternal Spirit, who saw the end from the beginning, hath so ordered it that the whole Scripture ministers unto all generations of His people, that as the fathers cannot be made perfect without the children, so the children who are privileged to see the better things provided for them by God are gathered unto the fathers, and blessed with the ancient household of faith; and when the purpose of God is at last fulfilled, then Abraham, Isaac, and Jacob, kings and prophets, who saw the glory afar off, the church gathered *since Pentecost*, and called especially to know the fellowship of Christ's sufferings, shall rejoice together and praise Jehovah, "Jesus Christ the same yesterday, and to-day, and for ever." As there was diversity in the dispensations and the gifts, the service and the suffering, and yet one Lord, one Mediator, one Spirit, so will the glory also be manifold and yet one glory, even the glory of God and of the Lamb.

The incident of the meeting of Melchizedek and Abraham which is mentioned in the book of Genesis belongs unto the history of God's people, which, both in itself and in its record, is under the immediate guidance of God and of the Holy Ghost.

We have seen already what the meaning of the appearing of Melchizedek was unto Abraham himself—what is immediately implied in the historical record apart from its typical aspect. This Melchizedek, who was king and priest in one person, and the name of whose residence was Salem—that is, peace—who possessed the knowledge of God, as of the Lord Most High, who is supreme above all kings and above all gods, who is high above all things that are created, came as the representative of the primeval dispensation, which is greater and more comprehensive than the dispensation that commenced with Abraham, and is therefore a type of that restoration of all things, of that universal reign of Truth and Love which shall commence with the appearing of our Lord Jesus Christ. He came as the representative of the first dispensation, and as the type of the ultimate dispensation, and he blessed Abraham, the father of Israel and of the faithful, in the name of God, bringing unto him in bread and wine the symbolic representation of all the blessings pertaining to a vigorous and joyous life which, according to the goodness of God, were in grace vouchsafed unto Adam's children, although they had forfeited life through their transgression. Abraham, the man whom God called His friend, who was chosen, honoured, and blessed of the Lord, acknowledges this royal priest as his superior; he receives his blessing, and he gives unto him tithes.*

But now the apostle tells us that in this record we have to consider not merely that which is mentioned, but that which is not mentioned. Different speculations have been entertained in the church with regard to the actual historical person Melchizedek. The sole reason why I allude to it is to remind you how utterly useless these speculations are, and not merely useless, but entirely in

* The only feature of the narrative which the apostle does not explain is that Melchizedek meets Abraham *after his victory by faith.* Here is a figure of the final blessing, the possession of the purchased inheritance, and the perfect enjoyment of communion with Christ. They who overcome shall inherit all things ; they shall be met by the Lord, who said, "I will not drink henceforth of this fruit of the vine, until that day when I drink it new with you in my Father's kingdom." (Compare Rev. ii. 17 ; iii. 21 ; Luke xxvi. 29.)

contradiction to the scope of this very passage. Some have thought this Melchizedek was Shem. As far as chronology is concerned, there is nothing impossible in this hypothesis; for Shem lived not merely up to the days of Abraham, but even into a later period. Others have thought that this Melchizedek was a descendant of Japhet. Some again have supposed that he was an Amorite. But the Scripture *purposely* does not mention who he was. Genesis abounds in genealogies, and in full and minute genealogies; but the genealogy of this man is not given. If we knew who he was, should we not counteract thereby the meaning of the Holy Ghost in this instructive omission? If he was Shem, then we know who his father was, and when he lived, and how old he was; and this is just the very point which the Holy Ghost does not wish us to know. Thus has it pleased God to leave this man that he should stand out *in Scripture* as a man without father, without mother, without descent, having neither beginning of days nor end of life; as a man having a priesthood inherent in himself, of whom we do not know the parentage, of whom we do not know the successor. It is equally obvious that this Melchizedek is not a theophany, an appearing of the Lord Jesus Christ Himself. For he was made like unto the Son of God; that is, he was made in the inspired record to be a similitude, or pattern, or illustration of the Son of God. In all the appearances of the Word of God or the Son of God, in all theophanies before the incarnation, there is something either in what the mysterious One says, promises, or does, or in the worship that is given unto Him, or in the names and attributes which are applied to Him, which shows most clearly and distinctly that He is the Lord Jehovah; whereas there is nothing of this kind in the record of Genesis; all we are told is, Melchizedek was one of those still left upon the earth, who retained the primeval knowledge of God, who worshipped Him, and who ruled in righteousness. With regard to all other circumstances, our *ignorance* is *knowledge.* The negative element is a positive element. Let no man attempt to supply that which the Holy Ghost purposely has left out; for, in the first place, he must be unsuccessful; in the second place, if he were successful, it would only militate against the purpose and the word of God, and only hinder us from learning those lessons which the Scripture intends us to derive.*

* "We are not to know anything of the historical Melchizedek; for he is ordained of God for us 'a wonderful man' (Zech. iii. 8), as type and illustration of the One who was to come."—STIER.

Instead of indulging in morbid and fanciful speculations about the historical individual, let us look at the important spiritual realities which in the inspired commentary are given us in this parable of type. Let us learn also from this instance and the other New Testament comments on Old Testament types that the typical meaning is always deduced from what *the Scripture itself says concerning them.*

Now, in this Melchizedek we see, as in a type foreshadowing, these things: In the first place the dignities and functions of priest and king combined in one person; in the second place, righteousness and peace joined together; in the third place, a priest who is greater than Abraham, and therefore above the Levitical priesthood, which, as Abraham's descendants, are represented by him; in the fourth place, a priest who has neither father nor mother, without beginning of days, or end of life, who therefore has a priesthood inherent in himself, to which there can be no successor, a priesthood which is based upon an eternal or indissoluble life; and in the fifth place, this royal priesthood which, different from the priesthood of Aaron, is appointed and confirmed with the divine oath.

Looking upon Melchizedék simply in the way in which he is spoken of in the Scripture—not the historical individual Melchizedek, but the Melchizedek whom *Scripture* both by its statements and omissions makes a similitude of the Lord, an illustration of that fulness which is in Christ Jesus—we may hope in the light of the apostolic epistles and of the doctrine of the new covenant to see how beautifully the perfection of the heavenly priesthood of our blessed Lord is prefigured in this eminent type.

1. What is meant by king? what by priest?

What is the idea of kingship and of priesthood? For it is evident that in this world there are many kings and many priests who give us a false and, if not an erroneous, yet an inadequate idea of what God means by royalty and by priesthood. For the things and relations which are seen on earth, and which are imperfect and temporal, are according to realities which are in heaven, and which are perfect and eternal. Even in the case of the illustration of father and child, we must not transfer earthly things to heavenly things, but we must rather transfer heavenly things to earthly things. There is a true, eternal, and perfect fatherhood; and thus we must also learn from God's word what is implied in kingship and in priesthood.

Now, the idea of kingship was to some extent announced in the creation of Adam, who was of God (Luke iii. 38), and who was appointed lord and ruler over the earth, over the beasts of the field, and over the fowls of the air. (Comp. Ps. viii. and Dan. ii. 37, 38.) A king then is a man in the image of God, who represents upon earth God Himself, and unto whom, direct from God, without the intervention of any other, there is given power and dominion that he may rule according to the mind, according to the goodness and the wisdom of God.

By priesthood is meant communion with God—that which brings unto man the love of God—that which brings unto God the worship and service of man. It need scarcely be added, that kingship and priesthood cannot exist without prophetship; for how can there be rule in the name of God, or how can there be a mediation of the love of God to man, and of our worship and obedience to God, unless there be in the first place a manifestation of God Himself, a revelation of His character? Nay, as this very revelation of God is the basis, so is it the very essence and the very fruit of all kingship and priesthood; in which aspect the office of the prophet is the most comprehensive and ultimate of the three. These simple ideas combined amount to this—there is a mediation between God and man; this mediation is to bring unto us in the first place the knowledge of God (we require a prophet); in the second place the love and favour of God, so that we can have communion with Him (we need a priest); and in the third place the life and the power of God, so that we can serve, obey, and glorify Him (we require a king; in New Testament language a head, source of life). And this the Church of Christ has always taught; everything that Christ does as a Mediator is summed up in these three offices. He is prophet, priest, and king. There is no fourth; neither will any one of these, or two of these, suffice. These three, by a necessary, essential, and inherent unity, go together.

Moses, as we have seen, combined to a certain extent the three offices; hence as the mediator of the old covenant he is a figure of Jesus, the Mediator of the new and everlasting covenant. But in the history of Israel we nowhere see the royal and priestly dignity united; for, as the apostle reminds us, the priests were of the tribe of Levi; the kings were of the tribe of Judah. He who was a priest never could rule over Judah and Israel. He who was a king never could perform priestly functions in the sanctuary, still less go into the holy of holies. When king Uzziah, contrary to the ordinance of God, interfered with the prerogatives of the priesthood, he was smitten with leprosy; that is to say, he was made an outcast, so that he was not able to approach God and to mingle with the congregation of Jehovah. What a wonderful thing it is then, that that which formerly never could have been combined was, in the primeval age and before the children of Abraham were born and the Abrahamic dispensation commenced, shown to exist in u ity—that Melchizedek, who was a priest, was also a king. "David who as the king over Israel after God's heart was himself a type of his great Son, given to him by divine promise, got possession at last of Jebus* according to God's command; he founded

* There seems little doubt that Salem is identical with Jerusalem. "In Salem is His tabernacle, and His dwelling-place in Zion." (Ps. lxxvi. 2.)

the sanctuary of the Lord upon mount Zion, and in connection with it his royal throne. He thereby to some extent restored the ancient Salem of Melchizedek; he appears as it were as a successor of Melchizedek, a king appointed by God, whose sceptre goes forth from Zion, where is also the ark of the covenant, the glory of the Lord."* It is on this historical basis, that the prediction of the future royal Priest rests, illustrated by the Melchizedek-type; it is from this point of view that the eternal priesthood and glorious reign of the Son and Lord of David are seen by the psalmist. In like manner we read in the prophet Zechariah, that the Messiah, the man whose name is the Branch, is to build the temple of the Lord: He shall bear the glory, and shall sit and rule upon His throne. With the terseness characteristic of this prophet, who condenses the previous Messianic predictions, he declares of the Son of David, "He shall be a Priest upon His throne."

The fulfilment is in Christ. It is fully explained to us in the New Testament. That simple and most comprehensive expression, "The Lamb in the midst of the throne," shows us that when this High Priest entered into the holy of holies He entered also as King into the palace.† He

* STIER, slightly altered.

† Jehovah is Israel's King. Hence, the temple (היכל) means both palace and sanctuary. In the New Covenant Jesus is represented as seated on the throne of God; and with greater simplicity,

went not merely into the sanctuary, but ascended and sat down on the throne of the Majesty on high, there to be a king and ruler over God's creation. Jesus by His blood entered into the heaven of heavens, and because He humbled Himself unto death He was not merely made a priest to represent us before the Father and to bring unto us the benediction of God, but all things were put under His feet, all power was given unto Him in heaven and in earth; He is ruler over all things, and head over all things unto the church, to the glory of the Father. He commands in heaven and on earth. All the elements obey Him, all angels and principalities, thrones and dominions, worship and serve Him; He is the Governor, the Prince of the kings of the earth; He has the keys of Hades and of death. Such is His power. And why is He King on God's throne? Because He is *Priest.* By reason of the obedience unto death, He was enthroned King in the universe of God; and in exercising this kingship now He exercises it in the *spirit* of priesthood. At present the kingship of Christ is in the background; the priesthood of Christ is prominent. Thus it is that He overrulés all things for the good of His elect. Thus it is

and leading us more fully into the perfection and sweetness of our filial relation to the Father through and in the only-begotten Son, the Lord speaks in the gospel of John of His going to His Father's house, there to prepare a place for us. (John xiv.)

that He stays the execution of vengeance and of judgment, in order that the chosen of God may be gathered in, and that the Church of Christ may be perfected. At present His royalty is not manifested, but His high-priestly compassion and mercy are continually set forth. The gospel of the Good Shepherd is preached now, who having sought and saved the lost sheep laid it on His shoulders and carried it home, there to abide in perfect safety, greeted by the love and joy of the Father and all angels; the gospel of the faithful Shepherd, who gathers the lambs with His arms and carries them in His bosom; of the compassionate and merciful High Priest, who prays for us that our faith fail not, and who upholds us with His all-sufficient grace and perfect sympathy. But when He shall come again, when the High Priest shall come forth out of the heavenly sanctuary, then shall He show unto all the world that He is King of kings, and Lord of lords; then shall His royalty be made prominent; then shall He be seen as the Son of man, unto whom God has given an everlasting kingdom and a dominion which shall have no end. Now the King is seen as Priest; then the Priest will be seen as King. The wrath of the Lamb will be revealed, and instead of the rod of the Shepherd will be seen the rod of iron. And after the judgment the King will reign with justice, mercy, and equity, as Psalm lxxii. describes.

How does He exercise His High Priesthood? He exercises His High Priesthood *royally*. He *sits down* on the throne of God. By that very attitude He shows that He is not an Aaronic high priest; for the high priest went into the holy of holies only once a year, on the day of atonement, and then only for a short time, standing there before the glory of the Lord, which he was not to see clearly lest he die; but this High Priest, when He enters into the sanctuary, by the very entrance shows that He is Lord of all, that He is King of glory, that He is equal with the Father. In His humanity He is enthroned as the Lamb that was slain; He exercises the High Priesthood with royal power. His intercession possesses omnipotence. The government is on His shoulder, and the Father heareth Him alway. Omnipotent royalty is in His Priesthood, priestly love and tenderness in His royal power and glory. He is still meek and lowly in heart, with infinite tenderness and compassion. He rules over His people by His indwelling Spirit. What a wonderful combination is here! What perfection in Jesus! He is Priest and King—He who is also the Prophet, the Son of the Most High!

I delight to think that the Sonship of Christ is the basis of all our hope, and that in that first announcement of our epistle, that God speaks to us now in His *Son*, all Scripture doctrines and consolations are contained. None but the Son of God can be the Mediator. From this eternal and essential Sonship flow all blessings of redemption. Here is the source of grace and glory. Because He is the Son of God, He is Prophet, Priest, and King, to bring us nigh unto God.

2. Melchizedek, that is, as the name signifies, the king of righteousness, lives at Salem, which signifies peace. In the Scripture everything is of importance; we cannot read and interpret the Scripture as any other book, since Scripture is not like any other book, even as no other book is like the Scripture. The Scripture is among books what the man Christ Jesus is among men: as Jesus is God and man in one person, so is Scripture a divine word and a human word; and hence it is that only through the interpretation of the Spirit in the Scripture can we understand the true meaning of the word. In God's light we see light. Scripture is its own interpreter. Only diamond cuts diamond. And when the inspired apostles see significance in names of eminent persons, we see in it nothing arbitrary or fanciful, believing as we do in the wonderful and perfect structure of the Scripture record.

These quotations and expositions of Scripture in Scripture are, as has been remarked, "grapes of Eshcol—examples of, not exceptions to, the fruitful Carmel, whence they come." Thus, who can fail to see the significance of the name Seth, who was given instead of Abel, one who was firm and enduring in the place of him who vanished? or of the name Joshua, who brought Israel into the promised land? or of Saul, the king asked of the people, and David, the man loved of God? or of Isaiah, who spoke of the salvation of God? The names Melchizedek and Salem are to teach us that Christ Jesus is the King of Righteousness and the Prince of Peace. "Righteousness" is one of those fundamental words in Scripture, without the true understanding of which it is impossible to understand its teaching. The experience of Luther, narrated by him in his preface to the epistle to the Romans, and frequently throughout his writings, is well known. While he understood by "righteousness" something which man offers to God, the Scripture remained to him a sealed book, and his soul was without peace. As soon as he discovered that the Scripture "righteousness" is righteousness, which God in His infinite mercy, according to His holiness and justice, gives to man, he understood the way of salvation, and rejoiced in the grace of God.

The righteousness of God, of which both the law and the prophets witnessed, is now revealed from faith to faith. It is now manifested. There is no righteousness by the works of the law; the gift of righteousness is by Jesus Christ unto all who believe.

"King of Righteousness" seems to be a title which properly belongs only unto God. For unto Him alone belongeth righteousness. Yet does prophetic Scripture speak also of God's righteous Servant; of David's Son, who loveth righteousness; of the true Solomon, whose reign is a reign of righteousness and peace. The prophetic word teaches also that this righteous Servant shall justify many by His knowledge; it announces that the Lord will bring man His righteousness, and that Jehovah-Tsidkenu will be the name of Israel's Redeemer, who bringeth safety and help to His chosen people. As in the prophet Isaiah (liii.), so in the prophecy of Daniel, the bringing in of everlasting righteousness is connected with the atonement for sin. (Dan. ix.)

The fulfilment is in Christ Jesus. He is the righteous Servant of God. He came to fulfil all righteousness; He obeyed the law perfectly; in Him the Father was pleased. While He was on earth, though no man could convince Him of sin, yet His purity, His holiness, His righteousness were not recognised, for the world knew Him not. He was made under the law. He went to be baptised of John, and submitted Himself to all the ordinances of God. He concealed His divine glory and righteousness. He was accused of blasphemy, of breaking the Sabbath, of not honouring the temple. He was at last numbered with transgressors, and died the death of reproach outside the camp. But it was by this death that He brought in everlasting righteousness. It was by His thus "going to the Father," by His entering through the cross into that glory, where the world seeth Him no more, that there is now "righteousness" unto and upon all that believe. In His resurrection God declared both the righteousness of Jesus and our justification in Him. And now we behold Christ in heaven, the Righteous One and our Advocate. (1 John ii.) He is the King of righteousness. The government of the everlasting kingdom is based on *redemption-righteousness.* Because of His obedience unto death He is exalted Lord; because He is the Lamb that was slain He has power to open the book and the seals thereof.

It is true, that it is of God that Christ is made unto us righteousness (1 Cor. i. 30), even as it is God who made Him, who knew no sin, to be sin for us, that we might be made the righteousness of God in Him. (2 Cor. v. 21.) God is righteous when He justifies those that believe in Jesus. But when we speak of the Lord our righteousness, we refer not to the divine attribute of righteousness, but to the righteousness of Jesus, the Mediator, the Substitute—of the Redeemer-God,

Jehovah, in whom all the seed of Israel shall be justified and shall glory. As God commends His love in Christ's death on the cross, so God s righteousness is the righteousness which in Christ is ours. By the obedience of one, even Jesus, we are made righteous. We possess the righteousness of God and our Saviour Jesus Christ. (2 Peter i. 2.) Even as eternal life is the gift of God, and Jesus saith, *I* give unto my sheep eternal life, and *I* am the resurrection and the life; so is it with the gift of righteousness; it is of God, it is in and through Christ, it is Christ's righteousness, and it is Christ Himself.

Christ is the perfect righteousness in which believers stand, and with which they are clothed. Christ is likewise the *King* of righteousness, by renewing our hearts and giving unto us His Spirit. Hence He says: "Except your righteousness shall exceed the righteousness of the scribes and Pharisees, ye shall in no case enter into the kingdom of heaven." Christ speaks of *our* righteousness. In like manner, although Christ is the Light of the world, and the true and only light, He commands us: "Let *your* light so shine before men." If we are clothed with Christ our righteousness, we ourselves become righteous in our mind, and work righteousness. This aspect of truth is emphasized by the apostle John, when says, "He that doeth righteousness is righteous." He adds the necessary and salutary warning: "Little children, let no man deceive you." The same Lord who clothes us with His righteousness renews us also after His image. Justified by faith, we are quickened unto the new life of obedience. Jesus is our Lord and Master, our King, who by the Holy Spirit fills us with the love of righteousness, and enables us to be followers of Him, and to do the will of the Father in heaven.

Melchizedek is at Salem. Jesus is also, and by virtue of righteousness, the Prince of peace. Without righteousness there cannot be peace. But the Lord Jesus came to bring peace, to make peace, to be our peace, and this according to the holiness of God; so that glory abounds to God in the highest, because justice is satisfied, the divine law honoured, and the conscience purified; and even Satan the accuser, who has the power of death, can no longer lay anything to the charge of God's elect.

How perfect is the peace which the risen Saviour gives to His people! It is His own peace, which the Head gives to His members. It is a blood-bought peace. It is God's peace, ordained by Him and beloved of Him as His chosen rest—a peace which passeth all understanding, and which is secure from all the interruptions and adverse influences of the world. Jesus has made peace between God and man (the

Father Himself, the God of peace, sending Him for this purpose to His "enemies"); peace between angels and reconciled sinners, between Jew and Gentile. In Him all things which are in heaven and which are on earth shall be gathered together. (Eph. i. and Col. i.) He is the Peace and Bond of the whole creation. Blessed are all who dwell in Salem, who are in Christ.

3. Melchizedek, greater than Abraham, is also greater than the Levitical priesthood, and is thus a type of Christ, who is above Aaron, and whose priesthood is perfect.

Abraham represents all Israel. The doctrine of federal representation is deeply rooted in Scripture. By Adam's disobedience many were constituted sinners. In his fall all men fell. Through the transgression of one, sin and death entered into the world. Such is the truth revealed to us in Scripture, and confirmed by universal experience. And the darkness of this mystery is irradiated by the brightness of the great mystery of the Second Adam.

We can praise God that there is such a federal representation; for the gift of God is eternal life through the righteousness of the Lord Jesus, the federal Head of all who trust in Him. Nor is the gift as the offence, but exceeding abundant is the grace of God, which instead of merely restoring us to our former condition of creaturely innocence, unites us with the Son of God through the Holy Ghost, who from the glorified humanity of Jesus is given unto us.

We see this same law of representation here. Isaac was not yet born. The whole nation was therefore as yet in Abraham. And the tribe of Levi was, in the person of the father of the faithful, paying homage and acknowledging the superiority of Melchizedek. Abraham received Melchizedek's blessing. He paid tithes to him. It seems, from the expression used by Jacob (Gen. xxviii. 22), that the offering of a tenth was from time immemorial one of the ways in which believers honoured the Most High. Hence we may argue that, in receiving the blessing and in offering tithes, Abraham (and in him Aaron) acknowledged the priesthood of Melchizedek.

For we must bear in mind what is implied according to Scripture in this expression: "He was blessed of him." Abraham, as the apostle points out, had already received the promises. The Most High had already revealed to Abraham the gracious purpose, that in his seed all families of the earth should be blessed; and he had received repeated assurances of this great and comprehensive promise. (Gen. xii. 2, 3, 7; xiii. 16.) How great the blessing is which God promised to Abraham we may learn from such passages as Gal. iii. 14. Who then is this royal priest, better and greater than Abraham, the father of the faithful and the blessed of the Lord? We know with what profound veneration the Hebrews regarded their father Abraham, and how reverently and fondly they cherished the remembrance of all that is written concerning his faith and the favour he found with God. It is therefore with great emphasis that the apostle says: "Now consider how great this man was, unto whom even the patriarch Abraham gave the tenth." Melchizedek typifies the Lord Jesus, who, although a Son of Abraham, yet says of Himself: "Before Abraham was, I am;" who is not merely the offspring, but the root of David. He who was promised to Abraham is Himself the blessing of God, the Mediator through whom all divine gifts and promises are bestowed, and in whom all spiritual blessings in heavenly places are given. In Him Abraham and Abraham's children are chosen. He is that greater One who blesses the patriarch. Herein is also typified that Jesus is above the Levitical priesthood. When He was on earth Jesus was subject to the law, and observed all its ordinances. He commanded the cleansed lepers to go and show themselves to the priests. Thus it behoved Him to fulfil all righteousness. But He is the Lord, and His is an eternal and perfect priesthood. For whereas the Levitical priests died and succeeded one another, thereby also showing their imperfection, Jesus, as is witnessed in the 110th Psalm, liveth for evermore. (Heb. vii. 8.)

But if the priesthood is changed, if instead of the Levitical priesthood there ariseth according to the type of Melchizedek and the prediction of the 110th Psalm "another priest," then the inference is inevitable that there is also a change of dispensation; *there must needs be also a change of law.* This was a very important statement, and we can scarcely realise the effect it was calculated to produce on the minds of the Hebrews. The unbelieving Jews accused Stephen that he had spoken against this holy place and the law, and that he had been heard to say that Jesus of Nazareth should destroy that place, and change the customs which Moses delivered them. (Acts vi.) We must remember how difficult it was even for believing Jews to understand the liberty of the gospel, the change of dispensation, the character of the new covenant; for they also were zealous of the law. (Acts xxi. 20.) But now the same argument by which the apostle had proved to the Galatians, that apart from the law the promise given to Abraham was fulfilled unto all who believe, is presented to the Hebrews from another point of view, and with equal clearness and cogency. For the Levitical priesthood is evidently imperfect. It was weak and unprofitable (*v.* 18); that is, it could not bring perfection, else "another priest" would not have been predicted. But as the law was based upon the Levitical priesthood, so the change of priesthood necessarily involves a change of dispensation. Jesus, the great High Priest, is the end of the law unto righteousness; and in the liberty and power of new covenant blessings, of which the gift of the Holy Ghost is the chief, the righteousness of the law is fulfilled in us, who walk not after the flesh, but after the Spirit, who are not under the law, but under grace.

4. Melchizedek is introduced in the narrative of Genesis without descent. In the book of Genesis genealogy holds a very prominent position. The genealogical records in the word of God are of importance, although we frequently may not see their value or significance. There are many things in Genesis, and in Scripture in general, which will only be understood when Jesus comes again to fulfil all things, and when, according to the purpose of God, known to Him from the beginning, the nations are brought to know and to serve Him. Then shall we understand why all these genealogies are given at length. In the book of Genesis are enumerated also tribes which do not appear afterwards in the history of redemption. God has entered them in His book to show that He has counsels of love and peace with regard to them.

Now, with regard to Aaron, we know the name of his father and mother; we know how old he was, and how he was buried. And so important is the genealogy of the priests, that in the book of Nehemiah we read that those priests who were not able to trace their descent, and about whose genealogy there was the slightest doubt, were excluded from the Levitical services. This strictness was necessary; for these men were priests, not by reason of anything inherent in them, but simply because God had set apart that tribe, and therefore their descent from one who was unmistakably and certainly a priest was their only authority, and their only position. There is nothing of the kind in the Church of Christ.*

But Melchizedek appears in the inspired history as a Priest solely by divine appointment and right.

* Those who introduce the legal element of a successional office into the Church of Christ, a shadow which has passed away, an old thing which has vanished and decayed, must remember that as the genealogy of the Levitical priesthood was kept with perfect accuracy, and the slightest flaw or break in it would unfit a person for the priesthood, so the so-called apostolic succession must be made out with perfect and unbroken regularity, to have any value or significance. That it is scarcely possible to do this is admitted nearly on all hands. Even if it were, the argument of this epistle, and the teaching of all the epistles, show that the New Testament ministry is spiritual, and not after the method of a carnal ordinance. "By their fruits ye shall know them." The last council of the "successors of the apostles" proves that, whatever historical evidence may be adduced for an unbroken series of ordinations, the true apostolic authentication, the power of Christ's Spirit, was lamentably absent.

His priestly dignity is personal; his position is directly God-given; his priesthood is inherent. It is not derived and inherited; for he who is the first person in Scripture called priest, is introduced "without descent," without father, without mother. There is neither end mentioned of his priesthood, nor successor.

Let us look now at the fulfilment. Jesus is the "everlasting Father." The very Scriptures, which describe Him as a child born, as a Son given, which dwell on His humanity, declare to us His eternal divinity. He has no beginning of days, nor end of life. His is now a continuous, not a successional priesthood, not after the law of a carnal commandment, but after the power of an endless, an indissoluble life.

For He, the eternal self-subsistent Word, that eternal Life which was with the Father, became man, and of His own free will laid down His life for the sheep. Through the eternal Spirit the Son of God offered Himself, and so that life which was manifested on earth was solved. The Saviour actually died, He gave up the ghost. He was crucified because of the weakness which in His mercy He had taken upon Him. According to the counsel of God, He who was God's own Son, sent in the likeness of sinful flesh, was a sacrifice for sin, when in His death God condemned sin in the flesh. But when Jesus rose again from the grave, after He had been offered for our offences, and had in His death conquered death and put away our sins, He, as God and man in one person, entered into that life which is indissoluble; for who or what power can solve it? He died unto sin once. The condemnation of the law, the power of Satan and of death, the guilt of sin and the wrath of God—all was met on the cross. Hence Jesus is declared now to live to God for evermore. (Rom. vi. 10.) Thus the glorified Redeemer, when He appeared to the beloved disciple, said: "Fear not; I am the first and the last [without beginning of days or end of life]: I am He that liveth, and was dead; and, behold, I am alive for evermore." Because He *was dead*, His is now an endless, an indissoluble life. In the power of this resurrection-life He exercises His priesthood; for in Him is fulfilled what no single type could set forth, what all types combined do not adequately illustrate. He is God and Man, Sacrifice and Priest, Righteousness and Life, Atoner and King, interceding Advocate, and the Dispenser of blessings. The life upon which He entered by His resurrection is life for us, because in Christ's death our death is abolished, and we are raised together with Him. And the sanctuary whither He has ascended is heaven itself, the very throne of God, whence He rules over all things, according to the power which is given unto Him in heaven and in earth. Continuously, without interruption and without successor, He is our Priest, applying to us the efficacy of His sacrifice, and by the Spirit appropriating to us the blessings purchased with His blood. He is our Priest in the power of His endless life. Thus we know the power of His resurrection. God's power to us-ward who believe is exceeding great, according to the working of His mighty power, which He wrought in Christ when He raised Him from the dead, and set Him at His own right hand. (Comp. Phil. iii. 10; Eph. i. 20.) We are partakers of Christ, Christ liveth in us, and therefore our life is endless, indestructible, incorruptible. Neither things present nor things to come; neither this present earthly existence nor the death of the body, which may be before us; neither powers, nor principalities, nor angels; neither height, nor depth, nor any creature, can separate us from the love of God which is in Christ Jesus; for our risen Lord is Priest according to the power of an indissoluble life.

Here let us pause. These truths are truths of the greatest solemnity. Why were the Jews so unwilling to receive them? Was it not partly because it was too solemn and too overwhelming to believe that the end of all things had come; that the last times had begun; that the days of the Messiah had been ushered in; that the day had commenced, the very day which shall end with the appearing of the great God and Saviour, and with the establishment of the reign of righteousness and peace upon the earth? And is not this hesitation natural to us all? Do we not shrink from entering into the full and realizing faith of what is revealed unto us in the Gospels and in the Epistles, because it is the beginning of the end? The Son of God has become man; the Son of God has died upon the cross; the Son of God has entered as man into the holy of holies. The blood of Jesus Christ is in the heavenly sanctuary. The powers and influences of the Holy Ghost are going forth now to gather a people unto Himself. He is waiting until the command is uttered by the Father to appear again, and to change all things, and to make all things new. We are living as it were upon the very threshold of that new dispensation, the new heavens and the new earth wherein dwelleth righteousness. The most awful and stupendous sacrifice has already been made. Christ has suffered and entered into His glory. We have now to wait for nothing except the consummation, Jesus, apart from sin, appearing unto salvation to them that look for Him. But the reality, the substance, the earnest of the inheritance, behold, all is given even now to every one that believeth. This very instant that I speak, Jesus as man, as the Lamb slain, as the merciful High Priest, is at the right hand of God. Believe in Him and you are justified, a child of God, an heir of God, and joint-heir with Christ Jesus.

Oh, if we know these great, these awful, and these real solemnities, what manner of men ought we to be! Have we tasted the power of the world to come, of that kingdom of heaven, which has come already? Have we received a life which alone is worthy to be called life—not the life of the senses, not the life of the intellect, not the life of emotion, not the life of fluctuating and sentimental religiousness, but the life which comes out of the fountain of life, even from Jesus, and from Jesus only after His death and His resurrection? How blessed is it for poor guilty sinners to know that the King of righteousness and peace is the Lamb, and that the Lamb has all power! He was dead; then all my condemnation is gone. And He liveth; therefore we also live. And He is alive for evermore; and we also, who bear now the image of the first Adam in humility and bondage, shall bear the image of the second Adam in liberty and in glory.

CHAPTER XVI.

THE WORD OF THE OATH AND THE SON PERFECTED FOR EVERMORE.

HEB. vii. 15–28.

THE characteristics of the eternal Priesthood of Jesus, inferred by the apostle from the inspired record of the typical history of Melchizedek, both in its statements and omissions, are, as we have seen, that Jesus is Priest and King; that in Him righteousness and peace are united; that He is above Aaron, and that He is Priest for ever after the order of an endless life. All these points receive additional illustration and confirmation from the fifth characteristic—the *oath*—by which Jesus, according to Psalm cx., was made Priest.

The legal dispensation was connected with the Levitical priesthood. Without mediation it was impossible that God should enter into covenant-relation with sinful and guilty men; and therefore even the first covenant was made not without blood. The apostle argues that if there is a change in the priesthood, there must necessarily be a change in the dispensation with which that priesthood is connected. When the apostle speaks of the Levitical priesthood and of the first dispensation in such strong terms as that it was weak and unprofitable, we must remember that here, as well as when he speaks of the law of Moses, he looks upon them as separate from Christ, who was the substance of the shadow; he addresses those who viewed the law and Levitical ordinances apart from their vital connection with the promise of Christ and with the true sacrifice. The believing Israelite, taught by the law and the prophets, looked forward unto the coming of Jehovah, and the redemption that was to be accomplished by the Messiah; he saw in the ordinances pictures of eternal and heavenly blessings; and although under the dispensation of the law still in the spirit of servantship, kept under the guardianship of the schoolmaster, he obtained through faith the forgiveness of sins, and looked forward to that everlasting inheritance which God had promised unto the fathers. But when the Jews looked upon the law as a source of righteousness and life, forgetting its true character and significance; when they regarded the Levitical priesthood and the temple and the offerings apart from Christ, looking upon shadows and types as substance, then it was that the apostle, in all the epistles where he touches upon this subject, is constrained to show unto them that the law, the tabernacle, the sacrifices, the priests viewed in themselves, were in no way able to give righteousness or peace or life unto the soul; that they were entirely weak and unprofitable; that they were sent only for a temporary purpose, in order to prepare for the introduction of that which shall never be moved, and in which there is true substance and blessedness everlasting. In this way the whole dispensation of the law and the Levitical priesthood were merely parenthetical. They were never intended to remain. They were only, as the apostle explains it of the law in the epistle to the Galatians, the schoolmaster, the tutor, appointed for a time until the child had reached a certain maturity, in order that then it might obtain real possession of the blessing, being made free by the Spirit of sonship through faith in Christ Jesus.

The apostle announces a great principle in the words, "The law made nothing perfect." There was not a single point in which the law reached the end; for the end of the law is Christ. The law is in itself by its very nature fragmentary and temporary; it is necessarily imperfect. This is an essential characteristic of the dispensation. The law was a revelation and condemnation of man's guilt, and, secondly, a shadow of things to come. The law showed unto the people that God was holy, that man was sinful, and that therefore a perfect mediation was necessary, to bring us into the presence of the Most High. The law typified this mediation; but all types are by the very nature of types mere shadows, and therefore not able to give the real substance except by anticipation. The imperfection of the law appears in these three points especially:

First, The forgiveness of sin. In the old dispensation believers were comforted by the revelation of God's mercy, and by the promise of the Messiah. But, as was shown by the continual repetition of sacrifices, the true atonement was not yet made; everlasting righteousness was not yet brought in, and therefore the conscience was not yet purged from sin. The apostle explains in the epistle to the Romans, that although God forgave and pardoned the sins of the Israelites before Christ died upon the cross, yet they were remitted only through the forbearance of God. (Rom. iii. 25.) It was in a temporary manner, in view of the future atonement. But now that Christ has died, He has become the Surety of the new covenant, which has better promises, and the first blessing of which is the forgiveness of sin. In this dispensation we now have no longer any conscience of sin, because he that has come unto Jesus Christ, who died once for all, has received the absolute and entire remission of sins, and needeth not but that his feet should be washed daily, that his trespasses should be acknowledged and confessed to Him who is faithful and just to forgive us our sins, and to cleanse us from all unrighteousness.

Secondly, Access unto God was not perfected under the old dispensation. Abraham, Moses, David, and all the fathers, prayed unto God, and knew that God was the hearer of prayer; but their access to God was imperfect, because they were not yet able to enter into the holy of holies, seeing that the way into the sanctuary through the rent veil of the flesh of Christ was not revealed yet. Before Jesus came, the worship of the Old Testament saints was not in liberty of the Spirit. They had received the spirit of bondage, and not the Spirit of adoption. They could not pray as the children, who are identified with the Man who is their Lord and Head, the Son incarnate.

The third imperfection was this: They had not received the Holy Ghost as an indwelling Spirit. This is explained in the apostle's epistle to the Galatians. The more we study this section of the Melchizedek priesthood, the more shall we be convinced that the same mind that argues in the Romans and the Galatians about the law, explains here the superiority of Christ over the priesthood of Aaron. If a law could have been given through which life could come, it would not have been necessary for Christ to die upon the cross. Then righteousness would have come by the law; but the law, the dispensation of Moses, was not able to minister life, that is, to give unto us the Holy Ghost (Gal. iii. 2, 21); for the Holy Ghost was not yet, because Jesus Christ was not yet transfigured. (John vii.) The Spirit of God is from eternity to eternity one with the Father and the Son; but the Lord Jesus refers to the Holy Ghost as the Spirit of the anointed One, who, according to the promise of the Father, dwells in the church. He was not yet given, because Jesus was not yet glorified. The Spirit was to be sent from Jesus the Son as our Lord and glorified Head. It required that indissoluble (resurrection-) life of the High Priest, of the Victim slain upon Calvary, and raised again by the power of God out of the grave. It is from our risen Lord that *life* is now given to believers; the Spirit dwells in our hearts, and we have fellowship with the Father and the Son. Such is the threefold privilege of believers in the present dispensation—perfect forgiveness of sin, perfect access unto God, and the indwelling of the Holy Ghost.

But the law made nothing perfect. For perfection is true, substantial, and eternal communion with God through a perfect mediation; and this perfect mediation we have obtained in the Lord Jesus Christ.

Now, the apostle says that all this is quite evident from the word of God in Psalm cx. David in the Spirit declared the oath of the Lord: "Thou art a Priest for ever after the order of Melchizedek." If "after the order of Melchizedek," he puts aside the order of Aaron. If "a Priest for ever," then there must be perfection in this priesthood; that is to say, this priesthood is continuous, untransferable, unchanging; it brings that ultimate blessedness which endureth for ever, perfect and substantial communion between God and us.

And this ordinance is by an oath. The Lord hath sworn. Thus it is written in the psalm. The apostle deduces a most important argument from this expression; and if, as the Lord Jesus Himself points out, David was "in the Spirit" when he penned this psalm, we have no difficulty in accepting the teaching of the apostle. Are we to judge the expressions of Scripture like the expressions of other books, in which sometimes words are used thoughtlessly, accidentally, superficially, without any further or deeper meaning? This be far from us, if we have indeed learned the mind of God. The priesthood of Aaron was not instituted with an oath. That which is connected with an oath can never be changed; for

God is immutable. And in the same way as He swore unto Abraham, "Surely with blessing I will bless thee," in order that by two immutable things in which it is impossible for God to lie we may have abundant assurance of hope; even thus is it that because the High Priesthood of Jesus can never be altered, because it is based upon the eternal decree and counsel of God, and because it is essentially connected with the very nature and purpose of God Himself, it is introduced with an oath. The Lord hath sworn, and will not repent.

For this royal priesthood was set up in Christ before the foundations of the world were laid. Here is revealed to us the mystery of His will, according to His good pleasure which He hath purposed in Himself. (Eph. i. 7–9.) Christ, the Lamb without blemish and without spot, the Sacrifice; Christ the High Priest, Christ the Heir of all things, was foreordained in the eternal counsel of God. His royal Priesthood is an eternal one; even as eternal life was promised by God, that cannot lie (the nature of oath), before the world began. (Titus i. 2.) Thus are believers chosen in Him unto glory, and thus the gospel of grace is connected with eternity; whereas the law, which deals with man's works, belongs in its very nature to the region of time. God's own purpose and grace was given us in Christ Jesus before the world began. (2 Tim. i. 9.) This is the Priesthood of the Oath, of which it is said: It will never repent Him.

In this declaration the apostle beholds the disannulling or abrogation of the legal dispensation which was connected with the Levitical priesthood, and, in the second place, the introduction of a better hope by which we draw near to God. This oath shows that Jesus is the surety of a better dispensation.*

Let us look now at the contrast between the priests of the Levitical dispensation and this Priest according to the order of Melchizedek. They were many; He is only one. Their priesthood was successional—the son followed the father. Christ has a priesthood which cannot be transferred, seeing that His life is indissoluble. They were sinful, but He is holy, pure, and spotless. They offered sacrifices in the earthly tabernacle; He presents Himself with His blood in the true sanctuary, which is high above all heavens, which is eternal. He appears in the very presence before the face of God. In Jesus Christ, the eternal Priest after the order of Melchizedek, all is fulfilled which

* διαθήκη occurs here for the first time in the epistle. As will be more fully explained in connection with chapters viii. and ix., the word means dispensation, covenant, and testament. The Levitical priesthood is connected with the law, the *old* covenant, temporary and imperfect, with a *worldly* sanctuary; the Melchizedek priesthood of our Lord with the *new*, eternal, and perfect covenant, of which Jesus is Mediator and Surety (compare viii. 5; ix. 15), and with the *heavenly* sanctuary.

in the preparatory dispensation could only be shadowed forth imperfectly and by a variety of ordinances. It was impossible to illustrate adequately by any type or combination of types that which is infinite, that which is eternal, that which is both divine and human. All the types taken together are not intelligible to us, and will not bring us to a right conclusion and a right understanding of Christ, unless we always bear in mind their necessary imperfection. Jesus is the sacrifice; but what sacrifice could be a type of Christ? The animals that were slain were only passive in death. It is quite true that they were to be without blemish, and in that way they showed forth that Jesus Christ was perfectly holy. But that offering up of Himself, the giving Himself unto God in our stead, the laying down His life for the sheep, the coming to do the will of God the Father who had sent Him, the obedience of faith and love,—this could never be typified. Again, the sacrifice was slain, simply to obtain the blood. Remission of sin was through the blood. It was the blood that was brought into the holy of holies. And this blood existed separately from the sacrifice which had ceased to live. This also was a very imperfect adumbration of the reality. By His own free will, in obedience to the Father, and out of love to us, the Lord Jesus gave His life as a ransom for our sins.

With the blood, Himself, the living Jesus, Priest and Sacrifice, entered into the holy of holies, there to abide as our righteousness and life. On the cross He was the victim; in the holy of holies He is Priest, not after the order of Aaron, but after the order of Melchizedek. All that was prefigured by the sacrifices, and all that was prefigured by Aaron, the Lord fulfilled; and having fulfilled all, He entered upon His true, real, and eternal Priesthood, which is after the order of Melchizedek. For although He intercedes for us, and bears us on His heart, as was typified by Aaron, His Priesthood itself is now not after the order of Aaron. And although He is Priest after the order of Melchizedek, He has not entered yet on the fulfilment of the priestly reign typified by the priestly king who met Abraham.*

Christ, in virtue of His priesthood, can save completely (in a perfect, exhaustive, all-compre-

* We still look forward to the ultimate fulfilment of this type. After the final victory over all enemies, over all kings and great powers of earth gathered against the Lord's people, when idolatry is destroyed for ever, and the Most High God alone is worshipped, then shall heaven and earth be blessed in the priestly reign of the Lord Jesus. The King of righteousness and peace shall bless the seed of Abraham, and all the meek who inherit the earth; while the glorified saints, who have overcome in Christ's name and strength, inherit according to His promise all things. Then all things, both which are in heaven and which are in earth, shall be gathered together in one, even in Christ; and God, the possessor of heaven and earth, be blessed, while His blessing flows unhindered through all parts of His dominions.

hensive manner) all who through Him come to God, because He ever liveth to intercede for them.

Let us remember the importance which is attached in all epistles unto the resurrection-life of Christ. He who was our Paschal lamb liveth now, and our only hope is in the risen Lord. There are many Christians who dwell on the crucifixion of Jesus in a one-sided way. We cannot dwell too much on the glorious truth that Jesus Christ was crucified for our sins. Yet it is not on the crucifixion, but on Christ the Lord, that our faith rests; and not on Christ as He was on the cross do we dwell, but on Christ who was dead and is risen again, and liveth at the right hand of God, making intercession for us. What does the apostle Paul mean when he says, "If we have been justified through His death, *much more* shall we be saved by His life"? There is a "much more," there is progress, there is a climax. When Jesus died upon the cross He put away our sins, but this was only removing an obstacle. The ultimate object of His death upon the cross was His resurrection and ascension, that through suffering He should enter into glory, that He should be the perfect Mediator between God and man, presenting us unto God and bestowing upon us all the blessings which He has purchased for us with His precious blood. He has obtained eternal redemption on the cross. He applies the blessings of eternal redemption from the holy of holies. Therefore do we testify every Lord's-day that Christ is risen. If Christ was not risen we should still be in our sins; and if such a thing were possible, though we might be forgiven, we should be dead and without the Spirit. The law brought neither righteousness nor life; Christ brings both righteousness and life: for He died in our stead, and He lived again to be our life. Thus the apostle says, in the epistle to the Romans, "Who will condemn? It is Christ who died, yea rather, that is risen again, who is at the right hand of God, making intercession for us." The Father Himself loveth us; it is the Father's good pleasure that Jesus should thus intercede for us. It is of His own free love and sovereign grace that Jesus intercedes for us, that thus the life which through death He has brought unto us might be in us abundantly, and that all the spiritual blessings in heavenly places, which are in Him, and all the temporal blessings which we require for our safety, comfort, and usefulness, may be bestowed upon us by the love of the Father, and through the indwelling of the Holy Ghost. The Lord Jesus, who through death entered into glory, brings us to God as to His and our Father, and brings God to us by the indwelling of the Holy G'ost. Thus is His Priesthood perfect.

Consider now the perfection of Christ's Priesthood, and of that better covenant or dispensation of which He became Surety and Mediator.

There are three things that Scripture teaches. God is holy; man is sinful; Jesus is the perfect Mediator. In the old dispensation great stress was laid upon the first two points—God is holy; man is sinful. Therefore the godly Israelites prayed: Oh that God would send forth His salvation! Mediation was foreshadowed. Perfection was promised, the true Sacrifice, the gift of the Spirit. Israel was taught of God the nature, depth, and condemnation of sin. The law was the full, comprehensive, and profound commentary on the consequences of the Fall. It revealed to the Jews man's deep-seated estrangement from God, his depravity and corruption, the sinfulness of the very root and fountain of our life. The holiness of God and man's sin and sinfulness were thus vividly impressed on God's ancient people. The sins committed in ignorance required also atonement; the sinfulness of the flesh was constantly brought to their remembrance. Thus they longed for the fulfilment of God's promise, the true Atonement and the indwelling Spirit. In the new covenant the emphasis is laid on the perfect medi tion of Jesus; and from the stand-point of perfect acceptance we are to see the holiness of God and the sinfulness of man. Let us not cherish less profound views of God's holiness and of the nature of sin than our fathers under the less perfect dispensation of the law. In the light of the heavenly sanctuary, where Jesus is as our High Priest, we can never say that we have no sin, or that we have any confidence in the flesh, or that we have not to mourn over and to condemn the evil that is present with us, and the opposition of the old man, who constantly warreth against the new.

The Lord Jesus is the perfect Mediator. The Levitical high priests were sinful men, and required to bring sacrifices for themselves. But the Lord Jesus was holy, harmless, undefiled. In His relation to God the Lord Jesus was holy (ὅσιος); from His very birth pure, and in His whole life manifesting His inner perfect love to the Father, and conformity with His will. In relation to man He was harmless. He went about doing good; He loved with perfect love, forgiving and enduring all things. With regard to Himself, though living in a world of sin and temptation, He was undefiled. He touched the leper, and the leper was cleansed. He came into contact with death (herein a contrast to the Jewish priest), and conquered death; He took the little maid by the hand, and she arose. He came into contact with the tempter; He remained undefiled. He was "separate from sinners." The description given of the righteous man in Ps. i. is fulfilled in Him. The only sinless one in the world, He was always alone with God.*

This Lord is "exalted above the heavens." Jesus went into the holy of holies, which was typified in the tabernacle. Above all created heavens, above angels and principalities, Jesus is now in the true Sanctuary, in the presence of God, and there He is enthroned our perfect High Priest. His position in heaven demonstrates that when He offered up Himself He put away sin for ever, even as it sets forth His divine glory. For who but the Son of God can sit at the right hand of the Majesty on High? As it is written, "Be thou exalted, O God, above the heavens."

And now the apostle turns again, in a most emphatic and conclusive manner, unto the key-note which he had struck at the beginning of the epistle. The law of Moses constitutes priests that were changing continually. But the Word which came with the oath after the law consecrated for evermore as High Priest Him who is the *Son.*

* And yet, although thus in reality separate from sinners, He attracted and befriended the poor in spirit and contrite in heart. Sinners drew near to listen to His gracious words. He received them and ate with them; and at last He was numbered among the transgressors. Let us learn from Jesus the true separation unto God, which manifests itself in humility and in love to sinners, as contrasted with the self-constituted Pharisaic separateness, in which there is neither communion with God nor the attractive power of divine grace drawing men to God.

(Comp. the same emphasis on Son, Heb. i. 1, 2.) Only the Son could be the High Priest, and He *became* the High Priest. Through His incarnation, through all the experiences of His life of sorrow and of faith, through His death upon the cross, through His resurrection and ascension, Jesus is perfected for evermore a High Priest at the right hand of God. He is our one and only royal High Priest, eternal, heavenly, God and Man in one Person.

True peace or communion with God must combine three things. There is no perfect mediation, and there is no real communion with God, unless it fulfils three conditions.

In the first place, the mediation must go low enough. A ladder is of no use unless it comes down exactly to the point where I am. Unless it is there where I can place my foot upon it, it is of no avail. Hence mediation that does not reach down into our fallen, guilty, and lost condition—a mediation in which there is no expiation—a mediation that does not remove the wrath of God, that does not take away the curse of the law, that does not blot out the writing of ordinances that is against us, that does not bind and conquer Satan, who has the power of death—I say, a mediation that does not go into this depth is no true mediation for a sinner. But Christ's mediation is based upon His sacrifice on the cross; and therefore it descends to my lost and guilty condition. How can I receive it without repentance, without godly sorrow, without self-condemnation, without the crucifixion of the old man, and of all the flattering hopes which may be built upon self?

The second point is, the true mediation must go high enough; it must bring me into the presence of God. Only that which is pure and that which is living can be brought before God. Hence I need righteousness and life. The Lord Jesus is our righteousness, and by His resurrection and the indwelling of the Spirit He is our life. In Him we are accepted, and filled with the Spirit of life. We have access by Christ unto the Father. Here is our perfection. It is not in ourselves, but in the Lord, who is at the right hand of God. It is not a progressive perfection, or a gradual diminution of the evil and God-opposed character of the flesh. Through all the days of our earthly life the flesh warreth against the Spirit, yet is there no condemnation to them who are in Christ Jesus.

And the third requisite is this: As the mediation must go low enough, reaching us in the depths in which we are, and as it must go high even into the sanctuary of God, so it must go deep into our very hearts. As we are brought unto God, so must God be brought unto us; for the Christ that lives *for* us must also live *in* us.

Christ, who is our High Priest at the right hand of God, sends the Spirit into our hearts; for to be carnally-minded is death; but to be spiritually-minded is life and peace.

Of which things this is the sum: Christ the Son of God died *in our stead* on the cross; Christ lives *for us* in heaven; Christ lives *in us* by the Spirit.

CHAPTER XVII.

RETROSPECT.

HEB. I–II.

REVIEWING the teaching of the first seven chapters of our epistle, let us recall some aspects of truth brought before us with regard to—

1. THE SCRIPTURE.
2. THE GLORY OF THE LORD JESUS.
3. THE CHRISTIAN LIFE.

1. The Scripture: its authority, inspiration, and practical character.

No other church appears to have been in so perilous a condition as the congregation of Hebrews to whom our epistle was addressed. The abuses which had crept into the Corinthian churches, their discord and divisions, their pride and conceit, the flagrant sins into which some of their members had fallen, were grievous indeed; and the apostle addressed to them words of sharp rebuke, not free from piercing irony, though characterised throughout by his tender and loving spirit. The error into which the Galatians were ready to fall was of vital importance, and the apostle expostulates with them in tones of eager and intense anxiety, warning them that if they do not stand in the liberty of the gospel, but return to the stand-point of law, Christ is become of no effect unto them. And while the character of false teachers and corrupters of the doctrine of godliness became more apparent among the congregations to whom the second epistle of Peter and the epistle of Jude are addressed, yet do we not behold anywhere a congregation in so imminent danger of apostasy. It is therefore remarkable that, although in this epistle the Hebrews are exhorted to obey them that have the rule over them, to submit themselves to those who are called to watch for their souls, and to remember those that preached the word of God to them, yet this is done only in the concluding chapter, while the main argument of the apostle is to obey the word of God, to hold fast in loyal and persevering faith the Word which was spoken of God in divers portions and ways to the fathers by the prophets, which in these last days was spoken unto us in the Son, and which was declared by the apostles, who had seen Him on earth. Identifying the gospel message with the written Word, with the Scripture, which was received in Israel as the record of divine revelation and as the oracles of God, the writer of our epistle bases all his arguments and exhortations on the inspired testimony. It is most instructive to notice how the individuality of the writer is kept in the background, how the authority of Scripture is kept prominent. And if the so-called successors of the apostles and some communities lay much stress on central authoritative legislation, by which all doctrinal and practical questions which agitate Christian congregations are to be settled, it is well for us to remember how little the apostles themselves thought of exercising such a mechanical authority, and how they relied exclusively on the power of the Word applied by the Spirit to the heart and conscience.

If it was thus in the apostolic churches, ought it not to be still more so in the present day? Scripture is the only authority in the Church. We are to be guided and moulded by the Word, not by antiquity or the opinions of men, however eminent, or the traditions and customs of churches, however venerable. The church is the bride, and it is hers to obey the Lord, and in all things to carry out His commandment. She has no light of her own; like the moon, she is to reflect the light of the sun. And as the church, so the individual Christian is to abide in the teaching of the Word. Avoiding all subjection to the opinions of men, to the charm of novelty, to the authority of those who are distinguished by their gifts of learning or their character of devotedness, let us seek always the teaching of the Holy Ghost through the Scriptures, that so we may receive truth from God, that we may be taught of Him who alone can teach to profit, and whose teaching is accompanied with the light of peaceful assurance and with vital power. From early childhood we may thus know the Scripture, and be made wise unto salvation; and from the least to the greatest the members of Christ's church may possess that true, individual, and direct teaching from above, by which alone we can retain our liberty and abide in the humble, docile attitude of disciples of the one Master.

The word of God abideth for ever: "Every plant, which my heavenly Father hath not planted, shall be rooted up." Whether it be doctrine or practice, nothing can stand except it be of God; and of plants, not planted by God, it is not enough to lop off some branches in order to prevent their too luxurious growth, but according to the declaration of the Lord, whose love is as infinite as His truth, they must be rooted up. The Reformers, in so far as they were enabled to return to the Scripture, were acting according to the commandment of the gentle and loving Saviour; and their zeal was spiritual and salutary, and for the true welfare of the church and the nation. We cannot be reminded too frequently and too emphatically of the authority of Scripture, and of the relation in which every Christian stands to the word of God. According to the Scriptures, Christ died; and according to the Scriptures, Christ rose again. And as the apostles preached from the Scriptures the gospel in its most elementary and fundamental aspect, so all divine truth, which is necessary and salutary for us, is taught by the Spirit through the prophetic and apostolic word.

The Scripture is the record of God's revelation to His chosen people Israel. God revealed Himself in word and deed, in doctrine and in the works of His redeeming grace and royal rule, in promises and in types. Hence it is impossible to separate in a mechanical way the divine and eternal element from the lower and human, the historical and subjective. In the history of Israel, the institutions and laws of the chosen people, the character, conflicts, and development of patriarchs, prophets, and kings, God reveals unto us His truth, and reveals to us Himself. When the inner life of God's saints is unveiled to us, as in the Psalms, the Book of Job, the Lamentations of Jeremiah, and indeed throughout Scripture, so that, as Luther says, "we see into the very hearts of these men, and not merely behold paradise and heaven itself there, but also death, and even hell," we possess in these apparently purely human and subjective delineations the teaching of the Holy Ghost, who presents to us truthfully and perfectly the conflict in human souls between God's grace and their sin and weakness, and provides us with a guide-book in which all possible difficulties and errors are noticed, and the true remedies and correctives indicated. Hence no Scripture is purely human and temporary; all Scripture is divine and eternal. It possesses vitality, fulfilling itself continually, and containing throughout the revelation of God's character and of God's salvation.

In Scripture all lines of thought and history, of type and prophecy, converge and meet in one point, the Messiah. Christ is set forth in the words, deeds, and persons of prophets, priests, and kings. He is typified in the tabernacle with its God-appointed furniture; His advent is heralded and His work proclaimed, not merely by the living voice of God speaking to the patriarchs and prophets, and not merely by the response of faith and prayer of the saints, but even by the creatures whose blood was shed; by the inanimate symbols, as the ark, the laver, altar; by the Sabbath, by the feasts and fasts, and the year of jubilee. Yea, the very infirmities, failures, and sins of prophets, priests, and rulers, whose offices were bestowed by God for the glory of His name and the ood of the nation, only increase the desire of the God-fearing, that the perfect Mediator may appear, even the Son, in whom God speaks, and through whom the divine favour and rule are brought perfectly unto His people.

While God-manifestation or Christ-manifestation [Revelation] is thus the central and crowning object of the Scripture, this great purpose could only be fulfilled gradually. Each succeeding need of man was used by God as a new opportunity of manifesting His character, and of unfolding the vast resources of His gracious counsel. Hence Scripture gives us the *history* of the chosen seed, the people whom God formed for Himself, that they might show forth His praise. It reveals to us Israel in bondage, Israel in the wilderness, Israel worshipping, Israel entering the promised land, Israel now conforming to the nations, now conquering in faith. In all these various aspects is Israel represented, that we may learn thereby the ways of God, the character of the world, the trials and difficulties of the believer, the source of weakness and defeat, as well as the source of victory and strength. Thus while God reveals Himself throughout, it is in such a way that it suits our weak vision, and that it supplies all the guidance, correction, and encouragement which we need during our earthly life.

Our epistle illustrates these truths concerning Scripture in a remarkable way. We read in Acts xvii. 2, 3 that it was the manner of the apostle Paul to reason with the Jews out of the Scriptures, opening and alleging that Christ must needs have suffered and risen again from the dead, and that "this Jesus whom I preach unto you is Christ." In this he only followed the method of the Lord Himself, who after His resurrection began at Moses and all the prophets, and expounded unto them in all the Scriptures, the things concerning Himself.* This was the method of all the apostles. Like their divine Lord, the apostles regarded the books of Moses and prophets as one; they speak of "the Scripture," and of "all Scripture." The references to Scripture in our epistle, by which doctrines are proved as by an ultimate and all-sufficient authority, show that the writer regarded the whole collection of books as of equal importance and dignity. In a very marked way the Scripture is quoted as *God's* word; He is the true and one Author, though many holy men were His messengers and instruments.

For Scripture is not merely the record, it is the *inspired* record of revelation. Scripture teaches of itself (directly, and still more frequently and strongly indirectly) that it is given by inspiration of God. The choice of biographies, narratives, genealogies, prayers, proverbs, the manner in which these were recorded, the very omission of

* Luke xxiv. It is striking that this is specially recorded in the gospel of Luke, whose Pauline character is acknowledged by all.

circumstances—all this was not according to human selection, wisdom, and skill, but according to the mind of the Spirit, who, searching the deep things of God, and foreseeing the end from the beginning, has caused holy men to write in such a manner that the truth of God is revealed in fulness for the instruction and comfort of all generations. To the Holy Ghost we trace Scripture. It is perfect, all-comprehensive, and pure. The Scripture is above every age; for it is written by the eternal Spirit; and our wisdom is to receive Scripture teaching with absolute child-like faith, and to receive Scripture teaching according to its own method, not mixing it up with the enticing words of human wisdom, and the thought and terminology of temporary schools.

While the authority and inspiration of Scripture as a testimony of Christ are vividly brought before us in this epistle, the practical character of the Word is continually urged. The Spirit is still connected with the Scripture. By it He still teaches, guides, and comforts the hearts of men. The Word is living, because the Holy Ghost applies the Word, and the voice of God is heard by the soul. Especially are the exhortations of Scripture attributed to the Holy Ghost. As the Holy Ghost saith, "To-day if ye will hear His voice, harden not your hearts." For the Spirit of God, though one with the Father and the Son, identifies Himself in His condescending love with us. As He maketh intercession for us, praying within us, and, as it were, becoming a suppliant with us, expressing our desires and wants, so when God speaks to us, the Spirit continually urges us to listen and to take to heart, as an affectionate mother encourages her child to attend and to mark the important and beautiful instruction of the teacher.

The Scripture is the mirror in which we behold the human heart, with its unbelief, its selfish and carnal thoughts, its tendency to hypocrisy and to rest in mere shadows. The apostle reminds us that by this Word, as by a sharp sword, all that is confused and mixed in our thoughts and hearts is severed, the heavenly separated from the earthly, and the thoughts and intents of the heart discerned. He shows us that the Word brings us into the presence of Him from whom it comes, and with whom we have to do.

Thus while the Word reveals Christ, it judges everything in us that prevents our walking by faith in Him. Solemn and stern as its voice may be, the blessed result, to the faithful and humble who tremble at the word of God, is, that by it they are directed to look off unto Jesus, to look up unto Him who is the way of life above to the wise, and that thus they are kept from the evil that is in the world.

The Word speaks to the heart. The voice of the Lord is powerful and full of majesty; the heart adores and is filled with awe. The voice of the Lord is full of love and tenderness; the heart trusts and rejoices. The voice of the Lord declares mercy; and the heart forgives them that have trespassed against us. The voice of the Lord promises peace and glory; the heart feels the festival of generosity, and becomes cheerful and patient in giving sorrow.

Of a living Christ and to living souls does the living Word speak, that we may walk *with God.** All Scripture, given by inspiration of God, is profitable for doctrine, for reproof, for correction, for instruction in righteousness, that the man of God may be perfect, throughly furnished unto every good work. It makes us wise unto salvation; it gives us not that knowledge which puffeth up, but the wisdom which is from above, even love, that edifieth.

2. The person and work of Christ.

The great object of this epistle is to show the heavenly Priesthood of the Lord Jesus, the Messiah. But as all the offices of our adorable Lord are rooted in His eternal Sonship, and are most inseparably connected with each other, the epistle

* Luther's well-known expression, that the words of Scripture are not Lese—sondern Lebe worte; not words for reading, but for living.

brings before us in great fulness the doctrine of the person and work of the Messiah. In the first chapter the Messiah is spoken of as the Son. In relation to *God* He is from all eternity, the brightness of His glory, the express image of His substance. In relation to the *world* He is the Mediator by whom it was created, and by whom it is upheld. In relation to the *prophets* He is the Son, in whom is the perfect and ultimate revelation of God. In relation to the *angels* He is Lord, whom they worship and serve. In relation to the future world, or *the Messianic kingdom*, He is appointed Heir of all things. And this glory was not lessened by His humiliation, His sufferings and death; it was by His obedience that He entered into glory, that He ascended into heaven, and was exalted at the right hand of God. We behold the glory of Jesus, the Messiah, the Son of David, the Son of Man, of whom Psalm viii. and the prophecy of Isaiah witness, the glory of the Lord, unto whom all things are subject, and whose dominion is everlasting.

The first two chapters set before us the wonderful union of the divine and human natures in one Person. We rejoice that He who is the eternal Son of the Father, and the self-subsistent Word, has through sufferings and death entered into glory, and that Jesus is Lord above all, and our High Priest before God. He is the Mediator of the new covenant, greater than Moses; for Jesus is Son in the House and Lord over the House; whereas Moses, though faithful, was only a servant, and for this very reason in a preparatory and imperfect economy. (Com. John viii. 35.) Jesus is greater than Joshua; for in Him the rest of God is also our rest, even as through Him we shall finally enter into the everlasting Sabbatism. He is greater than Aaron; for, while fulfilling all that was prefigured by the Aaronic priesthood, He was consecrated a High Priest for ever after the order of Melchizedek; and after the power of an endless life He is the true Mediator, who in the heavenly sanctuary represents us before God, and communicates to us the blessings of the everlasting covenant.

But as the epistle unfolds the glory of the exalted Saviour, it dwells also on the humanity of Christ, and on His obedience and sufferings in the days of His flesh. In showing Christ's eternal divine glory, the first chapter of our epistle reminds us of the commencement of John's Gospel, it ascends into the loftiest height; but it is also like the Gospel of Luke—in which the beloved Physician reveals to us Jesus the Son of man, in a manner as vivid and touching as it is profound.

In no portion of Scripture are we so fully taught the humanity of our blessed Lord, the sufferings of Christ, and the sympathy of the glorified Saviour. And this is one great and important feature among many which renders this epistle so important and precious to every Christian.

Here we see His real humanity. Moved by a boundless, an infinite love, He took hold of the seed of Abraham; and because the children were partakers of flesh and blood, He likewise took part of the same. He was true, real Man, body, soul, and spirit. In His walk on earth He went through every sorrow, trial, temptation, that can oppress and pain the human heart. He lived by faith, putting His trust in the Father. In this epistle we behold the reality of His suffering in temptation, of His conflict and walk of faith, of His weakness and fear; we see how He became a merciful and compassionate High Priest, touched with the feeling of our infirmities, able to help us and sympathize with us in our difficulties and sorrows. The agony in the garden of Gethsemane, which is here described, shows us that Jesus went into all the anguish of death in dependence on God, submitting Himself, and learning obedience, though He was Son. Because His obedience, tried to the utmost, was perfect, He was exalted, and is now the glorified Man; and as Son of man, the eye of faith beholds Him at the right hand of power.

Jesus is in heaven a perfect High Priest. His

perfection is twofold. First, in that, having through the sacrifice of Himself obtained everlasting redemption for us, He was by His resurrection and ascension perfected—the High Priest who, in the power of an endless life, represents us before the Father, and brings to us the blessings of the heavenly sanctuary. Secondly, that through His experience on earth, He possesses a full knowledge of our difficulties and trials, of the power of temptation and the anguish of suffering, and regards with an infinite compassion, tenderness, and sympathy His people below, while His purpose is to keep them faithful, and to make them more than conquerors.

While, according to the purpose of the epistle, the emphasis is laid on Christ's Priesthood, and present glory at the right hand of God, His prophetic and royal office and His future Messianic reign are not left out of view. As the perfect Prophet or Revealer of God He appears already in the first chapter, and the royal character of His Priesthood is indicated, not merely by the name Melchizedek, but also by His session at the right hand of power. And though the object of the epistle is to confirm the Hebrews by showing them the heavenly sanctuary as the place of worship, yet the future reign of Messiah as King is indicated. This is meant by His being the Heir of all things, as Son of David, as Son of man, who by reason of His sufferings is enthroned Lord of all, the King of the whole earth, of whom all prophecy witnesses. Thus the epistle to the Hebrews represents the continuity of God's dealings with men, and with Israel especially. It shows the gospel of Jesus Christ, as preached by the Lord Himself and the apostles, to be the full culminating manifestation of the revelation of God to the fathers by the prophets; it declares the faith of God's saints from Abel to Abraham, and from Abraham to the Maccabees, as a looking forward to the ultimate kingdom and glory of Messiah, which is also our hope. Likewise it speaks of the new covenant as the covenant predicted by the prophet Jeremiah, as the covenant made with the house of Israel and the house of Judah—a promise containing spiritual and eternal blessings—but enshrined in and immovably connected with the *national* restoration in the land of Canaan, according to the purpose of God and the unconditional covenant made with Abraham, Isaac, and Jacob. (Jer. xxxi.)

3. The Believer's Life.

(1) We begin with the most important, the highest aspect, *worship*. As there is only one High Priest, Christ in heaven, so there is only one holy place, the heavenly sanctuary.* And by the blood of Jesus we have boldness to enter into the

* This is more fully brought out in chaps. viii.–x.

holiest. As the sacrifice was offered once for all, and the Lord is perfected for evermore, there is now the continued and uninterrupted favour of God resting upon us in Christ Jesus. We possess an unchangeable, perfect righteousness in Him. There is no more remembrance of sin, and we enter into the presence of God Himself in the full assurance of His love. In this epistle the chief point insisted on is *access to God*—worship in the holy of holies. We constantly fall into sin, and thereby our *communion* with God is interrupted, and our enjoyment of peace and light. If any man sin, the apostle John teaches us, we have an advocate with the Father, Jesus Christ the righteous. Through Christ's advocacy we are restored, and in answer to His intercession we are preserved, so that our faith fails not, and our souls are brought back into the paths of righteousness. But our epistle deals with the subject of the believer's *position*, of his standing before God, of his access to the throne of grace, and we are taught that in Christ we are perfected for ever. Boldly we may come to God, for His throne is a throne of grace. In the sympathy of the Lord Jesus we have the blessed assurance that, amid all suffering, temptation, and failure, sufficient grace and timely help will sustain us, and that as we are seated with Christ in heavenly places, so the love of God and the grace of our compassionate and merciful High Priest will uphold and succour us during our weakness and warfare on earth. The Christian is still in the wilderness, but his worship is in heaven.

We cannot come boldly unto the throne of grace unless we see the High Priest. By one sacrifice Christ hath perfected us, consecrated us, and brought us nigh unto God for ever. Christ having made purification of our sins, sat down at the right hand of God. We are accepted in Him. We possess a righteousness divine, perfect, eternal. Our sins and failures interrupt our communion with God; we are chastened and humbled; we must confess and repent; but our state before God remains the same. We always return to a throne of grace, to the Father and to the Saviour. Hence we worship, as accepted and forgiven, inside the veil, on the other side of the cross, so to say; not at the brazen altar, not at the laver, but in the holy of holies. And here I may appeal to the experience of the Christian, that it requires deep humility, self-abasement, and self-condemnation, to go with our sins and failures unto God as our Father, and unto Jesus as our Saviour and High Priest; to appear in His presence on the ground of perfect righteousness, and in faith of eternal and unchanging love; to turn from sin and disobedience, from forgetfulness and lukewarmness, unto God, believing that in

His love to us there was no interruption or diminution, that in the mercy and the intercession of our High Priest there was no pause or alteration, that the same favour, the same righteousness, the same eternal and infinite covenant-love was ours, while we were forgetting the Rock of our salvation and grieving the Spirit of promise by whom we are sealed. To do this is indeed hard and painful to flesh and blood, it is contrary to the carnal mind, for it exalts the grace of God and abases the creature. And if we come otherwise, if we draw near less 'boldly,' if notwithstanding our sins we do not come as those whose warfare is accomplished, whose iniquity is forgiven, and who have received of the Lord of free grace, and according to the eternal covenant, a double Benjamin portion, we fall back into the law, into the spirit of bondage, into the dark and lifeless region of works. True humility praises the glory of His grace, wherein He has taken us into favour in the Beloved.

2. Our perfection.

Christ, according to the teaching of our epistle, was perfected to be our High Priest. God consecrated Him to be the perfect and all-sufficient Mediator, who presents us to the Father, and who brings to us the blessings of the new covenant. After He had put away our sins by one sacrifice, He was, in His resurrection, ascension, and session at the right hand of God, perfected to be our royal High Priest. We are sanctified by the will of God through the offering of the body of Jesus Christ once for all. The Lord Jesus hath perfected for ever them that are sanctified.* All who believe in the Lord Jesus, and as soon as they believe, receive the blessings of the new covenant; their sins are forgiven, Christ is their righteousness, and they are consecrated or sanctified unto God; they have access unto the throne of grace, and as a royal priesthood they worship and serve. Christ is our sanctification, He is our perfection. We have been made the righteousness of God *in Him*, and this the moment we accept in humble faith the gospel, that He who knew no sin was made sin for us.

What other consecration can we speak of? The Son was consecrated (or perfected) for evermore, and the new and living way through the veil—that is to say, His flesh—was consecrated or dedicated for us; and we ourselves were brought nigh by His blood, and through faith we realized that we are not our own, but bought with a price. But the question may be asked, Is there not an inward sanctification of the Spirit? This aspect of sanctification is not brought prominently before us in this epistle, although the work of the Spirit in the heart is enumerated among the blessings of the

* Heb. x. 10, 14.

new covenant. Sanctification by the Spirit is essentially connected with our only (objective and) heavenly perfection in Christ; it has no other root and source; and as in idea it has no separate and distinct commencement, so in actual realisation its commencement is coincident with our justification.

If the question is asked, How does our acceptance affect our walk and our relation to sin? the apostolic answer is, How can we continue in sin, seeing that we have died to sin? But when did we die to sin? Was this separate from and subsequent to our believing in the Lord Jesus as the Saviour? No; but when we accepted the Lord Jesus as our righteousness, even then were we set apart unto God, severed from our former life, transplanted into the kingdom of God's dear Son. And how did we die with Christ? Was it by a subsequent and separate act of ours, in which our sin, or the flesh, or the old man, was, by a volition or energy of our own, crucified? or was it not (really) when Christ died on the cross, and (actually) when we believe that Christ died for us? And is not this death the object of our *faith,* and of faith from the very commencement of its existence? To the believer the apostle says: Reckon yourselves, realise by faith, and bear in mind that you have been crucified with Christ. And this is meant by the exhortation: Yield your members servants to righteousness, put off the old man, mortify the members which are on earth. It is not by a separate and subsequent act converted and saved men are to be "sanctified;" believers are to realize, that by the cross of Christ the world has been crucified to them and they to the world; that they have died with Christ unto sin.

The perfection of the believer is the same from the first moment of his spiritual life to the last, though his knowledge of it increases in depth and strength. Christ is his righteousness in heaven. In Him he is before God. There is no interruption or break in his acceptance and in his standing. In the light of this perfect love the believer discovers continually the true nature of sin and of the flesh. God condemned sin in the flesh, and therefore the believer looks upon the flesh as condemned. It cannot be purified. In us, that is our Adamic man, dwelleth no good thing. There is a fountain within us which cannot be cleansed, and out of which God-opposed evil thoughts continually ascend. Christ came in the *likeness* of sinful flesh, but His flesh was pure and holy. Whereas our flesh is sinful; when we are tempted, it is not apart from sin; for we to some extent, and though it be only for a moment, are pleased with the temptation. Besides, our sins of ignorance and omissions are many, and betoken the existence of sinfulness. And this sin, which dwelleth in us, we have to mourn over, to confess, and to fight against. Yet are we not in the flesh, but in the Spirit; for Christ dwelleth in us. Sin has no more dominion over us; for looking continually unto the Lord our righteousness, and reckoning ourselves to have died with Him, we are alive unto God. Still sin remains until we actually die, when beholding the glory of the Lord, seeing Him as He is, we shall be like Him.

According to the Scripture doctrine, there is one Christ and one faith and one life; and according to the Scripture doctrine, Christ Himself, and not what He effects in us, is the object of the believer's contemplation, and the source of his peace, strength, and joy. To look to our own state, and to put our own state of so-called holiness as an object and aim before our mind, is an unscriptural and hurtful thing. We are to behold the perfection of the Lord Jesus as our High Priest in heaven; and beholding Him, we judge ourselves, we have no confidence in the flesh, and rejoicing in Christ Jesus, we are renewed daily after His image.

God's ways are perfect, and they are simple. When Christ is received, all is received. The forgiveness of sins contains the only source and root of all godliness and true service. No subsequent supplement is needed. The apostles nowhere speak to the congregations of a higher Christian life, and of a second act of faith unto holiness; when they rebuke the sins and failures of the churches, and when they point out the remedy, it is always by showing the real meaning and power of the grace which at the first was preached unto them, and in which believers stand.

3. Lastly, let us remember the description of the Christian's life given in this epistle, in which various and apparently contradictory aspects are combined. If we really wish to walk with God, to enjoy communion with Him, and to remain steadfast in the faith unto the end, we shall realise in our own experience that rest and labour, peaceful assurance of our acceptance, and holy, vigilant, and anxious fear can co-exist. Knowing that God worketh in us both to will and to do of His good pleasure, we work out our own salvation with fear and trembling. Life-truths must be studied by living them. In theory it may be difficult to reconcile and combine the various aspects of spiritual realities and experiences; but when we do the will of God we come to know the divine character of Christ's doctrine. It is by faith, by a vital, trustful appropriation of truth, that we understand; it is in using the guide-book, in walking with God, that light shines on the path, and that we go on from strength to strength. Let us rejoice in the Lord, and let us rejoice always; yet let us remember that blessed is the man who feareth alway. "In the beholding of

God we fall not, and in the beholding of ourselves we stand not; yet while we are in this life it is needful that we behold both at once. The higher beholding keepeth us in joy and in the true love of God; the lower keepeth us in godly fear and self-abasement. Our good Lord would that we hold us much more in the beholding of Him, and yet not wholly leave the beholding of ourselves, until the time when we shall be brought up above, where we shall dwell with the Lord Jesus, according to our heart's desire, and be filled with joy without end, beholding Him as He is."*

* From *Reflections of Julian, Anchorite of Norwich*, 1326.

Printed in the United States
99497LV00008B/7/A